AFFAIRS OF STATE

THE EISENHOWER YEARS

AFFAIRS OF STATE

THE EISENHOWER YEARS

BY

Richard H. Rovere

FARRAR, STRAUS AND CUDAHY

NEW YORK

Published simultaneously in Canada by Ambassador
Books, Ltd., Toronto. Manufactured in the U.S.A.

American Book–Stratford Press, Inc., New York

For

E L E A N O R

A NOTE AND SOME ACKNOWLEDGMENTS

It is my hope that this book will serve as a useful chronicle. I submit it as a work of journalism, not of history. It is, in fact, quite literally, a *journal* of the period it is concerned with, and, as the reader will see, I have used the diarist's license to move from one thing to another without apology or plausible transition.

Most of the reports and comments republished here were written close to the time of the developments they describe and discuss—sometimes within a matter of hours—and I have chosen to retain the original moods and tenses. I cannot, however, disclaim certain of the advantages of hindsight. For one thing, I have selected only those articles and parts of articles that have retained their relevance. Much that I have written in the dusty aftermath of events has lost its relevance with appalling speed. Also, some of this material has been extensively revised. I have added clarifying identifications whenever I thought them needed, and I have recapitulated developments that were well known at the time I wrote. I have gone back over my notes and the materials I had gathered in reporting and included here much that I had not previously used.

In no case, though, have I yielded to the powerful temptation to employ hindsight to bestow upon myself a foresight I did not have at the time of writing.

I expect that at least a few readers will observe a serious imbalance in this book. It contains a good deal of material on the foreign policy of the Eisenhower administration and quite a bit on the activities of Senator McCarthy and those around him but not a great deal on the economic issues of the period. I regret the omissions; many interesting and important things receive too little attention here. But what receives a lot of attention seems to me worthy of it.

A word about the datelines: the letters from Washington and elsewhere appear under the date of composition. In a few cases, I have consolidated articles written at various times and for various periodicals with the items of correspondence. Still, the dateline is that of completion of the original work. With one exception, the articles that do not appear as correspondence carry the issue date of the magazine in which they were published. The exception is the last piece in the book. A much shorter version of this appeared in the *Reporter* for April 21, 1955. For this book, I have amplified and revised it so much that it is substantially a new piece of work.

The Letter from Washington dated September 22, 1955 was written for the *New Yorker* and scheduled for publication there but was withdrawn upon the news of President Eisenhower's illness. It is published here for the first time.

And a word about viewpoint: I have my own thoughts about politics and political personalities, and I suppose that some of my personal tastes and preferences show through. But I do not look upon myself as a partisan or upon this book as a polemic. In general, my effort has been to write about politics as much as possible in the manner of a critic making the effort, as Matthew Arnold put it, "to see the object as in itself it really is." I believe that it is at least theoretically possible to bring to public affairs the sympathy, interest, hope, objectivity, and rigorous discrimination that a conscientious critic brings to literature, painting, music, architecture, or any other form. Since I generally write hurriedly, and as close to the news as possible, I suppose my function is closer to that of a reviewer than to the more exalted one of critic, but I seek nevertheless to be guided by the best available critical doctrines. Every critic has his own tastes, or prejudices if you will, and would be scarcely a man if he did not, yet the fair and responsible ones are able to suspend them and to approach any given piece of work with a determination to learn what the performer hoped to accomplish and to render an honest judgment as to how well he succeeded and whether the success was worth the effort. It is my wish to make this approach to politics; I would like to succeed more often than I do.

Like every other writer, I have many people to thank. My heaviest obligations are to editors, and I have been lucky enough to have known some great ones. I welcome this chance to salute the memory of the late Harold Ross of the *New Yorker*. He died before any of these *New Yorker* pieces were published, but he encouraged me to persevere with the form and made it possible for me to do so. I owe a great deal to him—and fully as much to his friend, collaborator, and successor, William Shawn. The late Frederick Lewis Allen of *Harper's Magazine* was another of my mentors, and his successor, John Fischer, has given me valued advice and cooperation. Others I must mention are Gardner Botsford, Sanderson Vanderbilt, Ruth Flint, and Harding Mason of the *New Yorker*, Max Ascoli and Philip Horton of the *Reporter*, Lester Markel and Lewis Bergmann of the New York *Times*, Morris Rubin of the *Progressive*, Walter Taplin and Iain Hamilton of the *Spectator* of London, Basil Thornton of the British Broadcasting Corporation, and Erich Koch of the Canadian Broadcasting Corporation. I am grateful to the proprietors of the institutions named above for permission to publish material, constituting a considerable portion of this book, originally prepared for them, and originally copyrighted by them.

In preparing the work for publication in the present form, I had valuable advice and criticism as well as the most practical kind of assistance from Aimee Buchanan, John Peck, and Eleanor Rovere.

For reporters, there are always news sources. Some of mine are identified in the text. Others, I know, would not relish identification. I thank them all, and I must add my thanks to all of my friends in the Washington press corps. I am what is inelegantly known as a brain-picker, and I would not be able to function at all if my parasitism were not tolerated by those correspondents who from day to day are in touch with many developments that I follow only irregularly. I hope that sometime someone will do full justice to the contributions to the health and improvement of our society made by the regular Washington correspondents. They are a civilized group and a civilizing influence, and I consider it a reflection on the historians and sociologists that their influence has never been properly weighed and appreciated. For myself, I am full of gratitude for their generosity with their time and knowledge.

For enlightenment and reference, I rely heavily on the New York *Times*, the Washington *Post & Times-Herald*, the *Congressional Record*, *U.S. News & World Report*, *Time*, and *Facts on File*. They are my bibliography.

R. H. R.

Hyde Park, New York

Contents

1 Dwight D. Eisenhower

May 1950

There is again much talk of General Eisenhower for President. In fact, what might be called the second Eisenhower boom is under way. As a political movement, it is less formidable than the one the General put a stop to on January 22, 1948, when he announced that he was "not available for and could not accept nomination to high political office." It is natural that this boom should be quieter than the first and highly desirable from the point of view of those who favor the present movement. We are now almost midway between elections, and public interest in presidential politics is about as low as it ever gets in the four-year cycle. If the second Eisenhower boom were more formidable now, it would be less formidable in 1952. When water is brought to a boil too early, much of it passes away in steam.

Still, the boom is on in a small, promising way. It is reported in New York that the president of Columbia University will be the state's entry at the 1952 Republican convention. He is said to have been seeing a good deal of Governor Dewey, and the Governor is said to be favorably impressed. It is reported from the Middle West that Roy Roberts, the president of the Kansas City *Star* and a prairie Warwick who had a lot to do with the earlier boom stands ready to line up Eisenhower delegates when the proper time is at hand. Governor Warren is said to have the case of Eisenhower under advisement. The movers and shakers are thinking things over, and occasional feelers are put out to the public. Dr. Gallup has been around interviewing again —"successfully applying," he says with confidence, "the lessons

3

learned in 1948"—and he finds that Eisenhower would be far and away the most popular figure the Republicans could nominate. Eisenhower, Dr. Gallup says, is out in front among both independent voters and registered Republicans His nearest rival is his fellow educator Harold Stassen, and Stassen isn't very near.

To cite the polls in support of anything nowadays is to invite hooting and jeering. Yet even in their greatest failure, they were only a few percentage points out of the way, and if, suspecting that Dr Gallup's confidence in himself may be misplaced, we apply the 1948 margin of error to Eisenhower's 1950 rating and reduce his advantage accordingly (it might as reasonably be increased), his following is still impressive. All the claims of the poll takers are borne out by the shrewdest judges of political sentiment. The people like Eisenhower. Five years after V-E Day, no other public figure comes anywhere near him in the admiration of the country as a whole. The people not only respect him, as we have always known that they do, they think it would be a fine idea to make him President. That any politicians at all look with favor on Eisenhower is in itself proof that the masses do. Politicians are as a rule happier with a weak regular than with a strong irregular. But the voices of governors, national committeemen, and ward leaders have been added to the general clamor. In this season of Republican need and desperation, Eisenhower's chances seem excellent.

Nothing is easier than to apply simple logic to the Eisenhower phenomenon and to prove that it reveals the democratic electorate as an essentially frivolous body which worships success for its own sake and wretchedly confuses categories. Why on earth should anyone think Eisenhower would make a good President? What does he know about the United States? What does he know about anything that is related to the presidency except the running of the military establishment? Why should so many Americans think that this man, untrained and untested in politics and until recently quite uninterested in the subject, could make a suitable chief magistrate? Is the presidency a demanding job or isn't it? Does it require special knowledge and special abilities, or is it an office that any literate and halfway conscientious American can handle? If it is as demanding as we generally believe it to be, then clearly Eisenhower has no qualifications worth discussing and those who are so eager to have him for President are either contemptuous of the office or themselves ridiculously ignorant. That, at any rate, must be the verdict of simple logic.

Yet simple logic will not do. For there is a factor in the popular enthusiasm that largely redeems it and makes it more supportable and dignified. Eisenhower is not just the victor in great battles; he is, in the public view, a great personage. To the American people, a general in politics is never a mere personality but always a personage. By serving the country as a whole, he assumes a status above partisanship, above self, above all merely passing issues and concerns. "To a greater or lesser extent," Dorothy and Julius Goebel, Jr., have written in *Generals in the White House*, an uncommonly cogent essay on the American character, "every general who ever became President owed something to the public anxiety that the place be filled by a personage." The Goebels run through our history to prove that we violate our antimilitarist political traditions not in orgies of gratitude and hero-worship but in a search for men of vision. We have chosen generals to lead us only when the political scene was so dominated by party and faction that the ancient ideal of the chief executive as a man "pre-eminent for virtue and ability" seems to have been lost sight of and we have been offered nothing but men pre-eminent for the stripes of factional warfare they have earned. When a big man is wanted and the parties have none to offer, the people may turn to the military, which is one of our few institutions that stand, or seem to stand, above mean partisanship. Not every general we have chosen has turned out to be what the people wanted, but that is another story.

Eisenhower is, in the public view, a personage, and we are today in the midst of a crisis without any crisis leadership. Would Eisenhower run? No one who knows him seems to doubt it. Many think he is running hard right now. He is no longer bound by his eloquent strictures on military men in politics, for he is no longer a military man but the head of a great university. In his two years at Columbia, he has discussed and debated public matters with relish. "Eisenhower is chafing under his academic robes," *Look* magazine reports. "He itches to get into the political fight." The article is called "Eisenhower is Open to a G.O.P. Draft." Its author assures us that he is able to make these assertions on the basis of interviews he has held with himself. "This is my opinion," he writes; "it's not based on anything Eisenhower has said." Perhaps so, but no halfway responsible periodical reports that a man itches unless someone has seen him scratch. *Look* is owned by an influential Republican family which once did much to advance the public careers of Wendell Willkie and Harold Stassen. It now finds that "a crucial problem lies ahead for the next President of the United States, for which Ike is singularly qualified. This is bringing unity to the now disunited Western nations facing Russia." It is not entirely clear from this whether *Look* regards Eisenhower as singularly qualified for the presidency or singularly qualified for solving the crucial problem, but the chances are that it would stand behind either interpretation.

What sort of President would Eisenhower make? We know surprisingly little about him, really. No less than five books about him have appeared since 1944, but all of them were written in tenderly patriotic moods by men who couldn't get at all the facts even if they wanted to. His own book, *Crusade in Europe,* is a document that sometimes comes close to splendor, but it is, like most battle chronicles written by battle commanders, a rather austere, chilly book that seldom deals in personalities and therefore tells us little about its author except that he is capable of producing such a book, which is a curious and paradoxical fact, since he is customarily anything but austere or chilly. On the controversial military-political decisions that were made in Europe, it is informative but not notably enlightening, for it is necessarily a defense of those decisions by the man who either made them himself or participated with others in making them.

Ordinarily, a candidate, or a candidate for candidacy, is offered to the voters in three parts: personality, record, and program. The people are told what he is like, what he has done, and what he thinks he might do. In Eisenhower's case, only his personality can be discussed with any real assurance. His record is mostly irrelevant, and he has no program. True, one can, after a fashion, project a program from his recent statements of principle, but that is not wholly fair either to him or to the principle. There is today, however, less mystery about where he stands than there was two years ago. In 1948, no one knew whether he was a Democrat or a Republican. For all anyone knew, he might have been a Greenbacker or a Social Credit crank. No one knew whether *he* knew what he was. All that was known, or at any rate believed, was that he could win an election. It was, indeed, the mystery of his beliefs that made the first boom the vast popular-front movement it was—a movement embracing Chester Bowles and Alf M. Landon, the Americans for Democratic Action and the remnants of the Liberty League. A cynical but unstated assumption of the first boom was that the General would adopt whatever kind of politics paid off best; that if he were interested in running at all, he would run with the hounds, once he learned who the hounds were.

The present boom is a strictly Republican affair. The Democrats aren't having any. In the past two years, Eisenhower has said a lot. He has said that too much government intervention will turn "the American Dream into an American nightmare." He opposes deficit financing. He believes that free enterprise is the underpinning of all freedom. He thinks we worry too much about security and too little about liberty. He is, then, a conservative. But conservatism covers a lot of ground nowadays, and has its own right and left wings, just as liberalism does. It is impossible to determine just where on conservative ground Eisenhower stands. In the bales of speeches he has made since 1948, he has not once addressed himself to a specific non-military issue. How much government intervention does he consider too much? Is he opposed to deficit financing in all circumstances? It he a Taft conservative, a Kenneth Wherry conservative, a Wayne Morse conservative? It is impossible to tell.

The one thing that is perfectly clear is his personality. It is not a vivid personality, but it is a distinct one. To borrow a term from linguistics, it is a standard-American personality. Eisenhower is forthright, pragmatic, gregarious, alert, even-tempered, calmly energetic, more shrewd than wise, generous, courteous but neither courtly nor grand, modest but never humble. He is unintellectual and probably anti-intellectual, but he is enormously respectful of learning and knowledge when he encounters them in large quantities. He likes poker and bridge, bourbon, dialect jokes, vegetable gardening, moralities based on the adventures of Mama Skunk and Papa Skunk, and singing "Abdul Abulbul Amir" to the thirty-eighth verse. When he talks about the formative years, all the standard elements of song, story, and myth are there: the mother influence, gentling and purifying; the father influence, hardening; the life of the large, poor family that destroys selfishness, builds self-reliance, and encourages a decent acquisitiveness; the inevitable paper route and all the other part-time jobs. There is even a Jack Armstrong in the Eisenhower story—a town bully with the fine bullying name of Wes Merrifield, bigger and faster than our man, whom Dwight fought to a bloody standstill in a vacant lot at Broadway and Third in Abilene, Kansas, almost the dead center of the country, in the summer of 1903, almost the dead center of American experience.

Now that he is out of uniform. Eisenhower's personality comes through a good deal more clearly than it formerly did. If we cast about for a familiar example of the same type, we come upon one almost instantly: Harry Truman. They are strikingly alike in all the essentials of taste, behavior, and outlook. The reason Eisenhower has seemed singular rather than typical is that he is a general. His type is common enough in the country as a whole, but it has been a half-century at least since it flourished in the top ranks of the Army. It stood out refreshingly in the recent war. Perhaps its most fitting symbol is the garment known as "the Eisenhower jacket." While MacArthur in the Orient moved around under a heavy load of braid and metals, or else walked truculently through palaces in a limp open-collared shirt, achieving great conspicuousness in either dress, and while Patton's tank helmet of lacquered plastic, his pearl-handled pistols, and his boots of burnished leather glistened so brightly in the sun that they could light up half-tone engravings on wartime newsprint, Eisenhower, with nothing to glisten but his smile, made a neat and unpretentious appearance before the high and mighty of Europe in the kind of jacket worn here at home by fastidious gas-station attendants. It was in its way a brave thing to do, because it was a risky one for a man whose success depended so largely on the kind of impression he made. Eisenhower is not, physically, a very imposing man. Unlike Winston Churchill, who can somehow look even more martially resplendent in a grease-monkey's suit than a commodore's, Eisenhower might have seemed merely drab in his sawed-off jacket and might have been mistaken, in news pictures, for an orderly instead of a Supreme Commander, but he carried it off superbly, and the jacket became a kind of symbol of democracy fighting its war in simple, tidy, utilitarian, unmartial dress.

Eisenhower was well thought of by the troops who fought under him. This can be said with absolute certainty. Censorship could have covered up almost anything but attitudes toward him as a human being; dislike of him, if it had existed in any large measure, could not possibly have been concealed. No one today could hope to wither the Eisenhower boom with the kind of remark with which Heywood Broun, almost single-handedly, withered the mild Pershing boom of 1920. "It would seem rather foolish to me," Broun wrote, "for any party that hopes to win an election to nominate a man who would go to the polls with the votes of four million veterans solidly against him." The veteran vote would not be against Eisenhower; it might even favor him somewhat more strongly than the non-veteran vote. His troops knew him only at a distance, of course, but the point is that the distance was not resented. Although Eisenhower was a hotel general, the safest and most walled-in commander outside Washington, his troops seem never to have found it in their hearts to despise or ridicule him. They never decorated him with any of the mockingly felicitous sobriquets (Patton: the Green Hornet; MacArthur: Flash Gordon) they so easily found for anyone they suspected of phoniness. Eisenhower was always either Eisenhower or Ike, and if he made capital of his famous greeting, "My name's Eisenhower," because John Gunther had told him it would make a good story, being so refreshingly out of military character, the fact must be put down as simply another example of the genuine and the synthetic being wrapped together in the same package. In his personal conduct, Eisenhower emerged from the war with everything to his credit.

Eisenhower's record consists of twenty-seven years as an obscure Army officer and eight years as a figure of international repute and importance. The eight years break down into four as director of the American and Allied military effort in Europe, two as Chief of Staff, and two as president of Columbia University. The twenty-seven years are almost entirely unexaminable, and many of the examinable later years reveal nothing that has any serious bearing on any political career he may later enjoy. There are huge gaps in the record. There are, for example, no satisfactory accounts of what Eisenhower did between the two wars or of the steps immediately preceding his sudden rise to the heights in 1942. The version the Roosevelt administration gave, and the version he gives in *Crusade in*

Europe, is that he commended himself to the President and to General Marshall by his performance in some make-believe battles in Louisiana in 1941; but that is not a very likely explanation of how and why a decision of global significance was reached. The facts, if we could get at them, would certainly be more complicated and possibly more to Eisenhower's credit.

If the first boom had succeeded, Eisenhower would have been the tenth general to have become President, but he would have been only the second—Zachary Taylor was the first—to have won the office on the strength of a career spent entirely in uniform. Washington was a delegate to the Continental Congress before he was a general, and he was president of the Constitutional Convention that created the nation whose first President he became. Jackson had been a celebrated lawyer, a senator, and a judge. The first Harrison was Governor of Indiana, the second a Senator from that state. Pierce served in both houses of Congress before his presidency, as did Garfield. Grant's civilian experience was slight—six unsuccessful years in business and farming and an interim period in Johnson's cabinet —but his successor, Hayes, had been a congressman and a governor.

Eisenhower's career has now been enriched by two years in mufti, and we can learn a few things about him from them, but we are still faced with twenty-seven unquestionably important years that lay between his graduation from West Point in 1915 and the massive job he undertook in 1942. In all the biographies, they are made to appear as years of steady ripening, years filled with accomplishments each more stunning than the last. "Almost from the day he left West Point," one biographer has written, "he [was] marked by his superiors as one of the dozen best bets among the younger officers to win a high command." From then on, the story goes, he grew steadily in intellectual stature, allied himself with the men of broadest vision in the Army, and improved every hour of leisure by studying military history and acquainting himself with the complexities of life beyond the reservation.

It is possible that all of this is true, but none of its squares with what can be verified. On the basis of the record as we have it, the period can be accounted for only as one in which Eisenhower was constantly moving about on routine assignments— now to a small command, now to coach football, now to teach —from one post to another—Fort Leavenworth, Fort Lewis, Fort Oglethorpe, Camp Colt in Panama, Washington, the Philippines. The one assignment that was not routine took him to France to write a guidebook on American war monuments there. If these were years of preparation and ripening, he himself could not always have known about it. One of the few revealing things he has said about the period is that there were times when sheer ennui and the pariah complex which most peacetime offi- cers develop drove him almost to the point of resigning his com- mission and going into private business or newspaper work. He may have spent his peacetime leisure with Clausewitz, but it is known that in the war years, before he knew he was going to become an educator or a man considered for the presidency, he spent what little leisure he had reading cowboy magazines. "His wife sends over regular shipments of Western pulps which he consumes with astonishing speed and intemperance," it was reported in 1943. There is, to be sure, nothing delinquent in spending one's years the way Eisenhower spent that quarter century. We might all be in the soup today if he and hundreds of others had not endured their pariah complexes, and in truth Eisenhower's boredom and despair do him more credit than his pious biographers do. Still and all, twenty-seven years spent this way and unexplained except by official exegesis tell us very little about a man who, in the view of many, may soon be tell- ing us and the world a great deal.

In considering the four great years of Eisenhower's life, we come on a disconcerting paradox. If we accept the very highest appraisal of what he did in Europe—that is, if we take the view

of a man like Drew Middleton, who covered Eisenhower's headquarters for the *New York Times,* that "Eisenhower was the
principal architect of victory in the West, the principal planner
and chief executive of the battles which broke the German
Army"—then it is impossible to accept his greatest achievement
as any sort of political recommendation. If, on the other hand,
we accept the very meanest estimate of Eisenhower—that of a
man like A. J. Liebling, who watched him in North Africa and
France and has written of him as a political general, a fixer, a
chairman-of-the-board sort of commander—then the military
record may offer some very serious recommendations. A bum-
bling incompetent of a strategist would be no less qualified for
the presidency than a military genius, and Eisenhower's case is
neither strengthened nor weakened by the results of inquiries
into his apportionment of gasoline and other sinews of battle or
by trying to determine whether he, Bradley, or Montgomery
was right about this campaign or that. To be gifted in the reconciliation of conflicts, however, to handle men as creatures of
passion and prejudice rather than simply as deployable forces,
and to be responsible for the political decisions that are part of
the conduct of every modern war—these things, obviously,
should carry weight in any political evaluation.

It is in the large political matters, however, that it is still
hardest to tell what was what and who was who. In matters of
pure strategy, this is not the case. There, Eisenhower's place
in the chain of command is clear. The American plan for invad-
ing the Continent across the English Channel had been worked
out by the President and General Marshall, and Eisenhower's
main job, in the beginning, was to urge the American case, in
which he personally concurred, on the British, who were
against it. Once it was agreed upon, Eisenhower became responsible for its planning and execution, and all on-the-spot decisions
were either in his hands or in the hands of men answerable to
him. But in the case of the North African and Italian campaigns
he was personally opposed to the plans, and he was ordered by

Washington to go ahead with them, which he did, subsequently commanding the operations he had originally thought ill-advised. In short, he did not have a determining voice in American grand strategy, but below that level all military decisions were up to him.

No such clear formulation can be made for his part in the political decisions. It is hardly likely that his political power would have exceeded his military power, but it is still unclear how much responsibility he bore for the decisions made on the lower levels. In political affairs, three forces were operating—Eisenhower, Roosevelt, and the State Department—and though the last two should have acted as one, we know that they frequently did not. Eisenhower has often been made to take the rap for the Darlan-Giraud affair, for the succession of unhappy arrangements in Italy, for the rejection of Churchill's many proposals to limit the areas of Russian occupation, and for a good many bungled matters in the administration of defeated Germany; but it would be logical as well as charitable to suppose that even where he accepted responsibility, he had in fact yielded to superior wisdom and experience, generally in the person of Robert Murphy of the State Department. In that case, however, he cannot be given credit for the more fortunate political decisions, of which there were more than a few.

There is one clearly dismaying aspect of Eisenhower's part in the Darlan-Giraud and Badoglio affairs. This was his inability to understand what the criticism of them was all about. For the accommodation with Darlan there were many defenses, not the least compelling of which was Eisenhower's estimate that the early casualties in the North African fighting might easily have been 18,000 instead of the actual number of 1,800 if we had not softened French resistance by making the deal. Certainly the long-term consequences of our Vichy policy do not seem to have been nearly as bad as it was once predicted they would be. Yet to have been utterly unprepared for criticism of the deal and not to have understood the point of the criticism when it came seems like evidence of an alarming political innocence and military insularity. Eisenhower was deeply offended, according to his Boswell, Harry Butcher, when the first reactions, which came from London, were cool; but he was, Butcher's diary says, sustained by his knowledge that his countrymen would be behind him. "The American acceptance was not explicitly given," Butcher wrote on November 15, 1942, a week after the first Allied landings in Africa, "but we knew we were all right with the homefolk when a swell message of congratulations for Ike and for the forces of TORCH was received from the President." (The President's congratulations happened to be for the military operation, not the political one. When the flood of criticism broke on Roosevelt, he disclaimed responsibility, saying that he had not been consulted in advance. But it wasn't Eisenhower who had failed to consult him; it was Roosevelt's deputy, Robert Murphy, who had turned up at Eisenhower's London headquarters two months earlier to explain how "under certain conditions, French resistance would fade.") This record contains little assurance that Eisenhower is "singularly qualified" for "bringing unity to the now disunited Western nations facing Russia."

Eisenhower returned to this country late in 1945 to become Army Chief of Staff, a position he held until 1948, when he moved to Columbia. There has never been any public accounting of his brief stewardship in the Pentagon. He served in a difficult period of demobilization, attempted unification, and the beginnings of remobilization. He appears to have been a reasonably competent Chief of Staff, but his performance is never spoken of as enthusiastically as that of General Marshall or of Eisenhower's successor, General Bradley. His two years at Columbia are open to inspection, and there is a good deal to be learned about him and his cast of mind from what he has said and done in this period. As a university president, he has been, in the view of most of those working and studying under him, anything but a success. Some strong alumni groups appear to like him, but there is intense hostility toward him on the part of the majority of both faculty and student body. Whether or not there are elements of unreasonableness in the hostility, it exists and it is a measure of failure.

Responsibility for the failure, it must be added, rests only partially on Eisenhower. If ever anyone demonstrated a confusion of values and categories, it was the trustees who made Eisenhower president of Columbia in the first place. He himself pointed out that his knowledge of education was negligible, that his own education had been inadequate, and that education was not his primary interest. He had often said, it is true, that when he was under the greatest pressure in Europe, he filled his mind with pleasant visions of keeping busy in his later years by administering the affairs of a small men's college in a small town somewhere. Such an environment and such a job might have been well suited to him if the fates could have arranged for him to enjoy an obscure semi-retirement. But they didn't. He became a world figure and a man upon whom a mighty nation was eager to bestow any gift he might ask. To expect a man in this exhilarating position, and a man with little background in general ideas and even less interest than background, to feel himself at home in the highly-charged intellectual atmosphere of an institution like Columbia and to find a satisfactory release for his energies in administering its affairs was absurd in the first place and never anything but absurd. Columbia's disappointment in Eisenhower, which is probably no greater than his disappointment in Columbia, stems not so much from any administrative ineptitude he has displayed as from his inattentiveness to the problems of administration. It isn't so much that he is a bad president as that he hardly ever functions as president. The only thing he has shown any real interest in is rebuilding Columbia's lost prestige in athletics. When he is expected to be attending an important faculty convocation, he is downtown in the railroad station giving the throttle of the New Broadway Limited its first pull. When he should be worrying over where to find a good man for Seventeenth Century French Literature, he is off addressing Moose or Elks in Denver. Eisenhower, knowing that his interest in education was not very serious, was at fault in accepting the appointment at the start, but by far the greater responsibility rests with those who, knowing both his limitations and the responsibilities of the job, invited him to accept the presidency.

Eisenhower's mind is, like his personality, standard-American. It is unschematic, distrustful of fine distinctions, given to overstatement, impatient with theory, eager to make translations into the realm of matter and things, concerned with the effect of ideas rather than with their validity. At Columbia, he has taken with great ease to the theory that the goal of education is social improvement. In his one statement on academic freedom, he has made the point that the colleges must be free to discuss communism in order to show how fraudulent it is. The conservatism he has been espousing lately does not appear to be the outgrowth of any rigorous search for wisdom on his part, and it has not been expressed with any great urgency or moral conviction. It does, though, appear to be the result of a fairly recent conversion. Although we still know little about the views he held before 1948, there seems to be a clear contradiction between some of the things he felt several years back and some that he now feels.

In 1945, for example, he addressed a national CIO convention in Atlantic City, and in the course of praising labor for its wartime production had a few things to say about labor's achievements in its own behalf. "Men of my generation," he said, "familiar in their youth with the specter of insecurity that haunted many a family whose meager shelter and clothing and food depended on the father's prolonged hours of toil and sometimes miserably small pay are living witnesses of what has been accomplished." No commitment is involved here, and the sentiment is perhaps just a ghost-writer's pleasantry for a labor meeting, but the sentence contrasts oddly and rather pleasantly in mood and feeling with the following excerpt from a speech delivered a short while back:

> We seek the illusion called security. We want to wear fine shirts and have caviar and champagne when we should be eating hot dogs and beer. I have seen all around the world many people lying beneath white crosses. They are there because they believed in something more than trying to be sure they would not be hungry when they were sixty-seven.

A good case can be made against the current preoccupation with mere security, and security is certainly not the most exalted ideal to which a creative society may aspire, but Eisenhower's statement of the case betrays a disturbing coarseness of taste and expression. Moreover, the case against security as a goal in life comes with exceedingly poor grace from a man who spent thirty-three years in the United States Army, which makes security its most tempting bait for recruitment and whose officers are more preoccupied with early retirement and the future's grocery bills than any other class in the country.

Even since Eisenhower has been in the public eye, it has been said of him that he has remarkable gifts of self-expression, that he handles the English language with grace and dexterity. "A master of precise and lucid prose," *Life* has called him—citing as a sample a battle speech ending, "Don't act like this was a boudoir!" Ordinarily, prose style should not influence us strongly. We have, God knows, put up with doughy rhetoric from our presidents in the past, and we could do it again without too much discomfort. But the way a man handles words is sometimes an index to the clarity of his thought. Eisenhower's principal claims as a stylist now rest on *Crusade in Europe*, which would be impressive evidence if we could be certain that most of it came from his hands, but would not be final evidence, since clarity in dealing with the materials of one's profession is hardly a fair test. No one can excel a good mechanic in using words economically and to good effect when a good mechanic talks about machinery, or a good farmer when he talks about crops.

If *Crusade in Europe* did come from Eisenhower's hands, it is difficult to explain his choice of words or his taste in ghosts for his other postwar writings. There is no evidence of freshness or succinctness of language in any of the addresses he has been making in recent years. He is as dependent on the political tautology and the battered ornament as the next man:

> The United States must stand forever in the forefront of those that strive for the common objective. Nothing must deter us from advancing the day when mutual respect will replace mutual prejudice in international relations; when mutual confidence will replace mutual fear. When that day comes the soldier's task will be completed. Until that day, his readiness to discharge his obligations is a matter of deepest concern to us all.

If Eisenhower's mind and talents rise above the commonplace in any field but his own, the fact has not been demonstrated. None of the people who have supported him as a presidential candidate has ever given acceptable evidence that the man is suited for the job or that he could develop the gifts the job requires. To say this much, however, is to say very little. Many men with no apparent qualifications have made excellent presidents. Either they had hidden capacities for leadership or they developed capacities in office.

In 1932, Walter Lippmann characterized Franklin D. Roosevelt in a sentence that has become one of the most celebrated of our time. He said that the Democratic candidate was a pleasant man who, without having any important qualifications for the office, would very much like to be President. Poor Lippmann has had the line flung back in his face a thousand times. He has been brayed at, pitied, and taunted for making so unperceptive a remark about so towering a figure. Yet for those who are able to disengage their mental images of the post-1932 Roosevelt and frame in their mind's eye only the brash candidate of that year, it is clear that Lippmann's characterization was at the time about as acute a summary of the facts as anyone could hope to make in a sentence. The Roosevelt of 1932, the isolationist and the man who thought that Herbert Hoover was being improvident with federal funds, had a passable but quite undistinguished record. His intellectual equipment was not then especially prepossessing, if in fact it ever was.

Lippmann's error was not in failing to see a child of destiny when one stood before him but in failing to accompany his observation with a necessary caveat. He should have said that men of destiny are often hard to tell from other men. The possibility that Eisenhower would make a good or even a great President is by no means to be discounted. If he either knew his business or could give the illusion of knowing it, his personality, dignified but approachable, would grace the office in one of the best of our traditions. If by the mere fact of his high standing with the people he could create an atmosphere of confidence and unity, he might be able to do the country an immense service. It is conceivable that he could do these things, but the question is whether it is wise to bank on the merely conceivable. It is a whole lot more than conceivable that Eisenhower as President might find himself in the same state of unpreparedness in which he found himself when he was made president of Columbia.

It gives one a rather unsettling and queasy feeling to imagine him confiding to White House reporters the sentiments he confided to reporters a few months after he had been appointed Dr. Butler's successor. "I hope," he told newspapermen at the time, "to talk with various officials while I am here and possibly get some advance inkling of what a college president is up against. I know nothing about it."

2   The Non-Titanic Struggle

Letter from Washington

June 12, 1952

Here, as elsewhere in the country, the Eisenhower-Taft contest is the center of interest; in its most recent and most rancorous phase—the battle over convention officers and over the disputed delegations—it has been very interesting indeed. Nevertheless, it appears to be something less than the titanic struggle many people had hoped and expected it would be. The common feeling is that while the General, in the nine days that have elapsed since the mustering-out ceremonies on the Pentagon steps, has given the country some clear and valuable insights into his political style—his way of handling and expressing himself—he has thrown a lot more warmth than light on the points supposedly at issue between himself and Senator Taft. His failure to illuminate is in itself a revelation of some importance. It shows that he understands and approves the uses of ambiguity and is, as advertised, a seeker of golden means and close harmony. On the level of temperament, this distinguishes him sharply from Senator Taft, who understands the uses of ambiguity but does not approve of them and sets a high value on doctrinal purity. But differences in temperament had been apparent for some time, and what people here were mainly curious about were the differences, if any, in doctrine.

So far, no one can say that his curiosity has been assuaged. The General has been as difficult a man to smoke out as Washington flame-throwers have ever encountered. No one yet knows, for example, where he stands on Far Eastern policy, which looks to be the largest question of the campaign. Walter Lippmann and the Washington *Post* seem persuaded that he shares their views, which are shameful ones in the eyes of most other Republicans. One gathers that Lippmann and the *Post* editors think he would immediately reverse the pro-Chiang policy, which they regard as the folly that is at the root of most of our troubles in Asia. Eisenhower has said nothing to prove them wrong—and nothing to prove them right. He has indicated a dissatisfaction with the Yalta agreements, but this scarcely constitutes a point of view on the Far East. He has defended the government's policy in Europe but has complained that it costs too much, which is exactly the fault Senator Taft has to find with it. On most domestic questions, he has taken a position that can fairly be described as Republican, but in just about every instance he has constructed for himself a large, easily accessible escape hatch. He is opposed to federal aid to education, for example, except where it is badly needed. He endorses the Taft-Hartley Act but not in detail. He favors a federal health program but not of the sort that would require the hiring of doctors by the government. In some respects, there has been a net loss in clarification since his return. While still in uniform, he gave it as his opinion, in a letter to some Texas supporters, that the state governments have a better claim to revenues from tidelands oil than the federal government. Early this week, though, in a meeting with some convention delegates from Massachusetts, a maritime province with no known petroleum deposits beneath its coastal waters, he said that a study of a Supreme Court decision favoring the federal government might lead him to change his view. Someone here has pointed out that the only issue on which it is easy to differentiate between the positions of Eisenhower and Taft is General MacArthur. Taft has promised to give MacArthur a government job. Eisenhower has promised to listen to anything MacArthur has to say.

3 Republican Convention

Letter from Chicago

July 12, 1952

General Eisenhower and Senator Taft are still here, and so are several other Republicans, including Honeybear Warren and her sisters, but they might as well all be in Buffalo or Seattle as far as most sweltering Chicagoans are concerned. One is aware of them only through the newspapers. The nominee had a talk with several Republican leaders this morning, among them Senator McCarthy, who, after seeing General Eisenhower, said he thought Senator Nixon would make a good vice-president. Another visitor was Representative George Bender of Ohio, the bell-ringer. The General listened while the Representative sang "Onward, Christian Soldiers," which he had rendered four times during the Taft demonstration. In the Conrad Hilton, formerly the Stevens, the world's largest and most complicated hotel and a standing challenge to an American Kafka, practically every bit of evidence that the Republicans passed this way has been dismantled or sucked up by vacuum hoses. The Russell-for-President committee moved in last night and took over the Taft-for-President headquarters. Democratic beaters are arriving by the carload to set up the Democratic convention—or what someone has called the second Betty Furness show—for week after next. But the hotel management says they are not arriving in such force as to make it impossible for the Hilton to play host to a couple of other conventions in the interim. Some life insurance men and some safe-driving instructors are foregathered here at the moment, and early next week this mecca of conventioneers will extend its welcome to Ralston Purina sales people coming in from every corner of the land. After them, the Democrats.

Unlike the Hilton management, Colonel Robert R. McCormick is more concerned with looking back on the Republican convention than with planning ahead for Ralston Purina. This evening, on the radio, he predicted that "the Republican Party in New England and the East will just rot away." Earlier in the day, in an interview published in the *Sun-Times*, his melancholy was national in scope. He said that the party not only in the East but throughout the country is in an advanced state of decay. Asked what he thought of its prospects for winning the November election, he told the *Sun-Times*, "Zero." This, however, is at variance with the view his own paper, the Chicago *Tribune*, took today. Its leading editorial described General Eisenhower as the candidate of Wall Street, Europe, President Truman, and Governor Dewey, characterizing the last as "the most unpopular figure in the Republican Party today," but it went on to say that the Democrats are so disorganized this year that Republican prospects "can be described as fairly bright." Confusion is everywhere. The *Tribune*, though, did not come out in favor of a Republican victory, and it is doubtful if its readers want one. In the advance editions of Sunday's paper, a Racine, Wisconsin, reader writes that he has been voting Republican since 1916, "but I will not vote for Eisenhewey. Phewey on Eisenhewey!" An Elmhurst, Illinois, patriot suggests that it would be better for patriots to "vote for neither side. Let us write on the ballot a name of our choice—any name—to indicate for all the world to see how many Americans remain loyal to the freedom of man and our Constitution." The gravity of the McCormick situation was acknowledged at a press conference this morning by Arthur E. Summerfield, a Chevrolet agent from Flint, Michigan, who has just become chairman of the Republican National Committee. Summerfield was asked if he had any plans for bringing McCormick and his followers into the campaign. He said it was a puzzlement and that he was "wide open to suggestion." He got no suggestions. Neverthless, he radiated confidence. He does not expect any critical number of Republicans to take the "Phewey on Eisenhewey" line. He anticipates victory.

The convention that closed last night followed the form charts almost as if fulfillment had been the intention of the delegates. The word from the convention touts who gathered at every arriving train last week was that Senator Taft couldn't possibly make it. The argument that he wasn't a winner had taken hold, it was said, and while the convention was destined to be long and sulphurously wordy, the nomination itself, assured for Eisenhower, would be speedy. This prognosis was shaken at times but never abandoned. It came closest to being abandoned last Sunday afternoon, when Senator Taft strode briskly into the exhibition hall in the Hilton basement bearing a large, tidy bundle of telegrams (some five hundred of them, as it turned out) which, he explained, were from delegates who had banded together in the Taft Delegates Club, a new organization whose first and only principle was to stay with Taft to the end. Taft flourished his bundle. He hefted it to show its bulk. He talked as though, in the face of this, opposition was ridiculous; a man with five hundred delegates, each of whom made it a matter of personal honor never to desert, could not possibly be beaten. It was a remarkable demonstration of the strength of this remarkable man; in fact, it was perhaps the most impressive display of personal strength made by any political leader in American history. (Considering the excellent standing that the principle of desertion enjoys in politics, the impressiveness of that display was borne out by the fact that two hundred and eighty members, or more than fifty per cent, of the club stayed with Taft after the end had been reached.) Still, it was felt, Taft could not hope to find a hundred additional delegates who would reject or be unmoved by the argument that Eisenhower could arouse the voters and that Taft could not. Moreover, being unable to increase his hard-core strength, Taft would lose the fight over contested delegations, with the result that some of the signers of telegrams would be en route for Texas, Louisiana, and Georgia by the time the first ballot was called. Though the Taft bloc, even when some of its members had been unseated, was of a size that should have enabled it to stop Eisenhower or at the very least to name the candidate for vice-president, it was felt that in this case it could not do either of these things. A serious attempt was made to head off Eisenhower with General MacArthur, but it came to nothing. It might have had more of a chance if MacArthur's appearance before the convention—an event that was vastly overprepared—had not been so disappointing to the delegates (he drew less applause than Herbert Hoover) and if the clamor for his nomination had not come from what was by far the gamiest collection of supernumeraries that could be assembled in a city of this size. In any case, the attempt got nowhere, and the common belief was that it had never had a chance of success. It had been apparent for almost a week that the majority of delegates accepted, with however much distaste, the results of the primaries and the private polls favoring Eisenhower and that in consequence Eisenhower's strength could only build up. It may be that the Taft people made some grievous mistakes. It may be that the public reaction to the televised hearings on the contested delegations affected the delegates as a whole and the temper of the entire convention, but the feeling one had here was that, come what may, Eisenhower was going to win the nomination because so many people had said he could win the election, and that seems to have been the case.

Nominating Dwight Eisenhower was an act of hard sacrifice and self-denial for most of the delegates here. It was clear from the time the first throngs began to gather in the lobby of the Hilton that a lot of them, including many who wore "I Like Ike" buttons the size of saucers, really didn't like the General at all and were supporting him only because they had been sold on the Taft-can't-win theory. There were some, to be sure, who truly admired the General and believed what they understood him to believe. But they were a minority, and an Eastern seaboard minority at that. They were easily outnumbered by the many who actively disliked Eisenhower and, as the week wore on, with Taft's defeat seeming more certainly certain every day, they became, paradoxically, less and less inhibited about saying so; they grumbled publicly over a fate that forced them to reward a man they regarded as a parvenu, an amateur, a boob, and a heretic of sorts and to destroy a man whose leadership they both acknowledged and enjoyed. But the dislike for Eisenhower at this convention was as nothing compared to the dislike for his associates and in particular the titular leader of the Republican Party, Governor Thomas E. Dewey of New York. There was no audible protest, no expression of shock or outrage, from anywhere but the inner circle of Eisenhower enthusiasts when, on Thursday afternoon—by which time it was apparent to everyone in Chicago that nothing, nothing at all, could save Taft—David S. Ingalls, the Senator's cousin and campaign manager, circulated one of the most extraordinary documents in Party history. It was a newspaper-size broadside that bore the heading.

SINK DEWEY!!

and read in part:

TOM DEWEY IS THE MOST COLD-BLOODED, RUTH-LESS, SELFISH POLITICAL BOSS IN THE UNITED STATES TODAY. He stops at nothing to enforce his will. His promises are worthless. He is the greatest menace that the Republican Party has. Twice he has led us down the road to defeat, and now he is trying the same trick again hidden behind the front of another man. [It was obviously so unsporting of him not to hide in front of the front.]

Behind Tom Dewey is the same old gang of Eastern Internationalists and Republican New Dealers who ganged up to sell the Republican Party down the river in 1940, in 1944, and in 1948. They are trying it again this year. . . .

Tom Dewey, his machine, and his cold-blooded, self-seeking ruthlessness have meant only sorrow and defeat to

the Republican Party. Until and unless Dewey and Dewey-
ism are crushed our party can never win and America can
never be made safe from the insidious efforts of the New
Dealers, whatever their party label, to take us down the road
to socialism and dictatorship.

Issued by
TAFT COMMITTEE
DAVID S. INGALLS
NATIONAL CHAIRMAN

In a convention at which demonstrations both of approval and
disapproval were mostly forced and flaccid, the demonstration
against Dewey during the credentials wrangle on Wednesday
night was marked by a monumental verve. Not even Senator
McCarthy's hoarse, ophidian mentions of Dean Acheson, in
what was undeniably the most effective piece of oratory at this
gathering, brought forth anything like the volume of catcalls
provoked by Senator Dirksen's reference to Dewey during the
floor debate over the contested delegation from Georgia, and the
booing when Dewey rose to announce New York's vote on that
question far outdid the cheers from the Eisenhower claque.
(The Governor, incidentally, seemed positively delighted by
every insult he received, flashing clean, toothy smiles that
seemed to say he was sure the Republic would some day honor
him for the enemies he was making that night.) And the anti-
Eisenhower and anti-Dewey sentiment was not wholly negative. Those who disliked Eisenhower, those who liked him but
not very much, and those who disliked what he appeared to
them to stand for but could not find it in their hearts to dislike
him as a human being felt, a great many of them, a deep and
genuine warmth for Robert Taft. They liked him as a man and
as a political combatant. They liked his record—particularly the
fact that it was long. They liked his looks, they liked his voice,
they liked his invalided wife. They liked him for the same reason that men everywhere like their old shoes and bedroom slip-

pers: he fitted, he was comfortable, he was so well broken in that it was no chore at all to put him on. They liked him for the things he said at Chicago. They liked him for sometimes carrying consistency to quixotic, impolitic lengths. In any event, he, Taft, was the man they liked, and there is not the least doubt that if they had felt free to follow their own impulses, they would have nominated Robert Taft by a resounding majority on the first ballot and would have worked their hearts out for him. Even in the New York delegation, where enthusiasm for Eisenhower was higher than in most, a good forty percent of the vote, in the view of well-informed members, would have gone to Taft if Dewey had not cracked down hard. (Mr. Ingalls, in his broadside, greatly overstated his case against Governor Dewey, but unquestionably Dewey's threat to wreck the political careers of the New York delegates who went against him—a threat attested to by at least a dozen honorable men and denied by none—was a bold and remorseless assertion of personal authority.) What was true in the New York was true in some degree of all the other delegations, with the possible exception of those from New England, who came to the convention with a formal majority for Eisenhower.

A man who seems to have typified the majority that carried Eisenhower to victory was a Nebraska delegate who was found in a chatty mood during one of the nominating speeches on Thursday night. He said he was the original Eisenhower supporter in Nebraska, a claim that would no doubt have been disputed by other Nebraskans on the floor that evening. At any rate, this particular Mr. Blank was an accredited delegate pledged to Eisenhower and revelling in the way things were going. When asked if it was truly his conviction that Eisenhower would make a better President than Taft, he said that while he thought it extremely important for the party to take advantage of the General's prestige among the American people, he could not in all conscience deny that Taft seemed to him a more capable man and a profounder student of public affairs; for himself, he said, he was forced to concede that he found Taft's outlook on life far more congenial than Eisenhower's. It was not, he went on, to be assumed even for a moment that he had anything against General Eisenhower or against his views insofar as he understood them; he was simply stating a personal opinion, and he supposed there was much to be said on the side of those many Republican voters who preferred Eisenhower and to whose wishes in the matter he was humbly deferring. Since the names of Taft and MacArthur had been frequently coupled in discussions here (at one point, there was even talk of a Taft-MacArthur ticket; early in the convention, George Sokolsky, the newspaper columnist, presented himself to many delegates to assure them that he had been authorized to give assurances of MacArthur's willingness to serve as Taft's Vice-President) Mr. Blank was asked if he felt about MacArthur as he did about Taft. He said he most certainly did, only more so. "I'm glad to have you ask me about that," he said. "The way I see it, General MacArthur is the third greatest statesman in the world today. I have it figured out—of course, this is only one man's idea of it—that Herbert Hoover is number one, Winston Churchill is number two, and Douglas MacArthur is number three. I haven't worked it out too much beyond that, but now that you bring it up, I guess I'd run Bob Taft right in after MacArthur, and there isn't any question about it, Eisenhower belongs somewhere right up close to Taft."

With the help of the Nebraskan and hundreds like him, Eisenhower was nominated. He won because it was said he could win. But the delegates were deeply galled by the very argument they accepted. They hated it because of what it implied about Bob Taft and the American people. They hated it because they hated its sources. They hated it because they found it humiliating. They hated themselves for accepting it. And to make matters far worse, they only half believed it. Exactly what, they kept asking the Eisenhower people, made anyone think that public-opinion polls were any more to be trusted now than in 1948? They were given for an answer some statistics showing that the polls hadn't been

so very far wrong back then, after all—a trifling matter of three
or four percent. Even allowing for that much margin of error in
the 1952 polls, the Eisenhower strategists said, Taft was licked
before he started. Very well then, the delegates replied, what evidence was there that Eisenhower—essentially another Willkie, another Dewey, in short another trimmer—could win? The polls at
this stage in 1948 showed Dewey way ahead, and still he lost.
They were told that while Eisenhower's election wouldn't be a
sure thing under the best of circumstances, he had a vastly better
chance than Taft would ever have; organization, hard work, spirit,
loyalty—these would carry Eisenhower over the top. But these
were precisely the gifts they were most reluctant to give Eisenhower, while they would willingly have given them to Taft, who
had earned them, who himself exemplified them, who would
appreciate them, who would know what they really meant, as
Eisenhower—an upstage type, in their view—might not.

For all of that, they accepted the hateful argument. Twenty
years is a long time to be out of office. Loyalty to the organization
was in the end more powerful than loyalty to an individual. Still,
it was a cruel world in which the two could not be combined.

In the unreal, schizophrenic world of the convention, though,
they could for a time be combined, and hugely enjoyed. The
stomping and shrieking for Senator McCarthy, the booing of Governor Dewey, the demonstration and, later, the reverent hush that
greeted Herbert Hoover's remarks—these were displays of basic
conviction that could be made while there was still time by people
who knew that in a few weeks they would be trumpeting the
news that the temper of the country had changed and that the
Republican Party, while proud of its grandeur and oldness, was
making the appropriate adaptations. It was a long, loving over-
the-shoulder look at the past by people moving into a future in
which they hoped to prosper in a material sense but in which
they knew, or thought they knew, that they would be cut off from
cherished associations. They were like emigrants about to sail for
richer shores but rueful, nevertheless, at the thought of departing

Napoli or County Kerry. This seemed to be their feeling about
the thing. Preparing to embrace Eisenhower, they poured contempt upon his friends; preparing to repudiate Taft, they embraced him. "My God, I love him," one said. "It kills me to have
to do this to him." This strange mood was heightened by the fact
that many of the delegates had known it before. It was the kind
of experience that ought to be unique—one ought to say goodbye
to a particular past only once in a lifetime—but wasn't. For what
has happened here is almost identical with what happened in
Philadelphia in 1948. Indeed, a good many convention veterans
say that the dislike of Eisenhower wasn't a patch on the dislike
of Dewey by those who nominated him four years ago. And twice
before that—in 1940, when Willkie became the candidate, and in
1944, when Dewey was given his first chance—these people had
resolved to catch up with the spirit of the times only to find that
it really didn't pay. For all they knew, as they moved along with
Eisenhower's nomination in the stockyards, they would find themselves going through the same dismal business again in 1956. It
was this prospect that made Senator Dirksen's gibe at Dewey one
of the most effective of the week. "We followed you before," he
wailed, his finger pointing straight at Dewey—the finger pointing
and at the same time limp, by way of emphasizing his weariness.
He stopped for an instant and let the finger, incomparably the
most articulate digit in the history of American oratory, do his
talking. Then when the crowd caught on, and the murmurs began
to mount to roars and anguished groans, he went on, "And you
took us down the road to defeat." It was then that the dam of
feeling burst. Much of that great reproach to Dewey was in fact
self-reproach. For what is feared here is not just that Eisenhower,
Lodge, Duff, and the ubiquitous Dewey will twist the Republican Party into an unsightly, unrecognizable thing but that there
won't even be any profit in letting them do so, and that for this
double tragedy everyone will bear his full measure of guilt.

The convention was rancorous, and it is safe to predict that the
Republican Party will be full of rancor for some time. Some people

here have said that from the point of view of holding the party together, the nomination and defeat of Taft would have been far less damaging than the nomination and victory of Eisenhower. The selection of Taft would at least have got him off the Republican conscience, where he is now bound to remain whether or not Eisenhower wins. As for the Senator himself, it cannot be said that he accepted defeat gracefully; it would have been out of character for him to do so. But he took it the best way he could, and just about everyone recognized that what he was taking was a great deal. For fourteen years now, he has provided his party with forceful leadership and has been one of the few men of genuine substance in Washington politics. Though he will try to adjust himself to Eisenhower's leadership, it cannot be easy for a man of his partisan zeal to take kindly to the idea of losing the prize he has sought so long and so often to a man who up to a couple of months ago had people wondering whether he was a Republican or a Democrat or neither. And to lose, as Taft feels he did, because of the votes of some Southerners who, even if they are now bona-fide Republicans, are extremely green ones, can only add to the blackness of his mood. His followers may have brought defeat on themselves, and he may have given them a helping hand now and then, but in the view of many people who are not, and never would be, counted among his followers, he was a better man by far than any of those in his camp, and even people who think he did not deserve to win have the feeling that his career somehow merited a better climax than the one to which it has now come.

As a production, the convention differed only in minor ways from the conventions of the past. In keeping with the spirit of the times, it set new records for color presentations and pledges of allegiance to the flag. These perhaps comprised its chief distinction as a spectacle. There are claims, as yet unauthenticated, that it was the most musical convention on record and that it was graced by more movie people than any other. Next to Governor Fine, of Pennsylvania, Cecil B. DeMille was the biggest social catch of the week, and many delegates, and even alternates, will treasure among their memories clasping his hand and hearing him say, "*This* is the greatest show on earth." DeMille apparently had no part in staging the convention. It had been widely expected that television would bring about new and interesting changes in the ancient rituals. It was prophesied, for example, that demonstrations for candidates would be staged for the viewing, rather than the reading, public. In the past, the single object of the convention demonstration was to keep going, in order to impress upon newspaper readers that the ardor of X's supporters was greater than that of Y's by so many minutes and so many seconds. Since it seemed unreasonable to think that the prolonged waving of banners reading "BRONXVILLE, NEW YORK, FOR EISENHOWER" would enchant the television audience, it was argued by some Republicans that floor demonstrations might be re-examined, with the idea of making visual attractiveness, rather than mere endurance, the first criterion. But this was not to be. The demonstrations were as they have always been, and so was just about everything else. The only concessions to the new medium—aside, of course, from granting permission for the televising of the credentials-committee hearings—were the use of the International Amphitheatre, instead of Chicago Stadium, and the introduction of the "teleprompter," or "idiot board," on the lectern. The amphitheatre was rented because the television people, for some reason, found it better adapted to their purposes. When the decision to use it was reached, a firm of Chicago architects drew up a plan that called for putting the platform in one corner of the auditorium and arranging seats on the diagonal. The advantage of the corner platform, it was thought, was that it would prevent Western Union messengers, reporters, Pepsi Cola fetchers, and minor functionaries from forming a constantly moving background to pictures of the speaker. Having the seats on the diagonal was incidental to the corner-platform plan, but it was argued as an extra point in its favor that it would lead to more interesting patterns on the screen. The plan had several other reasonable-sounding features, but it was turned down. It may be that the Democrats, now well along with their planning, will adopt parts of it, but this is considered unlikely. Meanwhile, the one sure thing is that another convention is headed this way. There is said to be a growing market among local people for lapel buttons that read "I've Had It!"

4 Republican Campaign

Letter from Minneapolis

September 6, 1952

The Eisenhower campaign is easily the boldest and most militant of all Republican efforts to recapture the power the party lost twenty years ago. The 1952 impeachments are harder, the promises more magniloquent, and the endearments showered on the voters more endearing than at any other time within recent memory. When General Eisenhower takes out after "wickedness in government," and he is almost certainly the only candidate in this century capable of using such a phrase, he is not satisfied with half measures. During this Republican campaign, more ground is being covered and more money is being spent than during any previous one. The South has been invaded once and will be invaded again, in early October, and there are sensational reports making the rounds that the candidate will find time to drop in on Maine, New Hampshire, and Vermont, states that have been treated to a political neglect as humiliating and as prolonged as that suffered by Arkansas and South Carolina. It is also reported that a radio-and-television advertising program unequaled in cost and intensity even by those of the detergent titans is in the offing.

Whether all this militancy, mileage, and money will carry the day is, of course, quite another question, and one on which ap-

praisals are exceedingly hard to come by. Most of the people now
traveling with the General, in both the journalistic and the political sections of his entourage, are veterans of 1948, and no aspect
of their behavior is more affecting than the constancy with which
they adhere to certain vows concerning prophecy taken in the
early hours of November 2nd of that year. Some things, however,
are matters not of opinion or of mind-reading but of simple nose-
counting. The desire to see General Eisenhower is shared by a
great many more Americans than desired, or in any event fulfilled
the desire, to see President Truman or Governor Dewey in 1948.
Early this week in the South, and late this week in the Middle
West, he was seen and rousingly cheered by throngs that local
police and newspapermen claimed were larger than any that had
ever before turned out in their communities for anyone. In this
last region, the largest turnout was the one for his drive through
this city and St. Paul. Even making a fairly generous discount of
the police estimate of three hundred thousand, the Republican
candidate was undoubtedly seen by a third of the total population of the two cities—which are, incidentally, predominantly
Democratic.

Americans in large numbers enjoy seeing and cheering General
Eisenhower, and many of them will go to astonishing and sometimes perilous lengths to get a good look. It is not uncommon for
people to risk injury from rotten branches and high tension wires,
and three times during the tour of Minneapolis and St. Paul, the
crowds broke through the police cordons, forcing the motorcade
to stop. In one city, the disorder was such that the General's body-
guard, a hulking man well versed in running interference, got
separated from his charge and had to rejoin him much later by
taxicab. All these demonstrations have been heartening to the
members of the candidate's staff and have persuaded them of the
good will his countrymen bear him. They are frank to admit,
though, that the public's eagerness to see him does not necessarily
match its eagerness to hear him and to receive his message. The
crowds that come out to watch him ride through their towns are

unfailingly impressive, but those that show up to lend an ear when he pleads for their assistance in unhorsing the Democrats are often rather thin. The General's managers have more than once had the distressing experience of riding through a town whose jammed streets and clangorous air have aroused glowing expectations of masses of enfranchised citizens clustered around the rostrum at the end of the route, only to find, when they got there, that the crowd was still back on the streets, cheering from the curbstones, the roofs, and the treetop perches. Very often, the gathering at the appointed meeting place falls conspicuously short of filling it; in Tampa, for example, which is a city of a hundred and twenty-five thousand and which gave the candidate a big welcome as he drove through it, the Eisenhower rally failed to fill even the grandstands in a stadium that, including the bleachers, accommodates about five thousand.

An easy reading of these disparities would be that the crowds in the streets are honoring the man who once succored all of free humanity and are neglecting to honor the party politician. This may actually be the case, but most of those with the General do not accept this view. It could perfectly well be that he is being honored in both roles by those who merely watch him and salute him as he passes by. It would be an entirely reasonable compromise with the electronic age for a citizen to get his first-hand look at greatness as it rides along the streets of his town and then repair to some quiet, comfortable place to learn, by radio or television, what greatness has to say. Because of radio and television, attendance at political rallies has fallen off sharply in recent years, but a small crowd can as logically be taken to show that there has been an organizational failure to rout out the faithful as that the faithful are few in number. In any case, what has been clear right along on this trip is that whether or not the candidate now has all the political support he seeks, his reputation hasn't suffered from his entry into politics. He has quite a foundation on which to build.

Eisenhower, though vigorous and hard-working, is, perhaps because of his greenness in politics, an extremely uneven performer. There are times when his indignation, which is the emotional keynote of his campaign, seems real and powerful and times when it seems contrived, exaggerated, and glaringly at odds with his true nature. There are times when he and his crowds reach impressive heights of buoyancy and fervor and times when the atmosphere is leaden. Strangely, these extremes can be reached without any change of message by the candidate. His now-famous "egg lecture" can elevate one crowd and leave another unmoved. (The "egg lecture" is one in which the candidate exhibits his horror at the thought that on a single chicken egg—a product of nature to which no government, as he sees it, made any sort of contribution —no less than a hundred different taxes may be levied. This seems a shameful fact to him, a fact which in and of itself proves that it is past time for a change, and he has dwelt on it in town after town.) The problem of striking a balance, of achieving consistency of performance and response is one to which the Eisenhower strategists have already addressed themselves. On the swing through the South, they arrived at the belief that the way to achieve spontaneity and verve was to have the candidate improvise his speeches. They felt that while Eisenhower, speaking extemporaneously, might not give as pointed and lucid an account of current Republican doctrine as he would when reading a speech assembled by careful students of the doctrine and elegantly laminated by Dr. Stanley High—the versatile theologian and *Reader's Digest* editor who heads up the belles-lettres division for the General, a job he formerly performed for Franklin D. Roosevelt and Thomas E. Dewey—he would project far more vigor and conviction if he put things in his own words and spoke in his own rhythms. Though this seemed too simple an analysis (if only because the talks the General delivered without text were very often recitations from memory of pieces the writers had composed for earlier occasions —a form of political address described by one Southern newspaper as "semi-off-the-cuff"), it is unquestionably true that as a rule Eisenhower, like most men, is better served by his own words than by those that others put into his mouth. Indeed, he is some-times very well served by his own language, which can be grace-ful in spirit even when its cadences jar and its syntax is irregular, and he has often been rather poorly served by Dr. High. Although Dr. High is in many ways a gifted craftsman, his *Reader's Digest* prose, a splendid instrument for dispelling the complexities of life and for making the most of whatever stray beams of light can be found in the encircling gloom, somehow never seems quite the right instrument for the elucidation of the prickly questions that the General is called upon to deal with. When Eisenhower is im-provising, he can occasionally put across, even to large audiences, a vivid sense of the blend of plasticity and firmness that has always been said to characterize his personality and to have been such a valuable asset to American diplomacy over the past decade.

There was a striking example of this in Chicago a while back. The General was addressing a meeting of the Republican precinct captains of Cook County; this is an aggregation of several hun-dred men and women whose interest in ideas will never amount to an ungovernable passion but who have a makeshift philosophy distilled from the news and editorial columns of the Chicago *Tribune*. With few exceptions—perhaps with none—they had keenly supported Senator Taft before the convention, and right afterward many of them, along with Colonel McCormick himself, had expressed the view that Eisenhower would be no improve-ment at all over President Truman and might even subvert Amer-ican institutions more speedily and aggressively than Governor Stevenson would. Despite these misgivings, they had come to be-lieve that in the interests of the rest of the ticket, if not in the higher interests of the party, it was necessary to go to work for the candidate, and they had gathered in Orchestra Hall to meet him and demonstrate their newly acquired enthusiasm. This was not one of the quieter Eisenhower audiences. The building shook with shouts of "We want Ike!" as a few months before it might have shaken with shouts of "We want Taft!" In the middle of his speech, the General shattered precedent by acknowledging his awareness that his audience had never found him an enchanting figure, and still did not find him one. He said he realized full well that Senator Taft—"your great Senator Taft," he called him—had been their first choice and that he, Eisenhower, was coming before them as a very poor substitute. This simple statement of manifest truth was greeted with cries of "No! No! No!" from all over the hall—cries that proved, as the inevitable switch of delegations to a convention winner also proves, that Russian politicians are not the only ones who like to deny and destroy evidence of past heresy. The General would have none of it. Raising both arms and signaling for a becoming silence, he put a stop to the shameful performance and then delivered a rather stirring impromptu discourse on the nature and value of loyalty. He urged them to keep faith with their lost causes and their defeated leaders as long as they continued to believe that the causes and leaders had been honorable, and he explained to them, in less polished but also less unctuous language than Polonius used in saying the same thing to Laertes, that enduring human agreements can be made only by those who do not indulge in self-deception. Stunned, they listened quietly to the rest of the talk and made no further efforts to tell the General he was their beau ideal of a candidate. Undoubtedly he still is not, but he was a lot closer to it when he finished than when he first appeared before them. He made them respect him, and it is conceivable that his blow for candor brought an end to Republican disaffection in a pivotal state. At the very least, a whole new moral frontier was opened up when the idea of political candor was well received by Chicago precinct captains.

That was a rare moment in the Eisenhower campaign; in fact, it was the only one so far when the General's personality, as one apprehends it from the history of the last ten years, seemed an operative part of his equipment as a politician. His nice-chap side comes through, of course, when he is greeting a crowd and exchanging grins for huzzas, but in spite of the fact that the esteem in which he is held by most Americans is based on his approach to people rather than on his approach to farm parity (after all, it was not until a few short weeks ago that anyone had the faintest notion of what his approach to farm parity might be, or even if he had an approach), he now gives the impression of being grimly determined to be a politician and, as such, to stick to political matters. It may be that some form of military asceticism, hitherto obscure in his nature, leads him to disparage the role of personality and to disapprove of exploiting it, or it may be that the qualities he is said to have displayed in welding together the armies of the West are essentially diplomatic ones and cannot be put on display in the ballparks, courthouse squares, and hotel banquet halls to which his new calling takes him.

At all odds, he appears in these unfamiliar places not as a man of unusual and distinctive personal attributes but as a Republican drummer, and in that role he is sometimes vibrant, sometimes almost listless. The chief variable is not the authorship of the speeches but the candidate's morale. As a campaigner, the General is a creature of moods, and his mood always seems to derive directly from that of the crowd he is facing. Whenever it becomes plain early in the confrontation that his audience is as scandalized as he is by reports of mendacity and worse in the federal government, he warms up fast, speaks fluently, and increases the crowd's and his own anger as he goes along. It has been said that he and his advisers settled on the issue of corruption and slovenly administration—he clearly means the second as well as the first when he speaks of "the mess in Washington"—because they discovered that it pays off so handsomely in all sections of the country, but this appears to be only part of the truth, if that. The issues of corruption and dereliction of duty have an enormous, almost overriding appeal to Eisenhower himself. He can treat a problem like finance rather casually—at one meeting he said he thought we could get "a sound money" by proper use of "the Federal Reserve Bank and all that stuff"—but he tenses up when he speaks of corruption. Evidently, no living thing is quite so low and verminous in his sight as the crooked tax collector. Eisenhower may be aware from his reading of history—a fairly specialized reading, by all accounts—that the crooked tax collector has plagued civilization since taxes were invented, but he sees no excuse for continued complacency about the fact. He is deeply affronted by the instances of fraud and bribery in the Bureau of Internal Revenue brought to light by Senator Williams, of Delaware, by whom he was given a speedy briefing on recent outrages just before he left on the Southern trip. But Eisenhower has been able to convey his sense of indignation only when the audience he is addressing has been entirely responsive. Thus, he aroused a Miami audience with a powerful sermon on corruption and sloth, and left a Little Rock gathering fairly cold with almost the same message, because, implausible as it may seem, Miami was clearly more inspirited by the prospect of putting an end to wrongdoing than the Arkansas yeomanry, who didn't respond too well to the discussion of any political issues. The Little Rock gathering showed a certain gratitude when Eisenhower paid an agreeable tribute to General MacArthur, who was born in their city, in a building, now a shrine, to which Eisenhower made a brief pilgrimage before delivering his address in MacArthur Park. But there was no real ardor, and in consequence the speech seemed flat compared to the one in Miami, and the meeting profitless. And so it was most of the way along. Eisenhower became what his crowds were—not, to be sure, in the demagogic sense of taking on their political coloration but in the sense of meeting their pitch of enthusiasm, whatever it happened to be.

Traveling with a candidate, one tends to see a campaign as simply the sum of all the speeches made and all the crowds encountered. Actually, of course, the effect of a speech on a particular crowd, and the effect of the crowd on the speaker, can weigh scarcely at all in the final balance. In the long run, a matter of considerably greater substance than Eisenhower's technique as a campaigner is his approach to the problems of party leadership that have been thrust upon him. One gathers that in the country as a whole no aspect of his political career is being more widely and hotly discussed than the entente cordiale he has sought and reached with those groups that take their leadership from Senator Taft and from such of Taft's associates as Senators Jenner, Mc-Carthy, Dirksen, and Cain. Naturally, this important development has also been the subject of a good deal of talk in the General's entourage, but it was received here not only with less surprise but also with less disapprobation than is being expressed in certain sections of the press and among some of the General's more high-minded admirers. Of surprise, indeed, there was almost none. For several weeks, the question had been not whether there would be a reconciliation but how soon it would be held and on what terms. Eisenhower himself, according to those who have served on his staff throughout the summer, has been figuring it since shortly after the convention. Before the convention, it is true, he had thought of himself not as a partner of Senator Taft's but as something of an antagonist. To a group of reporters in Denver last month, he said that he would have neither worked for nor accepted the Republican nomination if he had not believed that it was very much in the national interest to prevent the Taft forces from controlling the Republican Party and imposing upon it what he regarded, and doubtless still regards, as their mischievous notions of foreign policy. In those days, also, he talked a lot about his eagerness to pull the rug from under Senator McCarthy. But the General is well known for having some kind of precognitive faculty that advises him when the time for compromise is at hand, and before very long he saw that although his nomination had been a smashing defeat for McCarthy, Jenner, and the rest, it had in no sense shaken their hold upon the Republican organization in their home states, a fact strikingly affirmed by the primary vote in Wisconsin. Nor, for that matter, had it substantially reduced their power in the National Committee, whose new chairman, Arthur Summerfield, of Michigan, is by temperament and solid conviction a Taft man in spite of the fact that at the convention he was one of those who felt the party would have a brighter future with Eisenhower. What Eisenhower and most of those around him began to sense soon after the convention was that to continue to snub the Taft and McCarthy factions would be to run the risk of losing several states in November. (Since Dewey ran well ahead of most of the Taft men on the ticket in 1948, there was also a case, strongly urged on Eisenhower, for disassociating himself even further from them. But while this might have ingratiated him with independents, it would have hurt him with the Party organizations, and by most calculations the organizations are still the more worthwhile allies in a hard fight.) According to members of the General's staff, he was moved not by any feeling of deep need for the benediction of his former antagonists but rather by his desire for the cooperation of the precinct level workers in their states, and he set about getting this by the most direct means.

Whether Eisenhower, in coming to terms, has abandoned anything vital in policy has not been established in any of the statements issued so far. It is denied on all sides that he has made any binding commitments on Cabinet appointments, but it seems fairly certain that the very spirit of the agreement would call, at least during the early days of an Eisenhower administration, for a balance between the two wings. The General's immense debt to the Dewey-Lodge branch of the party will, obviously, have to be discharged in some tangible fashion, but the likelihood is that Eisenhower will increasingly have to cast about for people associated with neither of the rival factions and representing a point of view somewhere in between them. He has already done some of this in making up his staff, which, though it continues to be headed by Governor Adams, of New Hampshire, who has the look of a Lodge-Dewey man, is really characterized by men like Senators Carlson, of Kansas, and Seaton, of Nebraska, who may be partisan to one side or the other but aren't definitely known to be. The trouble is that these people aren't definitely known to be anything, and the further trouble is that there probably aren't very many of them.

The Eisenhower party will shortly be off by rail on a whistle-stop tour through the North Central states. This part of the campaign will last a comparatively short time, and it would appear that by the time another presidential year comes around, the railroad will be obsolete. (In a report from Stevenson headquarters it was announced that he will probably make only one or two train trips during this campaign.) By 1956, even the airplane may be outmoded, for if campaigning is chiefly a matter of getting the candidate seen and heard by the voters, then television is the answer. Clearly, in a country this size it is impossible for one man, no matter what kind of transportation he uses, to be seen in the flesh by more than a tiny fraction of the electorate. When television blankets the country, however, just about everyone will be able to form a visual impression of the men running for the presidency. Once that comes to pass, a "front-porch campaign" will not necessarily be synonymous with dignity or inactivity. For a time, unquestionably, candidates will continue to honor the antique customs of the country by traveling about and meeting with some of the people they hope to govern, but for such traveling they will sensibly use airplanes. It is true that the airplane lacks one great advantage of the Pullman: it makes it impracticable for committees of local politicians to accompany the candidate across their states and, by their association with him, increase their local prestige, strengthen their egos, and stiffen their resolution to get out the vote. Not even the largest commercial transport plane can accommodate both a candidate's staff and a committee of average size (and political committees are almost always of more than average size), and even if it could, it would, at normal cruising speed, be two or three states beyond the one that counted by the time the man of the hour had managed a handshake and a word of greeting for each of his guests. But this is a trivial disadvantage, and the Eisenhower people had scarcely encountered it before they came up with a satisfactory solution to it. By using only a small part of the time saved by air travel, the candidate can stay long enough in the large cities of each important state to meet and greet the local party workers over cocktails or fricasseed chicken at a reception of some sort. Eisenhower has done this time and again recently, and, so far as is known, there have not been any complaints about the fact that the meeting place was stationary.

The airplane and, eventually, television may help make the sales technique of American politics as up-to-date as those of industry and commerce, but in bringing about an end to railroad campaigning they are destroying an established, if not always edifying, art form. The back platform meeting, as it has developed over the years, has become a highly stylized type of entertainment. To violate its prescribed routine—to have, for example, the local beauty hand over the asparagus in between the appearances of the county coroner and the candidate for the assembly—would be as esthetically degenerate as it would be to put the acrobats in the wrong spot in a variety program. Several attempts have been made in the course of the Eisenhower campaign to adapt the old ritual to the air age, but they have invariably failed. The fault lies not with the campaign managers but with the nature of the materials. The rear platform is a natural stage, and if the railroad yard is not the pleasantest of places in which to hold a rally, it has certain attractions that an airport lacks. In most towns, it is easily accessible; its associations are all familiar ones; its dimensions are on a suitably human scale; its lighting by night is not only dramatic but warm. Almost nothing about an airport is right for political showmanship. When the local Eisenhower campaign committees attempted to hold airport meetings on the Southern trip and to conduct the usual back platform ceremonies on the ramp, almost everything went wrong. Safety regulations made it necessary to keep the crowd behind the wire fences, where it could not hear the exchange of greetings on the ramp or even see who was greeting whom. The din of airport activity was so great that almost nothing of any sort could be heard. In Birmingham, a large bag of Jim Dandy Hominy Grits, presented to the candidate by Miss Hominy Grits, appeared to the average onlooker so diminutive a gift as to be almost insulting. After a few other unhappy experiments in Florida and Arkansas, the whole idea of airport ceremonies was given up as a bad job.

The passing of the whistle-stop ceremony would be no cause for regret if it were not that it seems to be about the only phase of mobile campaigning that has anything at all to recommend it. Most of those who have been observing the Eisenhower campaign from close quarters, however—and, one imagines, most of those who have been taking part in it—look forward fervently to the day when everything will be done electronically.

5 Election

Letter from Washington

November 6, 1952

Washington has reacted to the news with what one takes to be the same proportions of surprise, delight, and dismay that are being felt and expressed elsewhere. Whatever the sentiments were that led the sovereign electorate to issue so clear and insistent a call for General Eisenhower, they seem to have been about as strong in one place as in another, and although this is in many ways not a typical community, it was right in the swim on Tuesday. The three hundred thousand or so who were able to vote, either because they live in enfranchised Maryland or Virginia suburbs or because they qualified for absentee ballots, seem to have divided very nearly as the rest of the country did. Civil servants may have many of the faults commonly attributed to them, but the theory that in this country they are meek, frightened defenders of any powers that be seems badly in need of revision. The vote in the four counties surrounding Washington, areas dominated politically by people on the federal payroll, was a trifle more heavily on the Republican side than the national vote, and a good many bureaucrats and sub-bureaucrats joined with sworn enemies of their breed in shouting themselves hoarse as they watched the scoreboards at the Republican victory celebration in the Hotel Statler ballroom on Tuesday evening. The President-elect enjoys as much good will among those who are shortly to be his subordinates as he does in the country at large.

In the relatively small group that must read the returns as a vote of no-confidence, there was, of course, shock and dejection. Several members of this group attended a victory celebration at the Mayflower. The Statler is Republican, the Mayflower Democratic, at least by the test of usage. The Mayflower ball turned into a wake, and there was an odd historic aspect to this, since four years ago the Democratic wake had turned into a ball, while with the Republicans it was vice versa. In 1948, the Democratic National Committee was so impressed with the portents of disaster, in the form of polls, that it decided to begin the lean years with sharp economies. It did not reserve the Mayflower ballroom. Instead, it arranged for a small gathering of the mournful in the committee offices. So depressed was the committee staff by its anticipation of the news that it did not plug in a radio. In fact, there was no radio in the place; Democratic ears would not that night be assaulted by the disagreeable noises. It was not till well along in the evening that a late arrival who had not been able to avoid broadcasts came in with the word that Truman wasn't doing so badly—ahead in several states, though of course the farmers were yet to be heard from. Someone thought a radio might not be a bad idea; might as well have a final laugh or two. A radio was found. Meanwhile the solid Statler walls were crumbling. Republican matrons were eating their corsages, Republican gentlemen were wilting their collars with nervous perspiration.

Everything changes. In the past forty-eight hours, though, the misery of some of the Mayflower revellers has been somewhat relieved by an anticipation of the pleasures and rewards of opposition, a political term meaning freedom from responsibility. Among policy-making officials in the branches of government that have borne the brunt of the Republican attack—the White House, the State Department, and the Defense Department—by far the commonest observation is that it may be great fun to belong to a party out of power, an experience that few of the leaders of the present administration, and few of their supporters in Congress, have ever known. To be sure, the people in the executive branch realize that it will be quite a while before they will be allowed to sit back and enjoy themselves in this role. Not only must they get through the next two months but many of them know that they will be in for some harrowing experiences in the period immediately following the inauguration. (The inaugural ball and other festivities, incidentally, will be financed with money put up by merchants for the inauguration of Governor Dewey in 1948 and left to gather interest in the meanwhile.) For there is no question but that the new government, which will not lack advertising talent, will want the country to look hard and long at some before-and-after layouts. There is certain to be a spate of congressional investigations—Senator McCarthy is in line to chair the Government Operations Committee, and he has always been interested in government operations—featuring the misdeeds of the Democratic administration. How long these go on will depend on how long the newspapers can be kept interested. Those who know the newspapers say that will be a pretty long time. But investigations will come to an end sooner or later, and some, at least, of the victims will then be able to establish themselves as critics, and even, perhaps, perform a useful public service thereby. It is in any case a prospect that a number of them find consoling in the lame-duck phase of their careers.

It has struck some people here that the President-elect, with a six-million majority and with a hundred and seventy-six electoral votes to spare, is in a position to be the most independent magistrate in recent history. He could have won without the aid of any of the fractional groups—the disaffected Southern Democrats, for example, or the nearly disaffected McCormick Republicans—who offered him their votes as if they were pearls of great price and who have already begun to clamor for his favors. It was a personal victory of unparalleled magnitude—so great, indeed, as to free him from his entire party, since it is apparent from the heavy vote for Democratic congressional candidates that he could have won as the candidate of either party or possibly of neither. Four years ago, when he was less well acquainted with the political system than he is now, he told his admirers that he would consider accepting the nomination of one party only if he could be assured of also getting that of the other. In a sense, he has achieved or created the kind of support he then talked about, and he can be liberated by it. As long as he retains anything like his present prestige, he can probably arrange for the eventual retirement of any congressman whose presence in Washington he considers a hindrance to his administration.

This is not to say that sooner or later he won't encounter formidable congressional opposition. He undoubtedly will. But for as long as he stands on the heights of public acclaim, he can put together clear majorities in Congress from both parties. Indeed, for the duration of the incoming Eighty-third Congress he will have to get his majorities that way, since the Senate is closely balanced.

Looking further ahead, most people feel that when the honeymoon does come to an end, General Eisenhower will discover that he must hold on to a considerable bloc of Democrats—including Northern ones—in order to get the things he wants. It is pointed out that even though Republicans like Senators McCarthy and Jenner now owe their political existence to the General, a time will come when they will find their existence as members of a going concern to be intolerable. These men are born oppositionists; they can make use of their peculiar talents only when they can take the offensive, and eventually, it is thought, they will have to break with Eisenhower, for whom as an individual, they have never had much regard. When the press is no longer interested in exploring the depths of Secretary Acheson's degradation, Mc-

Carthy will have to seek fresh prey. He could find it, no doubt, somewhere outside the government—in education, perhaps, or in the press itself. But the dramatic possibilities in these fields are scarcely worthy of his talents. It seems to those here who have observed the whole course of McCarthy's career and the careers of such associates of his as Senators Jenner and Welker that these men will ultimately have to take on Eisenhower himself, who stands for so many things they despise, and discover that his administration is riddled with subversives. It would be a risky business for them, to be sure, for they would doubtless be disowned by the responsible leaders of the party, but they can afford rebukes from high places more easily than they can afford going off the offensive. The feeling now is that while they may ride high in the early days of the new Congress, their days under an Eisenhower administration are limited. They could and would have made life wretched for Adlai Stevenson—a number of people, during the campaign, ventured the opinion that McCarthy, alone with himself in a voting booth, would vote for the Democratic candidate—but in a Republican administration they will, eventually, have no function. When they finally break, the struggle may be a hard and ugly one, but no one here has much doubt about who will win it. Even without any great amount of party support, McCarthy may be an effective operator. But he will have to do his effective operating, it is felt, somewhere else.

In general, the long-range trend of the Eisenhower administration must of necessity be away from the Taft wing as well as away from the McCarthy wing. In domestic affairs, Eisenhower himself appears to have few differences with Senator Taft and even to be a bit to the Senator's right on some questions. But the pressures will mostly be from the other direction, for although Eisenhower's triumph was a personal one, it was accompanied by a vote for congressional candidates that suggests no revolution or deep change in American beliefs about the structure of American society. In this respect, General Eisenhower is likely to share some of the experiences of President Truman, who will be leaving office with a set of views rather different from the set he brought to it. The country clearly saw its own image in General Eisenhower, and all the logic of history suggests that he will conform to that image.

6 John Foster Dulles

November 11, 1952

The late Wendell Willkie, ruefully eying the shards of his political career in the closing months of his life, often said that he owed his misfortunes to a dead diplomat named John W. Foster. Foster does not have a large place in history. He served eight months as Benjamin Harrison's Secretary of State, having been chosen as a stopgap replacement for James G. Blaine, who had resigned to have a final whack at the presidency. It was Willkie's half-facetious, half-serious contention that if Foster had never attained his brief eminence, his grandson, John Foster Dulles, would never have become inflamed with the desire to fill the office himself, in which event he would not have dedicated himself to the political advancement of Thomas E. Dewey. It amused and perhaps comforted Willkie to speak of his nemesis as a mere invention of Dulles's, the political agent, so to speak, of the firm of Sullivan & Cromwell, of which Dulles, until 1949, was the head. Perhaps, too, the interpretation of the political struggle as a contest between Wall Street firms helped to bring it all into perspective for Willkie.

Defective on the face of it, Willkie's theory nevertheless throws a certain light on Dulles's career. Dulles himself has often borne witness to the ancestral pull, exercised not only through direct lineage but through a connection by marriage with Robert Lansing,

Woodrow Wilson's Secretary of State. He has said, for example, that after the Bible and Shakespeare, his grandfather's *Diplomatic Memoirs,* in two volumes, is the work to which he most often returns. Since the Bible and Shakespeare invariably have an honorific status in inventories of this sort, the tribute to *Diplomatic Memoirs* is a remarkable one. Grandfather Foster plays a large part in Dulles's intellectual and esthetic life. Dulles's favorite work of graphic art is a Japanese chromo in which Foster is shown declaiming in the presence of ten attentive, admiring Orientals, participants in the Shimonoseki peace conference of 1895; the then ex-Secretary had been hired by the Chinese, badly thrashed by Japan in a war on Korea's dark and bloody ground, to get them the best deal possible. "He was called," his grandson has explained, "not just because of his individual qualities but because he partook of the great quality which possessed our nation at the time." At Shimonoseki, the Chinese were obliged to surrender Korea and Formosa to the Japanese. It was not Foster's only venture in Pacific diplomacy. As Secretary of State, he had drafted a treaty of annexation with Hawaii; it would have been ratified if the Democrats hadn't got back in office and thrown it out. In 1907, he was once more retained by the Chinese, this time to lead their delegation to the second Hague conference; his grandson, then nineteen and a Princeton sophomore, went along and became secretary to the delegation.

Later, in the Wilson administration, Dulles was recommended for a series of diplomatic odd jobs by Robert Lansing. When he talks of this rich background in affairs of state, he somehow conveys the feeling that history itself would be displeased by the republic's failure to take advantage of it. "Dulles was trained for diplomacy as Nijinsky was for the ballet," one biographer has written. After an interview in 1944, Forrest Davis made a remarkably bold argument in Dulles's behalf. "Seldom," he wrote, "has an American been so conditioned, groomed, and schooled for public service. In fact, we must go back to the early Adamses for a true precedent." Clearly, no precedent or even parallel could be found in such upstart houses as those of Roosevelt, Lodge, Harrison, Taft, LaFollette, Stevenson, or MacArthur.

It was, in any case, a fond destiny and one mindful of tradition and legitimate tribal pride that so arranged events as to make it possible for Dulles to be the architect of a great peace in the Pacific last year. For Fosters and for Dulleses, the Japanese treaty must have been an observance, a fulfillment. For the architect himself, it was doubtless a great stone in the edifice, one to be set alongside his service as senior adviser to the American delegation at the San Francisco conference and his participation in United Nations Assemblies. Still, the edifice was incomplete: he had not become Secretary of State. His hopes have risen quadriennially since 1940 and quadriennially been dashed. Dulles was not Dewey's inventor, as Wendell Willkie's wayward fancy had it, but he was for many years Dewey's influential friend, his preceptor, and patient guide to the world that lay beyond the numbers rackets, the vice syndicates, and the Court of General Sessions, while at the same time Dewey was Dulles's most influential friend, his leading promoter, and his preceptor and guide in the practical business of achieving in politics the ends that both sought. In a way, each was the patron of the other; like Johnson and Boswell, they were indispensable to each other's celebrity. Dulles would for a certainty have been Dewey's Secretary of State. Well before Dulles's recent triumphs, Dewey was settled in the opinion that Dulles was "the world's greatest statesman." Why Dewey did not step aside and recommend Dulles, instead of himself, for the presidency he never explained. Surely, "the world's greatest statesman" deserves the world's greatest job—and surely the world's greatest job should be graced by "the world's greatest statesman," when he is of the right nationality and has the proper requirements of birth, age, and party.

Dulles has never voiced any sense of injustice over this. He has, however, conveyed a sense of history being cheated by his own hopes deferred. Up to Election Day of 1948, he has written, many diplomats

> had expected that I would be increasingly responsible after that date for United States foreign policy under the direction of a Republican President-elect. As it was, November 3, 1948, found me merely a member of a party that had been defeated at the polls and would have no chance to reverse that verdict for four years. Both Mr. Vishinsky, the head of the Soviet delegation [to the United Nations], and Mr. Katz-Suchy, head of the Polish delegation gloated at meetings of the United Nations Assembly. They suggested that instead of being Secretary of State, I should now be going back to the private practice of law. . . . My influence and prestige, which had been high, had sunk to a low point. I had, indeed, serious doubt as to whether I could usefully continue to carry responsibility in the United Nations, for the very heavy tasks which had been assigned to me up to that time. I so indicated to General Marshall.
>
> Secretary Marshall was then himself about to return to the United States. He had been unwell, and there was pressing need for him to have a major operation. . . . That would leave the delegation without a chairman.
>
> Then, on November 18, President Truman designated me to be Acting Chairman of the United States Delegation. . . . [This] action . . . immediately restored my waning prestige and enabled me to carry to a successful conclusion the various matters that I was already charged with and to assume others in the absence of Secretary Marshall and Ambassador Austin, who, on account of illness, had also returned to the United States.

But the capstone was still missing. It has not been finally established that Eisenhower sees Dulles quite as Dewey does. But there is a widespread feeling that Dulles is out front at the moment. He will probably become Eisenhower's Secretary of State. Still honored by Dewey and by the other Eastern Republicans with whom he is generally identified, he is, thanks to his neutrality before and during the convention and to his author-

ship of the foreign-policy section of the 1952 Republican platform, one of the few members of the Eastern group whose
presence in the Cabinet would give no offense, or very little,
to Senator Taft. This favorable circumstance was not altogether
uncontrived. Whereas, in serving Dewey's candidacy, Dulles
regularly declined invitations to assist with the party's platform
—feeling, as he told one reporter, that participation might limit
his and Dewey's subsequent freedom of choice—he determined,
in 1952, to put aside such narrow concerns and serve the party
by composing a statement of principles acceptable to both of its
leading factions. He resigned from government service on March
25, saying, "I look forward to . . . expressing my views about
foreign policy under conditions which will not risk embarrassment . . . to any presidential candidate." Shortly thereafter he
was expressing views that turned out to be not only his but,
extraordinarily, Taft's and Eisenhower's, too, and it was with
the explicit approval of both that he undertook his work on
the platform. By his success, he achieved a unique standing.
Already a symbol of bi-partisanship, he became the leading
prophet and agent of bi-factionalism.

Dulles will bring to the secretaryship a good deal more than
an imposing pedigree. He is a shrewd, intelligent man. He has
acquired over the years a considerable knowledge of the world.
His experience in diplomacy may not be as formidable as some
of his biographers make out, for the services he performed as
a youth, apprenticed to his grandfather and to Robert Lansing,
were essentially trivial in character. From the end of the first
war until well along in the second, he had little to do with diplomacy. He kept up a lively interest in it, though, and headed
various private groups, chiefly of a religious complexion, making
recommendations on foreign policy. And of course his extensive
international practice, which involved negotiations with government officials in Europe and Asia, contributed to his information
on world affairs. But diplomacy is an essentially political task,
and Dulles had no experience with the political side of it until

fairly late in life. And he had no political responsibility at all. Oddly enough, Dulles, though every bit as fervent in his Republicanism as in his Calvinism, has up to now served only Democratic administrations: those headed by Wilson, Roosevelt, and Truman. He was a delegate to the San Francisco conference at which the United Nations was organized, several times an American representative in the General Assembly, and a consultant at the meetings of foreign ministers in London in 1945 and 1947, in Moscow in 1947, and in Paris in 1949. He has been an able and sometimes eloquent exponent of American policy. Eloquence, however, has never been his long suit. He is a lawyer with a lawyer's mind. He is better at briefs and contracts than in appeals to conscience, imagination, and heart.

He has become, unquestionably, a skilled diplomatic technician. Some admire the Japanese treaty as a piece of creative statesmanship, unprecedented in magnanimity and breadth of vision; others deplore it as an instrument whose faulty workings are concealed by a resplendent form. But the fact must be conceded on all sides that its negotiation by Dulles was an adroit piece of work. In the U.N. and in most of his other assignments, he has been a deft, patient, and widely respected performer. He has come to know a good deal about the machinery of the State Department and the mood of the United States Senate. If his background is not all it is advertised to be, it is still a fairly impressive one. Certainly there is no Republican available for the secretaryship who can be said to be better qualified.

Up to now, however, Dulles has been, in the official phases of his career, only an instrument of policy. How he might perform as a maker of policy is a question on which the record is at once baffling and disquieting. Although he has been articulate, almost to the point of garrulity, in rendering judgments on matters of policy, it is exceedingly difficult to make out the basic pattern of his thought or to determine whether, in fact, it has any pattern. Over the years, he has taken very nearly every view of the world and America's relation to it that has been available to rational men of the century. In his youth, he has said, he was fired by the Wilsonian dream, which he sought to serve as a young lawyer at the Paris conference. At some point or other between the wars, it lost its hold on him. In the late thirties and early forties, he was an isolationist. Though he took no active part in the America First Committee, he gave money to it as late as November 1941, and his speeches of the period reflect its torpid dogma. "Only hysteria," he said, "entertains the idea that Germany, Italy, or Japan contemplates war upon us." And: "I see no justification for our participation in the senseless cyclical struggle which, under our present world system, always goes on between static and dynamic forces."

The "dynamic" forces were, of course, the totalitarian ones; the "static" ones their antagonists. Dulles's critics have suggested the possibility that this view was a particularly convenient one for the head of a law firm dealing profitably (Dulles was often said to be the world's most highly paid lawyer) with a number of dynamic cartels. If the view was convenient, there is no evidence that Dulles adopted it for this reason. The most plausible as well as the most honorable explanation is that disillusionment with Versailles had led him, on the one hand, to exaggerate the injustices done Germany and, on the other, to despair of national states ever being able to create an order based on peace and justice. It was a common enough attitude and a morally defensible one.

It lasted only briefly with Dulles, though. When the war was on, when he and his protégé Dewey were hopeful of becoming war leaders, he was once more a Wilsonian. John Chamberlain was able to come away from a talk with Dulles and report that his views were "broadly those of Cordell Hull." "Both the present and the hypothetical future Secretary of State," Chamberlain wrote, "think in terms of a continuing understanding between the United Kingdom, the U.S., Russia, and China. And both hope to see the world covered eventually by a peace system based on a new league assembly, a world court, and a system of commonly accepted international law."

Dulles's recent books, articles, and speeches fail to dispel the paradoxes that seem imbedded in his thought. On the contrary, they add new ones. A note he recurrently strikes is that he is seeking "to find ways whereby the moral force of Christendom [can] make itself felt in the conduct of nations." He says he has cherished this principle for fifteen years. "In 1937," he has written, "I attended the Oxford Conference on Church and State. That conference persuaded me that there was no way to solve the great perplexing international problems except by bringing to bear upon them the force of Christianity." He then and there, at Oxford, saw that "the best thing I could do with the rest of my life" was to translate the persuasion into policy. But the persuasion had two versions in translation. The charismatic approach covered his period of America First isolationism and his period of regenerate Wilsonianism, one of which, certainly, must have been better informed by apostolic values than the other. The approach endures today, when the student of Dulles's career is confounded by his two distinct and plainly incompatible views of our present situation.

There are times when Dulles's sanguineness seems to know no bounds and times when his view of life is crabbed and denying. "We stand at a threshold beyond which lies a vista of opportunities that are immense and glorious," he said in May of last year. "The last five years have been years of achievement, and . . . our people have already surmounted a great peril." But in August of this year, he said that he, General Eisenhower, and Senator Nixon were in agreement that American foreign policy had "put this nation in the greatest peril it has ever been in [in] the entire course of our national history." The situation, to be sure, could have changed for the worse in the meanwhile, or Dulles could have changed for the wiser. But it seems clear from his contribution to the Republican platform that the five years of achievement, in which, as he saw it, peril

had been surmounted, were concurrent with the period of unparalleled danger. "The present administration," he wrote in the
platform, "in seven years has squandered the unprecedented
power and prestige which were ours at the close of World War
II." On account of this profligacy, "Russia . . . proceeds confidently with its plan for world conquest. We charge that the
leaders of the administration now in power have lost the peace
so dearly earned by World War II."

When he was serving the administration, Dulles made directly
contrary assessments. In 1949, he said: "Soviet Communist tactics
cannot prevail against such curative and creative programs as
we have been evolving over the past two years." And two years
after that: "The struggle for peace, freedom, and liberation is
being greatly aided by the effort the United States is now making. . . . [Today] the free world, with the United States in the
lead, is creating a force-in-being sufficient to hearten those who
love freedom."

No doubt astutely, the Republican platform takes advantage
of public anxiety and discouragement over the war in Korea.
It is curious, though, that Dulles, of all men, should so willingly
have undertaken to heighten these moods. No one in public life
was more inspirited than Dulles by our Korean intervention. Just
as the first American troops were going ashore at Pusan, he
made a Fourth of July speech at the base of the Washington
Monument. "What we are doing today," he said, "is in keeping
with the tradition of our past. We can say with pride that our
spirit today is the spirit of '76 and that our living today is faithful
to the principles on which our nation was founded." Korea was
not an occasion for ruffles or bugle notes in the Republican platform. "We charge," that document says, "that [the administra-
tion] plunged us into war in Korea without the consent of our
citizens through their authorized representatives in Congress.
. . . [It] committed this nation to fight back under the most
unfavorable conditions." Dulles was in Tokyo and fresh from a
tour of Korea when the Communists swept down across the

thirty-eighth parallel; he did not then apprise his government of unfavorable conditions. He cabled the State Department: "It is possible that the South Koreans may themselves contain and repulse the attack, and if so this is the best way. If, however, it appears that they cannot do so, then we believe United States forces should be used." A year and even two years later, Dulles's enthusiasm for the Korean war was still soaring. On June 30, 1951 *Time* quoted him as saying that "President Truman, with bi-partisan support, acted promptly and vigorously" in response to the appeal from the Republic of Korea. And on May 19, 1952, he himself wrote in *Life,* "President Truman's decision that the United States should go to the defense of the Korean Republic was courageous, righteous, and in the national interest." In the same article, he wrote, in regard to events subsequent to the American intervention, "I can testify from personal knowledge that the President and the Secretary of State [Dean Acheson] really want bi-partisanship and congressional cooperation in foreign policy." In the Republican platform, drafted only a few weeks later, he insisted that "in the main the Republican Party has been ignored and its participation has not been invited."

The life of a platform writer is hard and onerous. He is almost by definition a dealer in grotesqueries. To seek formulations, however, in which the two factions of a great party can submerge or bypass their differences is not necessarily a dishonorable job, and a man should be allowed something in the way of a moral discount when he is clearly speaking for others rather than for himself. Dulles has on occasion applied for such a discount. In Chicago, during the convention, he was asked by a reporter, who happened to be the author of these lines, how he could bring himself to condemn the Roosevelt administration for not defending the Baltic republics when they had been seized two years before we entered the war and at a time, furthermore, when he, Mr. Dulles, was urging us to stay out of the "senseless, cyclical struggle" to maintain national sovereignties; he replied that as an individual he could not do so but that as a platform writer he was merely stating the Republican case against the Democratic Party, which was committed to the principle of liberation by the Atlantic Charter. "They *weren't* liberated, were they?" he said, and of course the facts were entirely on his side.

The difficulty with Dulles is in knowing when the man is really speaking for himself. It would be a fairly simple matter if one could appeal from Dulles the platform writer to Dulles the practicing statesman, but the statesman will not allow us to do this. Last summer, when Senator Douglas of Illinois pointed out that in view of the fact that Dulles had secured passage in the General Assembly of the resolution calling for the withdrawal of troops from Korea, there was a certain incongruity in his accusing the government of dereliction of duty for having complied with the resolution, Dulles blandly replied that in sponsoring the resolution he had merely acted as the agent of his government. Citing the United Nations Participation Act, which requires our U.N. representatives to take orders from the President whether they like them or not, he insisted that he could not be held accountable for the terms of the resolution or for the arguments he made in its favor.

He was indeed right about the Participation Act. But in bringing it up, he raised a question, When is Dulles Dulles? He will not be judged by the Republican platform; in writing it, he was setting down a party's bill of particulars, not the verdict of an individual conscience. He will not be judged, except on some sort of selective basis, by his work in the General Assembly, where he was dutifully representing a government whose foreign policy he privately felt—or did he?—was putting this nation "in the greatest peril . . . in the entire course of our national history." By the agent theory, almost every Dulles we have ever known can be made to vanish from sight and judgment. The Dulles of the Japanese Treaty was an agent, and so was the Dulles of the Big Four meetings, and the bi-partisan Dulles of the State Department, and the Dulles who was a spokesman of Governor Dewey, and the Dulles who is now referred to in the press as a spokesman for General Eisenhower.

Somewhere, among all these Dulleses, is a private individual, a man, a conscience. The occasional glimpses we get of this hidden person are not reassuring. The chief moral and intellectual characteristic appears to be a thin and achromatic spirituality. Looking every inch the worldling—he has, as someone has pointed out, the face of a Founding Father but a wearied expression and a banker's bearing—he nevertheless hankers after what he calls "the spiritual society." In his books, where at least it should be presumed that he is speaking for himself, he is constantly belaboring us, his countrymen, for false values. Americans of recent times, he wrote two years ago in *War or Peace*, seem "to be less concerned with conducting a great experiment for the benefit of mankind and to be more concerned with piling up for ourselves material advantages." (In the Republican platform, Dulles, who has himself piled up an enviable quantity of material advantages, wrote that we should "measure our foreign commitments so that they can be borne without endangering the . . . sound finances of the United States.") Sometimes he is given to saying that none of our problems are essentially political or economic: "The trouble is not material. . . . What we lack is a righteous and dynamic faith. . . . There is confusion in men's minds and a corrosion in their souls." He has not gone much beyond advising us of our general sinfulness and we cannot know much of his own righteous and dynamic faith until he tells us which of the Dulleses embodies it. Perhaps we will unveil the mysteries when and if he becomes Secretary of State. He very much wants that job and seems likely to get it.

7 Interregnum

Letter from Washington
December 1, 1952

The President-elect has chosen his Cabinet and made his other major appointments with remarkable speed, and his selections have been greeted here with unremarkable politeness. So far the only persons to express much disapproval are Senators Taft and Morse. Senator Taft's annoyance is selective. He describes the choice of Martin P. Durkin, the Chicago steamfitter who is to be Secretary of Labor, as "incredible." He regards the appointment of Herbert Brownell, the New York lawyer who is to be Attorney General, as a personal affront. He has had some unkindly things to say about the appointment of George M. Humphrey, the Cleveland millionaire who is to be Secretary of the Treasury. His annoyance over Mr. Durkin and Mr. Brownell is understandable. Mr. Durkin is a Democrat and a fierce critic of the Taft-Hartley Act. Mr. Brownell was one of the leading architects of Senator Taft's defeat at Chicago. But his irritation over Mr. Humphrey seemed at first incomprehensible, for Mr. Humphrey is not only an Ohioan but an Ohioan who heads a corporation bearing the name of Marcus Alonzo Hanna. What on earth could Senator Taft have against *him?* It was learned that Mr. Taft had nothing, really, against Mr. Humphrey—except, perhaps, that Mr. Humphrey had gone over to Eisenhower early this year—but that his grievance was the traditional one of the congressman who has not been consulted about an appointment from his own district. Senator Morse's disapproval is not selective. He thinks the entire Eisenhower cabinet, like the election itself, is a mistake. He pronounced this harsh judgment before the entire cabinet had been named, and he might be willing to say a good word for Mr. Durkin, but on the other hand the fact that Mr. Durkin is collaborating with General Eisenhower might damn him in Senator Morse's eyes.

Most judgments have been neither as sweeping as Senator Morse's nor as specific as Senator Taft's. Generally speaking, the appointments seem to have been made, as political appointments generally are, with a view to keeping all factions happy. The incoming Secretary of State, Mr. Dulles, is a breathing, talking symbol of party unity. He commands the respect of both the Taft and Dewey wings and is perhaps the only man alive who does so. Charles E. Wilson of General Motors, who will be Secretary of Defense, is a Republican not closely associated with any faction, but General Motors was the greatest of the business enterprises more or less officially committed to the Eisenhower candidacy before Chicago. There might be some pettishness in the business community over the amount of patronage General Motors is getting—Arthur Summerfield and Douglas McKay, Postmaster-General and Secretary of the Interior, sell Chevrolets for a living and may therefore be regarded as General Motors satellites—but this is thought to be unlikely, for right now the business community is counting its many large blessings and is not much concerned about such matters as who runs the mails and who manages the affairs of Indians. Sinclair Weeks, who will be Secretary of Commerce, and Ezra Taft Benson, who will be Secretary of Agriculture, are representatives of the Taft wing. Despite Senator Taft's laments, the Taft wing has fared quite as well as the Dewey wing, which can count only Mr. Dulles and Mr. Brownell as representatives in the inner circle.

The interregnum is proving to be a difficult and unprofitable period. The President and the President-elect have met and conferred and established a kind of liaison team, and the transfer will be about as orderly as it is possible to make it. Most people, though, wish that the new administration could take office right away. There is a widespread feeling, shared by many policy-making members of the outgoing regime, that before very long someone ought to do something to shorten the uneasy period between election and inauguration. It was cut down by six weeks in 1933, when the Twentieth Amendment was ratified, but it is still a lot longer than it need be. In Great Britain and most other democratic countries, new governments are installed almost immediately after being chosen by the voters and certified by the proper authorities, and while our system, in which the changes in personnel are as a rule greater, requires some sort of transition period, it does not require anything like the present eleven weeks, which are rough on the nerves of those waiting to acquire authority and even rougher on those who must exercise it in the knowledge that they will shortly surrender it and who must either pigeonhole all decisions or pile up headaches for the new management by making decisions that will soon have to be unmade. A proposed revision in the change-over procedure that has found a certain amount of favor here is to keep January 20, a day that seems no better or worse than any other, as a kind of terminal date for the transfer of power and full responsibility—the date by which the new administration would be legally liable for everything—but to allow the incoming president to request and be granted inauguration at any time he chooses after December 1 or thereabouts. The scheme would necessitate earlier action by the Electoral College, which now registers its vote on December 15, and no doubt would give rise to a number of other complications, but the advantages would be numerous.

This is an unproductive time, but it is not necessarily an unindustrious one. Although the most interesting and important events have been taking place in the Eisenhower administration's headquarters at the Hotel Commodore in New York, Washington has been the scene of a good deal of activity, not all of it edifying. A number of committees of the expiring Congress have been at work, hurrying to finish up their business before they too expire. A House sub-committee led by Representative Ezekiel Gathings of Arkansas is investigating obscene literature—magazines, novels, plays, poems, picture books, everything—and another, led by Representative Eugene Cox of Georgia is studying tax-exempt foundations in an effort to determine whether any of them are subsidizing anything they shouldn't be subsidizing, specifically Communism. The Senate Elections Subcommittee, whose present chairman is Senator Thomas Hennings of Missouri, has been trying to look into the knotted affairs of Senator McCarthy and into the points at issue between him and Senator William Benton, who is soon to be an ex-Senator. The Gathings group is said to be making splendid progress with the pornographic matter that has been pouring in on it since it announced itself in the market for this sort of thing, but the Cox and Hennings subcommittees have encountered frustrating obstacles. In the case of Representative Cox, it turned out that the foundation about which he had the most serious misgivings pays taxes regularly and is therefore beyond the scope of his investigation, being, in fact, not a foundation at all as the committee defines one. In Senator Henning's case, the difficulty has lain chiefly in finding Senator McCarthy and getting him to testify. The subcommittee has been trying to arrange a meeting since early September of 1951. Sometimes McCarthy is too busy, sometimes he is too angry. He raises civil-libertarian objections to being asked to testify against himself or to being refused the right to cross-examine witnesses testifying against him. Lately, it has just been impossible to run him down. A few weeks ago, McCarthy went deer-hunting, and the quest, according to people in his office, took him so deep into Wisconsin's north woods that there was no possible way of letting him know that some of his colleagues in Washington would like a few words with him. He came out of the woods once to hold a press conference. He stole quietly into Washington on November 20, summoned reporters to his office, and announced that there was nothing, absolutely nothing to the rumor that he planned to abandon his scourging of subversives and others with questionable pasts. He also announced that he would be willing to cooperate with the new Secretary of State, who may or may not be cheered to learn this. He neglected, however, to let anyone from the Hennings Committee know he was in town, and by the following evening, when the Hennings people learned of his presence from the newspapers, he was already back in the forest primeval and beyond the reach, so his office said, of all the marvels of modern communications. The Hennings Committee is drawing up a report on McCarthy, but it is expected to be rather like the Odyssey without Ulysses.

McCarthy is one of a large number of senators and representatives who have held press conferences lately. In fact, it is an inconspicuous and unambitious congressman who has not returned to Washington at least once since Election Day to take advantage of the fact that the press corps has, for the moment, time on its hands. Senator Maybank of South Carolina came in last week to start a 1956 boom for Senator Russell of Georgia and to announce that for the next four years all true Democrats could look to a triumvirate consisting of Senator Russell, Senator Byrd of Virginia, and himself for leadership. "I think we will serve together as the caretakers of the party," he said. He also said he considered President Truman's career as a party leader over and done with. "What about Stevenson?" he was asked. "Oh, I never did hear much about Stevenson," he replied. Sounded out on Senator Maybank's views, Senator Russell said that he regards Stevenson as the "titular head of the party" and he explained that in proper political usage "titular" means "title without authority." This showed how flexible political usage sometimes is. Representative Joseph Martin of Massachusetts, who will be Speaker of the House next year, has held several press conferences, most of them devoted to straightening out his views on fiscal matters, which were full of odd twists. It was originally his notion that it would be the first business of the new Congress to present the breadwinners of the country with a handsome cut in taxes. He said that while he thought it important to balance the budget and hold down the national debt, time was not of the essence in these matters. They could be gone into later. He stuck by this opinion even after Senators Taft and Bridges said that, as they saw it, the statesmanlike thing would be to cut the budget before cutting taxes, but he did not stick by it after receiving a call from Senator Taft last week. Following that meeting, he announced that he was a convert to the Taft view. In the Taft view, as set forth by the Senator at a press conference last week, the budget, which is now running about eighty billion dollars, can be cut to seventy billion in 1953–54 and to sixty billion in 1954–55, by which time the Senator thinks it will be possible to cut taxes twelve or thirteen percent across the board. The Speaker of the House now goes along with this— "one hundred percent," he says. But Representative Taber of New York, the incoming chairman of the House Appropriations Committee, has said at a press conference that he is pretty sure the budget can be cut to sixty-five billion right away.

8   Harry Truman: Au Revoir

January 15, 1953

In just five days, one of the great periods in American history will draw to a most ceremonious close. When the President accompanies the President-elect from the White House to the Capitol steps, where the Chief Justice of the United States will administer the oath of office to Mr. Eisenhower, the event will signalize not only the end of the Truman administration, which has lasted just eleven weeks less than eight years, but of a twenty-year period about which the central fact is not that it has been dominated by Democratic administration but that it has been the occasion, for better or worse, for swift and irreversible changes in American life and institutions.

History, one imagines, will see Harry Truman in the setting of that period. He was an agent of the movement that brought about those changes, and he cannot be considered apart from it. (Nor will its measure ever be taken without due consideration of him.) But he rose to his present eminence, paradoxically, because he seemed at the start not to be an agent; because eight years ago he was not closely identified with the New Deal or for that matter with anything else that was at that time controversial. It gives one something of a start, it makes one reflect on the weight and pressure of circumstances to recall that Harry Truman's nomination in 1944 was a gesture of conciliation—in a sense, of appeasement—to those who last fall thrust federal power into the hands of the Republicans. By 1944, the New Deal had made powerful enemies, some of them being its former supporters, and in order to make these enemies feel better about things in general the New Deal nominated a man with a conservative record, a quondam Southerner, and put him in line for the presidency.

And this was not a deceit. There is no doubt that in his own mind in those days President Truman thought of himself as a conservative Democrat. It is a matter of record, for example, that he then held views on racial questions almost directly opposite to those he later came to hold. His views on trade unions were very different, too. Far from being an enemy of the philosophy that underlies the Taft-Hartley Act, he advocated, early in his administration, measures so punitive, so hostile to a particular union, that none other than Senator Robert Taft became, for a brief time, labor's champion. Truman's plan was to apply the Selective Service Act, the draft law, to striking miners. This so outraged the libertarian side of Senator Taft that he led the Senate opposition to it.

But it was not long before Harry Truman became caught up

in the current of events and ideas. The movement of the times swept around and about him and made him its own. In time, he acknowledged himself to be its agent, and he was in some ways a more militant one than his predecessor had been. Under him, the movement both prospered and suffered, coming in the end to what now appears to have been an inevitable climax last November. The New Deal revolution is over. It has ended, though, in rather a cheerful, gratifying way. It was upset by a generation that took its benefits and many of its central principles wholly for granted. Revolutions usually devour their children, but, as Murray Kempton has pointed out, this was a case of the children devouring the revolution.

To say that Harry Truman was the agent of forces greater than himself is to speak only a partial truth about him. No one knows, ultimately, whether men shape events more than events shape men. But we could not go on living if we did not believe that men have some power over events. And there were certainly events in Harry Truman's administration in which his personality, his style, his jaunty outlook on life seem to have had some determining influence. He did many things he could not have avoided doing, things that any president would have had to do. But he did certain other things that he might very well have avoided. And these are the things that he as an individual rather than as an agent will be remembered for. One thinks, for example, of the Truman Doctrine. One thinks of the Marshall Plan. One thinks of the North Atlantic Treaty. One thinks of the Korean intervention, of the decision to contain the war there, and of the recall of General MacArthur, an act that took courage whether or not it took wisdom. In the showdowns, in the crises of history he faced in staggering succession, he was not the sort to allow events to slide over him. He acted vigorously in what he took to be the best interests of the Republic. Vigor must never be admired for its own sake, but Truman has shown moral courage under pressure, even a kind of moral grace.

There is no doubt that the election was a repudiation of the

President. It was not a repudiation on a grand scale, not the sort of repudiation the Republicans suffered time and again in the thirties, but it was plain enough just the same that a majority of the voters did not like what they assumed Harry Truman stood for. A great many million Americans, however, still bear Harry Truman an affection that is hard to describe. It is difficult for anyone to understand this who has not traveled about the country with him and felt for himself the special kind of warmth that Truman can generate. It is not a passion, it is not really political enthusiasm. It is friendliness and sympathy and plain liking, the feeling that townsmen have for one of their own whom they know to have borne up well under great difficulties—borne up well and got, they think, too little thanks for it. Roosevelt, Eisenhower, Stevenson—these men have been for different reasons greatly admired and respected and perhaps even deeply loved by millions of Americans. Truman is the one man of his time for whom liking and affection are the proper terms.

Even at his most outrageous, he is a hard man to dislike. It is only fair to say that he has been on occasion every bit as vulgar as Senator McCarthy. "Why, this fellow," he said, only a few weeks ago, of the world figure he will be accompanying to the Capitol steps next Tuesday, "this fellow don't know any more about politics than a pig knows about Sunday." Had this come from McCarthy, men of virtue would certainly have cited it as another example of McCarthy's brutishness. Truman was not harshly judged for it, except by those who judge him harshly for anything; in fact, many thought it rather quaint and funny. And probably they were right to make the distinction. For there is a snarl in everything McCarthy says, and Truman is no snarler. He is not vicious. He may have been petty at times, but he has seldom been vindictive. He is in this respect a much purer man than Franklin Roosevelt, and those who had the most unsatisfactory dealings with him sensed this. Newbold Morris, a Republican reformer in a great tradition and a man elaborately schooled in the theory and practice of being a gentleman, was brought to Washington by Truman and told to investigate corruption in the federal government. He started to investigate and got from the Truman administration what can only be described as a double cross. Asked his view of the President at the end of this sordid episode, Newbold Morris said, "I like him very much, really I do." Truman had behaved badly, very badly indeed, but Morris, in common with many other Americans, found good will and extenuating circumstances, and he acknowledged that in most ways Truman was serving the country well.

This brings us to what may be the basic meaning of Truman's career. Whatever anyone thinks of him, he is a kind of vindication of democracy. Thanks to a series of accidents, he found himself President of the United States in a period of war and mounting national peril. By any reasonable standards, he would have lacked the qualifications for the presidency even in a period when no crises impended. It seemed a time for greatness, and he was not great. His difficulties were increased by the fact that he succeeded a man whom much of the world regarded as authentically great. Truman, however, bore up well. Indeed, it is not easy for anyone to see quite how a great man, had there been one, might have done very much better than he did. It is hard to imagine what might have been different today if Roosevelt had lived through his fourth term and been succeeded by a man of equal stature. What President Truman has proved is that a democratic society can get along without greatness when it must. Either that or that a merely good man can, in a free society, become a great man—or at least approach greatness.

9 Inauguration

Letter from Washington
January 23, 1953

The revellers, relatives, and well-wishers have mostly gone back home, leaving the Eisenhower administration, which at the moment appears to consist of no more than a hundred-odd men and women, to its opportunities, which are large, and its troubles, which are moderately numerous. There has been a good deal of talk about the grandeur of Tuesday's ceremony, about the splendid myths the ceremony embodies, and about its powerful, though not necessarily eloquent, testimony to the possibilities of democratic civilization. Some of the talk has been mawkish, but if the ritual is thought of in connection with what is going on now and will be going on for quite some time—the transfer to this handful of people of the largest bureaucracy in history—it is indeed an impressive thing. This particular transfer is unique on many counts. The apparatus the Eisenhower people are taking over is many times larger than any that has been transferred in the past. The government today has four times the number of civilian employees it had when the Republicans were last in power (2,591,000 as against 630,000) and its budget has been multiplied by about twenty ($85,400,000,000 as against $3,863,000,000). For the most part, the present personnel was recruited by other people for other ends, and one of the declared objectives of the new administration, one of the reasons its leaders were so eager to acquire control of this massive organization, is to disband large parts of it—to disperse some of those 2,591,000 and abolish their functions altogether. Whether this can be done is another question, and an engaging one, but at least that is what is intended and hoped for. The transfer is also the best prepared in history, there being no precedent either for the warm-up sessions in the Hotel Commodore bull-pen in New York or for the pre-inaugural conferences between the old and new authorities here in Washington. Moreover, the receivers are, collectively, the least professional and the least experienced group of government administrators to come to power in modern times. The Eisenhower administration will be a great experiment in the interchangeability of talents, the biggest opportunity the business community has ever had to test the application of business knowledge and business techniques to broader problems. The President is no newer to the game than most of his advisors. On his personal staff, the only man with any real experience in government is Sherman Adams, who served one term in Congress and was Governor of New Hampshire for four years. In his Cabinet, only John Foster Dulles has any inside knowledge of the workings of federal power. All the rest are greenhorns—none being greener than the most formidable executive of them all, Charles E. Wilson, whose assertion that what is good for General Motors is good for the country will be a staple of Democratic oratory for many years. In the non-Cabinet agencies, only Harold Stassen, the Mutual Security Administrator, has a background in public affairs.

It will be weeks, and perhaps months, before the full impact of the new administration on the vast organization it controls or on the life of this peculiar community will be felt. For some time to come, Eisenhower's Washington will be Truman's Washington without Truman. But the doings of the past few days have had an impact on the consciousness of most conscious people, and in spite of some ominous rumblings on Capitol Hill, and the Washington *Times-Herald's* decision on Wednesday that there is no place for President Eisenhower in the Republican Party, it seems reasonable to say that most people are thus far well disposed. The inaugural address, which was responsible for the

Times-Herald's defection, was appreciated by most and fervently admired by some. Even Senator Morse liked it, though he has now gone on to other things, most of which he doesn't like. There was no stomping in the plaza as the speech was read, and there was a certain amount of disappointment over its failure to deal with domestic affairs, but the President had chosen to address himself more to the world than to his countrymen, and this was perhaps the statesmanlike thing to do. The White House and the State Department have already received gratifying responses from the embassies—from those, at least, that could be expected to have anything gratifying to say.

There has been almost universal approval of the President's decision to hold regular press conferences. Some of his advisors had urged him against this, and it was widely thought that in his press relations, he would adopt the practice of Governor Dewey, whose press secretary, James Hagerty, is now installed as press secretary in the White House. Governor Dewey dislikes press conferences and holds them only at his own convenience, which is seldom. But the President, though it is doubtful whether he likes press conferences any more than Governor Dewey, evidently agrees with those who feel that they meet a need that is met by no regular institution of government. He has announced not only that he will retain the conference but that he may put it on television once a month or so, as a kind of White House panel show.

The fact that an opposition is already taking shape inside the President's party as well as outside it is perhaps a sign of the administration's vitality. In the weeks before the inauguration, everyone assumed that there would be a period in which all dissident voices would be stilled and the administration would be given a free hand even by those who, as a matter of principle, would like to restrain it. This period has certainly not yet begun in Congress, and some people, it is apparent, have decided that it shouldn't ever begin. Senator Morse is clearly of this persuasion, but he is not the only one, and his quarrel with the administration, though set forth in harsh words and many of them, seems less profound than that of several others. In general, Morse's objection is that the administration is too conservative and business-minded for his taste. But his differences with the new President stop, he says, at the water's edge, whereas the differences of a growing number of congressmen, mostly Republicans, begin to get serious only as they approach the water—or, rather, as they get out beyond the tidelands and the continental shelf. Thus far, party discipline has been effective in keeping congressmen who were affronted by the twentieth-century notes in the inaugural address from saying so publicly, but several of them have expressed their dismay privately, and it is felt that it can only be a matter of days before the argument breaks out on the floors of both houses. Some of it came strongly to light during the questioning of Harold Stassen, the Mutual Security Director-designate, by the Senate Foreign Relations Committee the day after the inauguration. This took place in a closed session, but a number of the senators regarded that as a mistake and thought the world should be informed of the proceedings. Some senators wished to know how the Eisenhower administration differed from the Truman administration; would Mr. Stassen please explain when and how the new President and his aides planned to give the country a new foreign policy? Mr. Stassen didn't think "new" was quite the right word, but there would, he said, be changes, which the senators would see for themselves when foreign-policy legislation came up to Congress from the executive agencies. This did not entirely satisfy the senators. What changes would they see, they wish to know. What, exactly, was difference in viewpoint between the unspeakable and happily departed Acheson and Harriman and the new firm of Dulles and Stassen? Mr. Stassen said the differences were enormous, even fundamental, but were of such a nature that it was rather difficult to put them into words at this time. Couldn't he put just one of them into words? Stassen said it would be terribly hard to do so, at least at this precise moment. The question was asked whether it might not be possible to measure some of the differences quantitatively—in terms, to be practical about it, of dollars. For example, did Mr. Stassen think it likely that the new administration would find itself able to save democracy with somewhat less than the $7,600,000,000 for foreign aid that Mr. Truman had requested earlier in the month? Just in round numbers, how much less would it take? Mr. Stassen was afraid he was not in a position to explore this question at this particular time.

Mr. Stassen's reticence, coming after the President's assertion that the country's present alliances, would not be disturbed but would, if possible, be strengthened, was a grievous thing to a number of congressmen. The Washington *Times-Herald*, however, drew its unhappy conclusions entirely from the inaugural address. The administration was only about ten hours old when the paper came out on the streets announcing the bankruptcy of the regime. The address, it said, "might have been written at Mr. Truman's order, for it amounted to little more than an endorsement of the foreign policies of the outgoing administration." In view of this, the paper said, "the one useful purpose it can serve is to remind the American people that in Congress they will have to preserve their freedom." Twenty-four hours later, the *Times-Herald*, considering the speech once more, found another message in it. "The message is simple and clear," it said. "It is that what happened to Truman can happen to anybody." The same issue carried a letter from a reader who argued that "the American people have committed a great wrong in denying Robert A. Taft his rightful place. Let us hope it will not be too late to right a wrong in 1956." The *Times-Herald*, of course, represents no sizable body of opinion here; it is a medium of self-expression for its publisher, Colonel Robert R. McCormick, of Chicago, and in taking this view of the Eisenhower administration Colonel McCormick was simply following an old pattern of behavior. It was recalled in the press galleries that in 1929, when the Chicago *Tribune* correspondent wired the first few paragraphs of President Hoover's inaugural address to the home office, the Colonel wired back, "This man Hoover won't do." The Colonel's pattern of behavior is a contagious thing, though, and in the years since Hoover it has affected more and more Midwestern congressmen. Senator Dirksen, for one, is highly susceptible to it, and there are others, from as far away as northern Michigan, who come down with each new symptom of it within a few days, and sometimes within a few hours.

Actually, it is thought here that a certain amount of McCormick-style opposition in Congress could turn out to be an asset to President Eisenhower. It could, among other things, resolve in his favor the doubts of a good many Democrats, and thereby increase the over-all size of his majorities. It would be a matter for serious concern to the administration only if it included Senator Taft and those who normally seek his counsel. This appears most improbable. Taft, in whose body there is not one sycophantic bone, seems to have decided that General Eisenhower's foreign policy, as outlined up to the present, merits his support, and his response to the inaugural address was quite different from that of the *Times-Herald* and some of his congressional colleagues. "It was," he said, "a great and inspiring beginning, a great and inspiring speech." It may well be that later developments in administration policy will displease Taft, as certain pre-inaugural developments did, but if that happens, he is likely to say so and to go on supporting the large part of the program to which he is committed. There are a number of people here who have argued all along that a split in the Republican Party was bound to come once it was in power, and that Taft would give leadership and direction to the rebel elements. But there are also people who, while agreeing that everything pointed to just the kind of disturbance the inaugural address seems to have caused, have held that Taft would be found siding with Eisenhower on the basic issues. All the evidence thus far suggests that this school has the better of the argument. While Taft has made no effort to conceal his distaste for Herbert Brownell, and for Governor Dewey's friends in general, he has been, up to now, a model of punctilio in his dealings with the party leadership. It is believed here that Taft has determined to make himself responsible for the success of this administration, and that while he will unquestionably use all his power to make it conform to Republican gospel as understood by him, he will not desert it.

10   Assistant Crusader: Sherman Adams

January 25, 1953

Sherman Adams, President Eisenhower's chief assistant in the White House, is a man cut from the same bolt of plain, hard cloth as the late Calvin Coolidge. He was raised in a Vermont hill village, East Dover, thirty miles distant from Coolidge's Plymouth. He looks a good deal like Coolidge—a wintry type, lean and bony, with a face that is all planes and angles. He is an exemplar of the Coolidge virtues. He is frugal. As governor of New Hampshire, he took his lunch to the State House in a lunch box. He keeps cool. In the campaign, when the uproar over Senator Nixon's financial arrangements broke out, and the candidate for President was being advised by fellow crusaders to do this and do that, to hurry up and do something right away, it was Adams who said: "Wait and see." Eisenhower took this advice. It turned out to be sage. Eleven thousand telegrams came in. Most of them urged the President to stand by Nixon. That is what he did. Coolness paid off.

Adams's career as a transplanted Vermonter closely parallels Coolidge's. Coolidge crossed the Southern border, went to Amherst College, became a Northampton lawyer and, in time, gov-

ernor of Massachusetts. Adams crossed the Eastern border, went
to Dartmouth College, became a lumber executive in Lincoln,
and, in time, governor of New Hampshire.

Adams, who turned fifty-four a few days before being sworn
into office, isn't as silent as Coolidge, but then neither was
Coolidge. The President who never used one word where no
word would do was largely an invention of amused correspondents. Coolidge talked, but he certainly wasn't gabby, and Adams
keeps his own counsel pretty much, a trait which will be an
asset to him and to President Eisenhower though in certain
other circumstances it can be difficult. A story has been widely
circulated to the effect that Mrs. Adams, seeking to punish her
husband for matutinal uncommunicativeness, once packed his
lunch box with sandwiches filled with strong soap and heavy
string. Mrs. Adams says that the story isn't true, but blames this
on her lack of enterprise. If she'd thought of making him soap-
and-string-on-white, she says, she would certainly have done so.
"He doesn't even talk much at dinner," she says.

The duties of Adams's new job are fixed neither by statute
nor by custom, and it is well that this is so. The purpose of the
job is nothing more or less than to lighten the burden of the
President, and how this may best be done is determined by the
nature of the burden, which changes from time to time, and by
the nature of the President, which may or may not change.
President Roosevelt used Harry Hopkins as a troubleshooter,
giving him one prickly assignment after another—now in politics,
now in diplomacy, now in mobilization. Harry Truman did something of the same sort with Clark Clifford, but he tended more
often to rely on men whom he could make personally responsible for broad areas of national policy, in the manner, for example, of John Steelman, who relieved the President of nearly
all concern over problems of industry and labor, and Dean
Acheson, who was given his head in foreign affairs.

Eisenhower and Adams are certain to establish a pattern of
their own. The President, it is being said, will not institute in

the White House the kind of military staff system he has been trained to use, and the description of Adams as the President's Chief of Staff is one that does not please the President, Adams, or anyone else in the administration. Nevertheless the President is a methodical person, a respecter of channels, a great believer in the doctrine of *expertise*. He likes fixed responsibilities for the men around him, and Adams, for one, is a man who likes his own duties to be settled and predictable. According to those who have observed the Eisenhower-Adams battery in last year's campaign, at the Commodore during the interregnum, and in these first few days in Washington, Adams is to be the organizer of *expertise* for the administration. He will, it is thought, have relatively little to do with the Cabinet, but he will be the undisputed boss of the White House staff, and he will have a great deal to do with those non-Cabinet departments—the National Security Council, the Bureau of the Budget, the Council of Economic Advisers, and all the rest—which nowadays constitute so large and vital a part of the executive branch.

Adams will be concerned, it is said, not with the policy of these agencies but with their efficient operation, with their relations one to another, and with communications between them and the White House. In order to get the President's ear, the heads of agencies will have to get Adams's ear first and persuade him that the business at hand is urgent enough to require the President's attention. At the same time, the agencies will be informed of the President's wishes by way of Adams.

All this suggests that Chief of Staff is not a bad term for Adams's role in the administration. More than the President's personal style and background seems to foretell such an arrangement; it suits Adams's style and background, too. Adams is not a policy man but an organizing man. Except for a single term in Congress, which ended seven years ago, he has no background in national politics and no special knowledge of any national issue, with the possible exception of conservation. Before he went into New Hampshire politics in the early forties, he was Timberlands Supervisor of the Parker Young Company, and it was not in fact until he became governor four years ago that he abandoned the lumber business for a full-time public career.

But if Adams lacks experience in some of the weightier problems the President will have to deal with, he has had plenty of preparation for the kind of efficiency-engineering that Eisenhower says he wishes to undertake in the executive agencies. He is an efficiency enthusiast. As governor of New Hampshire, he applied the administrative magic of consolidation and made eighty-odd state departments into forty-odd. "Sherm figured a way to slice the whole government in half," a friend says. Though the number of job-holders remains approximately the same, the bureaucracy has a much tidier appearance. Adams was an industrious governor. He made the job a full-time one, which it had seldom been in New Hampshire. He rose at five-thirty each morning, and breakfasting silently and speedily, was at his desk not long thereafter. He frequently opened the State House doors in the morning and was there to close them in the evening. Once he snowshoed five miles to a highway in order to go to work aboard a snow-bucker. Though he has mounted no snow-buckers since leaving Concord and doesn't seem likely to, he has continued his hard regimen. It is one thing, incidentally, that sets him apart from Coolidge, who was an inveterate snoozer and one of Vermont's more easy-going sons.

Adams will not be one of the administration's policy makers, but this does not mean that his views on policy matters will be of no consequence. He will, and indeed already has, made important appointments; he will probably spend more time with the President than any other member of the administration; as a middleman between the President and the executive agencies, he can scarcely avoid being something of a broker in ideas. What he thinks about major questions may be less relevant than what Mr. Dulles and Mr. Brownell think but it will be relevant just the same.

So far as his views are known at present, they appear to be in pretty complete accord with those of the President on domestic matters. He is a man of deeply conservative instincts. In the Seventy-ninth Congress, he opposed every piece of domestic legislation advanced by the administration. Only once did he side with Democrats; he supported the Marcantonio Anti-Poll Tax bill, which, though not an administration measure, received the support of many of the President's backers.

Adams may be in thorough accord with the President on matters of foreign policy too, but it would not be easy to prove this from the record. What the record seems to show is that if he does hold the President's view of the world, he holds it somewhat less intensely than Eisenhower does. In Congress, he favored the British loan of 1946, but he opposed just about every other measure of administration policy, including several with which President, then General, Eisenhower was associated.

If Adams now feels as strongly as the President about our role in the anti-Communist coalition, he did not, up to late 1951, find this outlook incompatible with a large measure of sympathy for Senator Taft's presidential aspirations. Adams never formally supported Taft, but he came very close to doing so. It is customary nowadays to associate him with those New England Republicans—among them, the Lodge brothers, Senators Saltonstall and Tobey and Margaret Chase Smith, and Governor Herter of Massachusetts—who were charter members of the Eisenhower movement. But the fact is that he was a latecomer to this group and had one foot in another camp—that of Styles Bridges, Owen Brewster, and others who were determined that the nomination go to Senator Taft. He was under great pressure from both factions, and toward the end of 1951 there was high tension among New Hampshire Republicans over which candidate their governor and party leader would endorse. According to Mrs. Adams, he decided for Eisenhower because he became persuaded that Taft couldn't win. Whether he ever resolved the question of the principles involved is not known.

His decision may have been an historic one. For if it was touch-and-go with Adams for several months, it was also, in the opinion of authorities on the New Hampshire mind, touch-and-go with the electorate. There is a tendency now to think of Eisenhower's sweep through last year's New Hampshire primaries as a political cyclone, a storm made up in the rising air, against which no ordinary political exertions could hope to prevail. But those who know most about New Hampshire politics believe that the primary there could very easily have gone the other way. Taft was extremely well liked in New Hampshire. Eisenhower was popular, too, but there was never any reliable evidence, before the voting, that there was any real preference for him. Indeed, some people, sturdy Eisenhower partisans to the man, argue that Taft in the early days enjoyed more favor than his opponent. "There was really no basis—none that we know of anyway—for our big claims about Eisenhower's backing," one of the men who made the claims said the other day. "We were whistling in the dark for weeks. None of us was sure Eisenhower could win, and I don't think there was one of us, including Sherm, who wasn't scared stiff when Taft came into the state."

What settled matters, these knowledgeable people think, was not Eisenhower's popularity but Sherman Adams's decision, which had, of course, been taken some months before, to support the General. That and Adams's hard work on Eisenhower's behalf. Adams put the whole power of his office behind Eisenhower. It was he who got after the Republican legislators (the New Hampshire legislature is one of the world's largest deliberative bodies, having 443 members or a little better than one legislator per thousand residents) and had them get out the village vote. And it was a series of attacks that Adams made on Taft, which Adams felt free to deliver after Taft made the monumental mistake of attacking Eisenhower personally, that assured Eisenhower of reaping the benefit of the organizing work done by the Republican legislators. This at least is the view taken by the best-informed New Hampshire Republicans, most of whom find it altogether easy to imagine a situation, happily averted as they see it, in which Eisenhower, having failed to enlist the support of Sherman Adams, failed to become President of the United States.

Eisenhower and Adams had not met before the General's return from Europe last year. They got along famously from the start, Eisenhower being impressed by Adams' brisk, capable way of staying on top of a job, Adams seeing in Eisenhower the political boxoffice he had been looking for. On salaryless leave from the State House, Adams was at the candidate's right hand throughout the campaign. He was, in a manner of speaking, executive secretary of the crusade.

There is some doubt as to whether Adams now has the job he really wants. It is said that he had hoped to be ambassador to Canada. He likes Canada and all the lumber there. He could, of course, have had the job if he had insisted on it, but he did not insist, and his wife thinks he will find Washington only slightly less congenial than Ottawa. His interest in lumbering is greater than any other, she says, but he also has a powerful interest in group singing. He once directed the Dartmouth Glee Club and is a veteran of many Vermont and New Hampshire choir lofts. "I imagine Sherm will join the choir first thing," she said shortly before they entrained for Washington. This would be in the National Cathedral, in which he sung tenor during his hitch as a congressman. Apart from this, life in Washington will be all work. Rising regularly at five-thirty, he finds it necessary to get to bed at half past eight or nine most evenings, and this will preclude much participation in Washington's formidable night life. In response to demands for information about her husband, Mrs. Adams, during their stay in the Commodore composed and circulated to the press a series of notes on her husband's life and character. It is a piquant document and perhaps one that the future will regard as important. In it, she described his retiring habits and certain other traits:

Always went to bed when he thought it was time—regardless of guests or what was going on. He always figured when he had put a long day's work in, he should be allowed to retire at a reasonable hour. I have found many others who agree with him in this matter, but few with the courage to go through with it. It used to bother me in the early years of our married life, but I came to realize it was a very reasonable conclusion.

Sherm is a great lover of simple things—true things—has no patience with the artificial—the unnecessary.

BUSINESS: Never brings his discouragements home, seemingly overlooks them. He drives himself endlessly and has found contentment in working hard at a job he liked, and for less remuneration than he could have had at a job away from his beloved mountains and his simple country life. With him it has always been the job that counts, not the salary.

COURAGE: Got himself out on a limb before coming out for General Ike—but he had a pretty good idea of the stability of the limb before perching thereon.

Heard him say a number of times of Ike—"He's a great guy."

"What is best for the greatest number of people" is one of his familiar sayings—and he is willing to devote his life to that accomplishment.

He likes to peel an apple and leave the peelings and bits of core most anywhere—has a passion for Gravenstines and Northern Spys—is fussy about his maple syrup, prefers griddle cakes (Mrs. Adams mix) to waffles—is very partial to raw oysters—broiled steaks (home style)—winter squash—boiled onions and shell beans. Prefers plain cooking—does not care for the "Guess what it is" dishes.

11 Things Happening

Letter from Washington
February 7, 1953

The administration seems to have a grip on itself, if not on all of Washington, and a sense of direction that was not apparent in the first two weeks. This week began with the State of the Union message, which was well received, and moved eventfully along toward yesterday's order killing all wage controls. Price controls go later. Yesterday was a big day. Wage controls went out, Clare Boothe Luce went in as ambassador to Italy, and the Reorganization Act was extended. Today the President signed his first law. It creates a new job: Undersecretary of State for Administration. There will be some changes made in the State Department. Things are beginning to happen. Before this week, pretty much everything was talk, and some of the talk was regrettable. Though Charles E. Wilson and his associates in the Defense Department ultimately came to terms with the law, they left a poor impression in Congress and in Washington as a whole. Mr. Wilson's cheery identification of General Motors with the general welfare was bad enough, but even worse, it was felt, was his description of his examination by so gentle and courteous a man as Senator Russell of Georgia as "quite a pushing around." No matter how many securities he agreed to unload, Mr. Wilson, it was felt, had certain shortcomings as a public servant. Harold Talbott, confirmed two days ago as Secretary of the Air Force, and Roger Kyes, confirmed earlier as Undersecretary of Defense, seemed as uncomprehending as Mr. Wilson when called upon to discuss the delicate matters involved. The first conflict of interest laws were enacted by the first Congress, but news of them has been slow in reaching Detroit. (One Eisenhower appointee, Robert Chapman Sprague, who was to be Undersecretary to Mr. Talbott, grasped the principle very well and has just announced that he will forego the job altogether rather than sell his holdings, which are estimated to be salable at $5,000,000, give or take a few hundred thousand.) In the first two weeks, there were other difficulties. The mixup over the President's request for reorganization powers caused widespread dissatisfaction in Congress, and John Foster Dulles's maiden speech as Secretary of State was not looked upon as one of his happier efforts. Of the four local newspapers, all of which supported the Republican ticket last fall, three took offense at Mr. Dulles's announcement of the policy of "openness, simplicity, and righteousness." The *Evening Star,* normally a model of editorial restraint, spoke of it as "gross oversimplification and wishful thinking." (The *Star* did not object to the righteousness, but it took the view that this country is in no position just now to hold out the hope of rescue to 800,000,000 human beings; this seemed to be what Mr. Dulles was offering.) Moreover, the speech, because it dealt harshly with the work of the previous management, wounded so many sensibilities in the State Department that the Secretary, just before leaving with Mr. Stassen for the ten-day tour of the European chancelleries, had to call a big outdoor pep rally to assure his colleagues that he considered them, as a group, not bad.

Mr. Dulles was not the only newcomer to cause hurt feelings among his subordinates. The first two weeks were marked by a whole series of White House and departmental orders in respect to matters like punctuality, dawdling, extended lunch hours, coffee breaks, and smoking in corridors, and the tone of these was such as to suggest that the new administration held the view that before its blessed advent, no one in Washington had ever done an honest day's work. Regardless of the merits of this opinion, the directives in which it seemed to be implied were impolitic because they bred nothing but resentment among people who, thanks to the workings of Civil Service, a noble Republican idea, will be carrying on a large part of the business of the present government.

But a new period began with the State of the Union message. The message did not, of course, deal with any of the specific sources of irritation, but it served the important purpose of directing attention away from personalities and in the direction of policies. The administration is now something more than Mr. Wilson's captain-of-industry brusqueness, Mr. Dulles's air of transcendent wisdom, and Mr. Sherman Adams's frosty puritanism; it is, finally, a collection of political remedies and procedures and ideas. These can be debated in and out of government and examined for their moral and practical worth, yet they cannot be resented in the way individuals can, for, coming as they do from the new President, they represent the will of the electorate, which it is the prime business of this city to respect and carry out.

On the President's part, this seems to have been an act of will undertaken in response to a clearly perceived need. In his conference with Republican congressional leaders on January 26, just a week before he addressed Congress, he revealed his plan to deliver a message that would have been in essence a restatement of the admirable generalities of the Inaugural Address. At that time, according to the party leaders, he had no intention of announcing, in the message, the new orders to the Seventh Fleet, the timing on the abandonment of controls, or any of the other substantive matters he eventually took up. The decisions had doubtless been reached by then. In fact, it is now known that the decision on Seventh Fleet order, or the "deneutralization" plan that is causing such a fluttering in Europe, had been reached by the President and Mr. Dulles very early. It was probably in the works before inauguration, and it was "leaked" three days before the speech. At any rate, on January 26, the President said he would not go into these matters in his address and no great pressure was then put on him to do other-wise. The congressional leaders—themselves as uncertain as any-one else as to what should be expected in the early stages of such a period as this—acquiesced in the proposal. Some, though, were outspokenly disappointed. As late as the following Thurs-day, Senator Taft, asked by a reporter to sum up whatever differences he still had with the President, said ruefully that he couldn't possibly do so because the President hadn't yet gone beyond the slogans and ambiguities of the campaign and added that, judging by the tonelessness and toothlessness of the forth-coming State of the Union message, he thought it would be quite a while before anything but ambiguities came from the White House. "I know he's under great pressure," the Senator said, "but I do hope he'll get down to business pretty soon." It was a hope that a good many people besides Senator Taft felt and it must somehow or other have been borne in on the President. In any event, he took the plunge, and in doing so gave his administration a character and identity it had not had, or had not seemed to have, up to that point.

Now there are policies and legislative proposals: rent-control extension; statehood for Hawaii, with Alaska's case to be consid-ered later on; revision of Taft-Hartley; revision of the McCarran-Walter Immigration Act; more social security for more people; federal aid to education here and there; farm price supports at the present 90 percent of parity; offshore oil for onshore states. Domestically, the policy is not bold or surprising or liberal—but it is policy, a legislative program, something for someone to get to work on. Foreign policy has fewer specifics but actually is more easily defined. Truman and Acheson were repudiated, as Senator McCarthy keeps saying, but there seem to be touches of Trumanism and Achesonism in the program of the Eisen-hower crusaders, as stated in the message—and this in spite of the President's request for "an appropriate resolution making clear that this government recognizes no kind of commitment contained in secret understandings of the past with foreign governments . . . permitting enslavement" and so on, in other words Yalta. The "new, positive foreign policy" seems to contain most of the old, positive features, at least for Europe. Mr. Dulles worried the British and French a bit by his threat to "give a little rethinking" to European matters if things don't soon pick up over there, but both he and the President spoke as heirs and continuers.

The "deneutralization" order, of course, changes certain things, particularly of an atmospheric nature. It is susceptible to a number of interpretations. The most obvious of these, which is that it was intended to have a direct effect on the military situation in the Far East, is the one that almost everyone discounts at the start. As a member of Admiral William Fechteler's staff pointed out a few days ago, it is quite some time since the Seventh Fleet offered any protection to continental China. Ever since late 1950, when the Chinese Communists intervened in Korea, Nationalist forces supplied from Korea and operating from small islands in the Formosa Strait have been making passes at the mainland, and a few strikes have been launched from Formosa itself. The raiders have not escaped the notice of the United States Navy, nor have they been intercepted by it. It has frequently been reported here, and never denied by the Defense Department, that the fleet has from time to time lent a friendly hand to the Nationalists in their efforts to keep in touch with sympathizers operating as guerrillas on the mainland, especially in the south. If the Peiping government is not reeling under the impact of Nationalist blows, it is not because the Seventh Fleet has been an effective shield but because the blows have been so feeble. It is believed here that the new administration's knowledge of the limited capacities of the raiders was one of the things that encouraged it to take this new step, which offered a spectacle, ideal for its present purposes, of drama without suspense. Both the President and Mr. Dulles have been committed, since the closing days of the campaign, to some new action in Korea. In his speech last week, Mr. Dulles said, "General Eisenhower will find the ways to make the enemy change his mind." Apart from the enlargement of our own ground forces in Korea, which certainly isn't to be done, there are only a few steps that could possibly be taken. There are in fact only the four steps urged by General MacArthur in the memorandum he sent the Joint Chiefs of Staff two years ago. These were: a naval blockade of China, bombardment of bases on the mainland, the use of Chinese Nationalist troops in the land fighting in Korea, and the encouragement of assaults on the coastal areas from the Formosa garrison.

What the administration appears to have done is choose the least risky of these steps, and the only step that seems consistent with, on the one hand, its promise to apply new pressures and, on the other, with its given word that it will take no action that would expand the Asian war or bring on a world war. The present move, of course, does not entirely satisfy both requirements; indeed, it can be argued that it does not really satisfy either one. The pressure to be applied is mostly theoretical and in any case not new. It may be that Chiang's striking force will be strengthened by the boost in morale the policy will give him and his troops, but apart from that there is no promise of anything in the way of additional power. Nor can it be claimed with certainty that the current action will not somehow or other spread the war. It is conceivable that it will be taken by Communist China or the Soviet Union as a pretext for new aggression; it is also conceivable that the consternation the policy is creating in Europe (Mr. Eden has advised Commons of his government's formal protest through the embassy here) and in parts of Asia will increase world tensions in such a way as to heighten the danger of conflict. But these contingencies are remote at present and will continue to be remote as long as there are no additional innovations in American policy. Since the Seventh Fleet has been looking the other way for two years it seems unlikely that Moscow or Peiping would use the legalization of its averted gaze as a pretext; anyway, a fiction serves them as well as a fact when they are in the market for a pretext. The distress the decision has caused among our allies appears to be a more serious matter, but while it could weaken us in the event of war, it is difficult to see how it could increase the immediate danger of war.

It should have, though, at least one benefit. It ought to clear up American thinking about China by giving us a true picture of whatever contribution Chiang Kai-shek is able to make to the free world. Most people think his contribution is scarcely worth talking about. If they are wrong, that will be fine, for our cause in Korea would certainly be strengthened if the Chinese Communists were forced to move some of their troops to the shores fronting the Formosa Strait.

There is among many people, though, a fear that despite the assurances Mr. Dulles and Mr. Stassen are giving in Paris and London, we may have to pursue this policy beyond a mere switching of the traffic light from red to green. Nationalist representatives in this country have already hinted that there will be requests for air and naval support for the contemplated landings. It would be simple enough for the government to ignore such requests as long as they came only from representatives of the Formosa regime, but sooner or later there is bound to be a clamor for them here, and it would be quite a reasonable one as clamors go, since a military policy that involves so slight an element of risk as this one seems to, must of necessity involve a large element of illusion. Once it is revealed that Chiang cannot win the war for us on the strength of our blessing alone, the administration will be confronted with further demands. Though President Eisenhower has expressed a certain amount of sympathy with the position General MacArthur took in 1951 ("I have always stood behind General MacArthur in bombing those bases on the Yalu from which fighter planes are coming," he once said in the course of the campaign), any one of them would bring his government into conflict with the United Nations, and he is doubtless too confirmed a believer in the coalition principle to relish such a conflict. But the elimination of approaches that would require the assent of the United Nations would intensify the pressure for more aid to Chiang, which the United States is free to give, and it is easy enough to foresee the steps that could lead in the end to a full-scale commitment to China. Nobody here doubts that President Eisenhower, Secretary Dulles, and just about everyone in the administration wants to avoid a catastrophe of that nature, and most people are convinced they will avoid it, but they feel that to do so will take a lot of prudent diplomacy and military planning.

12 Other Things Happening

Letter from Washington
February 27, 1953

Raymond Aron, a recent visitor to this city, is a distinguished Parisian journalist and in some ways a unique member of his profession in France at the present time. He is a supporter of United States foreign policy, which he regularly defends in his column in *Le Figaro* and in his political writing in other periodicals. Unlike many Frenchmen, he believes that the Soviet Union and its armies offer a clear and present danger to French sovereignty, and he feels that France should cooperate with the United States in resisting this danger. His point of view has led him into controversy with the many Europeans who believe either that the Soviet Union has no designs on Western Europe or that a choice between Russia and America is scarcely worth making, since both powers, as they see it, are totalitarian in spirit. Those who hold the latter opinion frequently cite the activities of Senator McCarthy and of various agents and imitators of his in Washington. M. Aron has patiently called the attention of these people to the fact that McCarthy is not the President of the United States and not an official of any executive agency but merely one member of a large legislature, in which many viewpoints are represented. And in reply to the charge that America is gripped by hysteria and that witch hunting has became a large American industry, M. Aron has said that on his own visits here he has observed comparatively little hysteria and very few witch hunts. He has said, further, that the term "witch hunt" is a highly misleading one, since the various congressional investigations have in the main been looking not for phantoms of any sort but for flesh-and-blood Communist agents, some of whom, in the past, have done material damage to American security. M. Aron has not pretended that everything about the United States is to his liking, but he has made strenuous efforts to allay European misgivings about the general drift of American society, which he regards as free and democratic.

This was M. Aron's view up to a few days ago, and in general it is still his view. On his most recent visit here, however, he acquired some misgivings of his own. He sampled the climate in Washington and attended some of the congressional hearings now taking place, in particular Senator McCarthy's investigation of the Voice of America. In an interview given shortly before his departure for Paris yesterday, he said that he was unable to see how he could honestly continue to defend the United States against those who maintain that our political life is characterized by fear and hysteria. He felt, as many people here do, that in the Voice of America hearings it was perfectly clear that Senator McCarthy's committee was seeking not to ferret out subversives—there have been no charges of Communist activity on the part of the Voice of America staff—but to win a cheap political victory against a group of dedicated anti-Communists. He also felt that it was now impossible to write McCarthy off merely as one legislator with a rambunctious man-

ner and an eccentric and easygoing approach to moral problems; on the contrary, the evidence he came upon suggested to
him, as it has to just about everyone here, that McCarthy has—
for the past ten days, at any rate—been a *de facto* official of the
State Department, a man who has simply to express his views
on any particular matter in order to have them translated, with
extraordinary and quite uncharacteristic speed, into a directive
flashed to American diplomats in every corner of the globe. Four
times in these ten days, McCarthy, whose ideas on diplomacy
M. Aron regards as not very useful in the struggle against world
Communism, has let his views on State Department issues be
known, and four times the State Department has made Mc-
Carthy's views American policy within a matter of hours. Under
the circumstances, M. Aron feels he must explain to his readers
that he misjudged the American situation in several respects. It
would be going too far to say that M. Aron is no longer persuaded of the desirability of Franco-American cooperation, but
it would not be going too far to say that one of our best and
most helpful friends in Europe has returned to his country very
much shaken in his beliefs and prepared to admit a high degree
of error in his earlier estimates of conditions here.

The shock experienced by M. Aron was no greater than that
felt by many other observers of events here. Two weeks ago, a
canvass on the subject of the most important problems facing
the administration would have brought forth a broad variety of
opinions. To some people, our Asian policy seemed the key
issue, to some taxation, to some the decline of farm prices, to
some the general pattern of relations between the executive
and the legislative branches. Lately, though, the key issue has
been Senator McCarthy's powerful challenge to the right of
the President and the Secretary of State to form and carry out
the foreign policy of the United States. In response to this challenge, the State Department has canceled two directives that
provoked McCarthy's criticism, temporarily suspended one employee who was critical of his ideas, and brought back to his old

job an employee whose transfer to a different job had displeased the Senator. (It is indicative of the pervasive atmosphere of panic that, by and large, these steps have *not* been taken at McCarthy's insistence or at the suggestion of anyone else in Congress; they have been taken, as it were, in mere anticipation of McCarthy's displeasure. It seems likely that McCarthy has been as stunned as everyone else by these evidences of his majestic power in Washington.) Three days ago, the State Department suspended Alfred H. Morton, the chief of its International Broadcasting Services, because Mr. Morton had sent to Washington from his office, in New York, a memorandum taking exception to the order, itself the result of a suggestion of McCarthy's, that the Voice of America refrain from quoting "controversial" authors. (Mr. Morton, formerly a high official of the National Broadcasting Company, was later allowed to go back on the job, presumably after a good dressing down by his superiors.) The department first announced that Mr. Morton had seen fit to "disregard" a policy directive, but it subsequently became clear that he had only registered a personal dissent as to its wisdom. He was suspended, however, and the point is that McCarthy did not ask that Morton be relieved of his duties, either permanently or temporarily, or even suggest that anything of the sort be done. In fact, it seems reasonable to believe that McCarthy had no knowledge of the fact that Morton did not see eye to eye with him, since, presumably, the department does not yet forward its correspondence to the Senator promptly upon receipt. But the department does know what the Senator thinks of people who disagree with him, and in no time at all Assistant Secretary of State Carl W. McCardle was telling reporters that Mr. Morton's temerity had been rewarded with a suspension. In all probability, McCarthy's appetite for victories would have been satisfied by the knowledge that the department has acted upon his advice in banning the "controversial" writers, and would not immediately have gone on to demand that those who disagreed be disciplined. Something of that sort could have been next week's victory. But the department gave him next week's victory this week, and so it has been going for what seems like an eternity.

In the past, it was not easy to measure the damage done by the Senator's tactics to American policy and prestige. It could be argued that he was mostly damaging private reputations and that some of these had been badly soiled by their bearers long before McCarthy came to Washington. Today, it is ridiculously easy to measure the damage. It is believed by the majority of people who have been familiar over an extended period with the methods of the Voice of America that much of its best work has been done in a section that is unappealingly known as the ideological division. This division has been for the past couple of years under the direction of Bertram D. Wolfe, a distinguished American scholar who has an intimate understanding of Soviet life, a good command of the Russian language, and what is probably an unsurpassed acquaintance with the writings of Marx, Engels, Lenin, and Stalin, as well as most of the lesser prophets of Bolshevism. Mr. Wolfe has been operating his division on the theory, widely adjudged to be a sound one, that most Russians will not be coaxed away from their leaders by the knowledge that some American workers own ranch-style houses equipped with deep freezes but that they may in time become embittered and disaffected by the knowledge that they have been betrayed by their leaders. It is no news to the average Russian, Mr. Wolfe has pointed out at various times in the past, that the Socialist paradise is not really a paradise. The Russians have been living wretchedly with this knowledge for quite some time. What may be news to a great many of them, though, is that the Socialist paradise is not even Socialist—that it is, in fact, about as far from the Socialist idea as any human society could possibly get. Mr. Wolfe's idea is that Joseph Stalin should be the principal target of our psychological warfare and that he should be attacked not as a man who would be no credit to Kiwanis International but as one who has consistently betrayed every decent ideal of the people he leads, and, beyond that, has betrayed practically everything he himself has said. The ideological division has been trying to get across to the Russians that just as Lenin was false to Marx, so Stalin has been false to Lenin and to himself. Mr. Wolfe has held that this is of far more importance than arguing that Stalin doesn't measure up to the standards set by Chester A. Arthur or Chauncey Depew. It is not, to be sure, a matter of record that the broadcasts prepared under Mr. Wolfe's direction have had any notable effect in the Soviet Union, but it has generally been felt that they had a better chance of advancing the aims of our diplomacy than most other approaches, and that in our great need they were at least worth trying.

Last week's order banning the quotation of Communist writers will obviously make it impossible for Mr. Wolfe's office to function along this line. To prove that Stalin has lied, it is necessary to repeat what Stalin has said, and this, of course, cannot be done under the terms of the new directive. There is one important exception. According to Assistant Secretary McCardle, Marx, Lenin, and Stalin may be quoted by the Voice of America if the quotations can be attributed to a "reputable" news agency or newspaper. Exactly what the point of this exception is no one here seems able to say, but it is clear that if our broadcasters must rummage through the newspapers of several decades back to track down a quotation they wish to use, the labor involved could place a new and severe strain on the national economy. Moreover, the moment at which a particular reference was pertinent could recede far into the past while the team of researchers was trying to establish prior use of it by a reputable newspaper or wire service. The general feeling here is that the directive puts the kibosh on one of the few potentially valuable efforts that the United States has been making in the field of psychological warfare. Most people find it impossible to believe that it will not in time be revoked, but there are no signs at present that revocation is so much as being considered. Even if that should come to pass, a great deal of irreparable harm may well have been done; the situation now is such that it would take an imprudent, not to say reckless, official to revert, even with permission, to a practice that had created such a storm and had led to the official chastisement and humiliation of so well-connected a figure as Mr. Morton. The appeasement of Mc-Carthy, besides crippling the Voice of America, gives substance to the already widespread notion that there is a totalitarian or semi-totalitarian censorship in this country, for the directive was accompanied by an order that "controversial" books and periodicals be removed from the shelves of the libraries we maintain in other countries. The mere removal of these books is not thought serious in itself, but the existence of the order is damaging in the extreme, since it suggests to all who learn of it that we have abandoned the principle of the free market in the world of ideas. And so we have, apparently, in this small but important area.

13 Robert A. Taft: Majority Leader

March 22, 1953

In his fifteenth year in the Senate, and in the year following his defeat in one of the great party struggles in American history, Robert A. Taft of Ohio has ascended new heights of power and prestige.

The old heights were themselves commanding. For well over a decade, Taft exercised greater individual authority than any other Republican in Congress. Almost from the day he entered the Senate in 1939, he was recognized as its foremost exponent of conservatism and nationalism. His knowledge, his energies, and his partisan zeal were unrivaled on Capitol Hill. Though his personality was seriously flawed—by pedantry, by stiffness, by impatience—he was able, by the sheer force of his example, by the vigor, if not always by the clarity, of his precepts, to wield vast influence in Washington.

By all the rules of politics, though, his influence should now be on the wane. Taft had enemies in the party. The enemies had power. They defeated him in Chicago last July, as indeed they had defeated him in every national convention since that of 1940. Taft is well acquainted with defeat. In November his party adversaries won control of the executive branch of government. In the circumstances, Taft, who will be sixty-four this year, might have been expected to suffer a gradual diminution of power. He had been outmaneuvered, outflanked, outranked; it would be going too far to say that he had been repudiated, but there was at least an element of that in the action of the Republican convention and in the subsequent verdict of the electorate.

Far from being driven to retreat, Taft stormed and occupied new positions of power. The military analogy commends itself on many grounds. What Taft has now he won for himself by superior combat strategy. It was not, as some people suppose, conferred upon him by General Eisenhower at the famous September meeting on Morningside Heights. Whether or not that meeting was properly described as an act of surrender on the candidate's part (it was indisputably an act of appeasement), the fact remains that the Eisenhower advisers never abandoned their desire to reduce Taft's authority. They felt they needed Taft's help in the elections, but they wanted for the future to be in a position to get along without it. In the Hotel Commodore headquarters in New York between election and inauguration, nothing was more fashionable, particularly among the younger members of the Eisenhower group, than to take a disparaging view of Senator Taft, to regard him as a man who, though perhaps deserving of a certain esteem for his years and for his courage, was hopelessly out of date and an obstacle to the progress of the Republic and of the party. Actually, they were scared stiff of Taft. In that period, and even in the weeks following inauguration, all sorts of clever-sounding schemes were afoot to strip Taft and his followers of their power. Of these, the most notable was Herbert Brownell's plan for changing the rules on patronage distribution by bypassing the Senate altogether.

Nothing worked. Taft has all his old power and more besides. Before this year, his influence in the Senate was that of a forceful, hugely respected individual. Some of his authority, it is true, derived from his committee assignments—particularly his chairmanship of the Republican Policy Committee—but on the whole his strength was independent of organization. As Arthur Krock has said, Taft is a MacGregor: wherever he sits, there is the head of the table.

In the Eighty-third Congress, he has organizational power, too. Moving in swiftly after the election, going quietly to work before the Dewey-Brownell wing had finished congratulating itself, Taft organized the United States Senate from top to bottom. He nominated himself for majority leader and put his followers in all the key positions. Eugene Millikin of Colorado, perhaps his most capable ally, is chairman of the Republican Conference, which is the party caucus. Millikin is also chairman of finance. Hugh Butler of Nebraska is chairman of Interior and Insular Affairs. Appropriations is chaired by Styles Bridges of New Hampshire. The Foreign Relations Committee, which since the days of the late Arthur Vandenberg has been the preserve of the party's internationalists, has been given a massive infusion of Taft sentiment by the presence of Taft himself and by that of William Knowland of California, Homer Ferguson of Michigan, and William Langer of North Dakota. Whatever became, people are beginning to ask, of Duff of Pennsylvania, Ives of New York, and Carlson of Kansas, those astute men who were for Eisenhower before Chicago? It is a good question. One hears little of them nowadays.

Taft's power reaches the House of Representatives in somewhat attenuated form, but even there it is impressive. Students of the organization of the legislative branch maintain that there has never been a Congress in which one man has the kind of authority that Senator Taft now wields. There have been powerful figures who have pretty well run one or the other of the two houses, but never a man whose influence is as bi-camerally pervasive as Taft's is today, less than three months after the opening session. He has given his attention to the most obscure House subcommittees, making sure that the slender Republican majorities can be used to the best advantage and that the pivotal positions go to Republicans of his own stripe. The majority leader, Charles Halleck of Ohio, is a regular in the Taft organization, and so are Clarence Brown of Ohio and Leo Allen of Illinois, who dominate the Rules Committee, the present-day seat of much of the power the Speaker of the House formerly had. Taft had no vote in selecting the heads of the House committees, but somehow or other the men he wished to see named were named. "Directly in the Senate and indirectly in the House," William Shannon recently wrote, "Taft is able to control the flow of legislation to the floor, the scheduling and timing of debates, and virtually the success or failure of any bill."

How will Taft use his hugely augmented power? The question is often asked in Washington, where it is recognized that there is still a conflict, doctrinal if not personal, between the President and the Senator. The President believes in coalition as a technique for meeting the external threat of Soviet Communism and for bringing about unity in the country. Taft is a lukewarm supporter of collective security, and in domestic matters he feels that the Republican Party can be true to itself only through a policy of rigorous conservatism. As conflicts go in American politics, this is a serious one. The Republican Party can contain adherents of both views, just as the Democratic Party can contain Adlai Stevenson and Herman Talmadge. But no mere election can dispel the differences.

In the period immediately following the elections, it was widely believed that a break would come sometime in 1953 and that when it came Taft would give leadership to the anti-Eisenhower forces. And when, in December, Taft denounced the appointment of Martin Durkin as Secretary of Labor, it seemed that the break would come early rather than late in the year and that the contest would be as hard-fought and rancorous as that which characterized the pre-convention period. It was felt that Taft was too chronic an oppositionist, too habitual a nay-sayer, to be part of a going concern.

The judgment turned out to be a mistaken one, but for a while there was every reason to think it sound. After Chicago, Taft withdrew to his father's old summer place in Murray Bay, Quebec. It may be unkind to say that he sulked there, but it would be hard to find a better word for it. He was bitter and resentful. Neither his party nor his admirers had any word from him. He played no part in organizing the Eisenhower campaign. Friends returning from Murray Bay reported that he brooded day and night over the cruel events of the summer and spring. One of the evening rituals at Murray Bay, they said, was a running commentary by Taft on a magazine article that dealt sympathetically and in detail with the injustice and ingratitude with which his career had been rewarded by convention. Taft, they said, had worn the magazine thin and had practically memorized the article. The situation was such that one old friend, Edwin Lahey of the Chicago *Daily News*, could report, after a visit to Murray Bay, that General Eisenhower's chances of getting Taft to help in the campaign are "about zero." Lahey suggested that it would even be difficult to persuade Taft to support an Eisenhower administration once it was elected. He said that Taft would want certain definite assurances and that he would want them "in writing." Lahey specified: a promise of no reprisals against Taft supporters, a promise "that the nominee is not going to repudiate the Taft-Hartley Act, even by indirection," and, finally, a vigorous assertion of Republican doctrine.

As the summer grew old, Taft's resentment lost its edge. He is not a spiteful or an uncharitable man, and in spite of what Mr. Lahey reported, it was probably always in the cards that he would come in the end to a reasonable and responsible position. The whole tendency of Taft's life has been to triumph in the end over his own unreasonableness and irresponsibility. By September 12 he was ready to come to terms with Eisenhower, but the terms were stiff and proud. He arrived at the Eisenhower residence on Morningside Heights with a firm, lucid, text—not a treaty, as some called it, but a manifesto—in his pocket. The General, a pliant man, agreed. That suited Taft, and from September 12 on there has never been any doubt of his loyalty, and now, although it still appears certain that there must be a contest sooner or later for control of the Republican Party, Taft's position is nowhere in dispute. He has rallied his followers and deployed them well, but it cannot be said that he has sought personal or, in his terms, factional advantage. He has differed with the President and has stated his differences openly—as he did on the "Yalta resolution" that was tabled after Stalin's death—but he has been clearly bending every effort to make the first Republican administration in twenty years, the administration he had such high hopes of leading, a thoroughgoing success. He will fight to get his way with the administration, but he will never fight to destroy it, as certain others certainly will. In that battle, when it comes, he will be at the President's side. He is already there.

He has assumed the responsibility for guiding the President's program through Congress. He makes no secret of the fact that he regards that program as fairly riddled with ideological impurities. "It certainly isn't all I'd like it to be," he told a visitor recently, "but I think I can go along with it most of the way. When I can't, I guess I'll just say so and be satisfied with getting myself on the record." He is more in agreement with it than many of his followers. In the dispute over whether a tax cut should follow or precede a reduction of expenditures, he stood with the President and rallied a majority to the budget-balancing side.

The Durkin appointment was by no means the only one that Taft has found hard to take, but, once having spoken his piece, he came to the President's support, and it is thanks to him that there has been relatively little Republican dissension over the personnel of the Eisenhower administration. He has failed in his efforts to keep Senator McCarthy from being a cause of anguish and embarrassment to the administration. This failure can be attributed partly to the encouragement he gave McCarthy in the past (it is doubtful if McCarthy would be around today if Taft had withheld his support in 1950), but it is also partly because McCarthy operates outside the party structure and in thorough disregard of the codes of political behavior which govern most of his colleagues.

At all odds, Taft has, in 1953, gone a long way toward vindicating the judgment of those admirers who have maintained that his independence and his candor entitled him to the respect of all men and that he could provide the conservatives of this country with the kind of responsible leadership they appeared to want. In the last period of the Truman administration, it was not easy to defend this judgment, for Taft's passion for thwarting the then President frequently overcame his good judgment and at times made even his candor seem more illusory than real. But since the opening of Congress, he has seemed to most people in Washington a model of political sobriety and responsibility, and there is at present no reason to suppose that he will be driven off the course he has set for himself.

This is not to say that his power in Congress will at all times be used to advance the program of the administration as it comes from the White House. He will unquestionably use it to bring the administration's program closer to what he thinks it ought to be. He is not the sort to borrow other men's convictions or to suppress his own for very long. ("I guess a lot of us had some reservations," he said after the President's State of the Union message, "but we're keeping them to ourselves for the time being.") He is an activist, a politician, and the administration will have to go on bargaining with him. Its program and in the end its record in history will bear the marks of this bargaining, as indeed it should, for the role of a congressional leader of the party in power is not that of a mere expediter of legislation prepared in the executive branch. It calls for criticism as well as assent, and Taft is not the man to disappoint in a role that calls for criticism. Taft will continue, one imagines, to stand somewhat to the right of most of the President's advisers and to be a good deal less enthusiastic than most of them about collective security. It is fruitless to dispute his contention that he is not an isolationist; the fact is that he has never had much sense of the urgency of coalition and has opposed it in practice more ardently than he has ever defended it in theory. It is reasonable to suppose that the policy will be more acceptable under Republican auspices than it was under Democratic auspices, and he will inevitably use his bargaining power to trim and scale down administration requests. At the same time, however, it seems evident that he will act in appreciation of the fact that it is not he but Eisenhower who has been called to lead the country and that, as a good party man, his own job is not to frustrate the President or to demonstrate his own superior wisdom but to counsel the President as wisely and as well as he can.

The Taft of 1953 differs in many ways from the Taft of the long Democratic dynasty. The combination of personal defeat and party victory has mellowed his outlook and softened his manner. The change can be observed just about any day that the Senate is in session and Taft is on the floor, playing his new role as majority leader. In fact, his very acceptance of this role is evidence of the change that has come over him. A year ago, it would have been difficult for anyone who knew Taft well to have imagined him in this tedious and unpleasant job. The office is one that requires no gifts of a high order. It has generally been held as a reward for enterprising mediocrity. The qualities it does require, apart from a good sense of parliamentary strategy, are tact, patience, and an ability to be agreeable to those for whom one has little respect. These are qualities which, up to now, Taft has conspicuously lacked.

But, driven by the gnawings of a masochistic Puritan conscience and whatever else it is that drives him, he sought the office and won it, and today the observer can look down from the Senate galleries and see what has every appearance of being a thoroughly overhauled, remodeled, and Simonized Taft. The Eisenhower administration may introduce new personalities and new ideas, but it is hard to imagine that it will introduce anything in the line of political spectacles half as arresting as Taft on the Senate floor. A man who has never suffered fools gladly and who has always been visibly impatient and nervous when duty required his presence in the Senate chamber, the scene of some of the world's most ridiculous oratory, he has now voluntarily taken on a job that requires him to be there most of the time, to coddle all manner of fools, and to indulge in exactly the kind of persiflage he so clearly detests. He is doing it, however, and doing it with no complaints and without sacrificing his other self-imposed tasks, in the interest of the party and also, perhaps, of reaching some place he has staked out for himself in posterity, and he is really quite a show. He is relaxed and genial. He moves about the floor wreathed in smiles, a friend to all men, almost a gladhander. He uncomplainly endures hours on end of Senate ritual and almost unendurable Senate oratory. He has become an adept, as he never was in the past of the overblown rhetoric of senatorial courtesy—"I gladly yield three minutes to my good friend across the aisle, the able and distinguished junior Senator from the great state of ——." (In an earlier day, the style of Taft's colloquies was crisp and unrhetorical. Samples: "That's stupid." "I think the Senator is talking tommyrot.") He is still assertive in debate, but his language is somehow less astringent than it was. His policy toward the opposition is one of comity.

In a sense, what has happened is that the private Taft has become the public Taft. There was always a striking and bewildering difference between the mulish, doctrinaire figure of the public image and the reflective, open-minded man one encountered as an individual among individuals. The private Taft was a literate, generalizing man, a true lover of ideas, who was perfectly willing to reconsider and listen to criticism of the views he would state to the public with such maddening self-assurance. He was a man only too willing to admit that life is a difficult proposition, that there are two or more sides to every question, and that it was entirely within the realm of possibility that he was mistaken on this question or that. But no sooner would he make these disarming admissions than he would take to the hustings and alienate a large number of his auditors by speaking as a man whose mind apparently could not entertain the thought that there was just the remotest chance of his being wrong or that things might be a trifle less simple and clearcut than he made them out to be.

Lately, though, the startling and engaging reasonableness of the private Taft has been put on the political display counters. Having publicly maintained for years that there was no possible way of seeing the Korean war except as he and General Mac-Arthur saw it, he has now come out and said that there is no course of action in which the advantages clearly outweigh the disadvantages. For years, Taft has privately maintained the view of academic freedom he has lately been advancing in speeches—that a teacher must be judged on his pedagogic merits, not on his political associations. As a member of the Yale Corporation, he has sturdily defended the right to teach of a Yale professor for whose views on public matters he has nothing but contempt, a man whom many people commonly adjudged to be more liberal than Taft have been urging the university to drop. But he withheld his views and concealed his efforts not so much, one

feels, because he feared that revelation would damage his political fortunes as because in his intense partisanship he was reluctant to say anything that would appear to align him with the
New Dealers and Fair Dealers whose opinions in general he
found insufferable.

Now, though, the pressures are off, the political suspense is
broken, and Taft's private judgments and political aims are no
longer in conflict with each other. His intelligence can function in
the service of what he conceives to be the common good. This intelligence operates within a fairly narrow range, but within that
range it is first-rate. His mind is cool, eclectic, pragmatic, and it
leads him very often to astonishing judgments. In a recent conversation, for example, Taft, who in the liberal demonology
is not so much Mr. Republican as Mr. Big Business, confessed to
certain misgivings about the number of business men who are
filling high places in the government. "You know," he said, "I'm
not at all sure that all these business men are going to work
out. I don't know of any reason why success in business should
mean success in public service. They're very different fields, and
anyone who thinks he can just transfer business methods to government is going to have to learn that it just isn't so." And Mr.
Republican, who is all kinds of abhorrent things in the demonology of British liberalism, turned for a moment to a consideration of affairs in the United Kingdom. "You've never heard me
criticizing the British for going Socialist," he said. "Their problems are entirely different from ours. In a country that size,
where there just isn't any hope of building anything like a self-
sufficient economy, the government's simply got to step in and
run a lot of things. All I've ever said is that there isn't any excuse for *this* country going Socialist."

If it is a fact that the private Taft is emerging from the
shadows, if the able senior Senator from Ohio gives the Republic
the benefit of the critical intelligence with which he makes his
own approach to matters affecting the common welfare, the
country will be greatly in his debt. It will have not only the mili-

tant conservative leader it has known for so many years but an astute and provocative social critic as well.

14 Republican Prospects

June 1953

In his first White House news conference, President Eisenhower spoke of the party of his choice as "these Republicans," and attempts were made to read deep meanings into what was surely an inadvertency of speech. So far as the President himself is concerned, the use of the third person could not have had much significance. He belongs to the Republican Party, and the Republican Party is where he belongs. He is a man of the right by instinct and conviction; his admiration for the business community seems to know no bounds. If he spoke of the Republican organization as something apart from himself, the explanation must be that he is a newcomer not only to party leadership but to politics generally. He has seen a lot of strange faces in the last year, and it is understandable that he should think of them as "they" rather than "we."

Yet the meaningless remark points to a meaningful circumstance. Whatever his own conception of himself may be, Eisenhower is not a Republican President in quite the sense that his predecessor was a Democratic President. Truman's party put Truman in power; Eisenhower put Eisenhower's party in power. It may be true that just about any Republican could have been elected last year. There were voters who wanted change for the sake of change and would have supported Taft or Warren or MacArthur or even Homer Ferguson on the Republican ticket. But it is almost certainly true that no other candidate could have achieved a majority comparable to Eisenhower's. Millions voted Republican because he was the candidate; they voted for him and not for his party.

Even with his six-million majority, Eisenhower barely managed to bring in a Republican Congress—Republican by seven votes in the House and in the Senate by the solitary, tie-breaking vote of the Vice-President. Had another candidate headed the ticket, the Eighty-third Congress would in all likelihood have been organized by Democrats. (In a post-election article in the Cincinnati *Times-Star*, Senator Taft, while frank to admit that he could not have commanded Eisenhower's popular vote, argued that he could have brought in more Republican congressmen. The case he presented was interesting but far from convincing.) To what would appear to be a critical number of voters, it is the President who has the mandate, not the Republican Party. In the public mind, unlike the presidential mind, the identification of Eisenhower and his party is far from complete.

This fact bears heavily on the Republican Party's future. Had it been returned to power on the customary terms, as it was, say, in the elections of 1896 and 1920, one could state the problem very simply. Its future, in that event, would be determined by the way it fulfilled its historic role—that of the party which represents the business interests of the country and manages the government in such a way as to promote the freedom and growth of those interests. When Harding succeeded Wilson, this was clearly what the country had in mind. It was what Harding meant by "normalcy," and the people wished to get back to it with him. They were eager, as Coolidge was, to press on with the American business of business. The discovery, at the outset of that period, that some Republicans were not single-mindedly devoted to the public welfare made little difference. The public welfare was a pretty hazy concept, anyway; what really mattered was the private welfare. Harding, Coolidge, and Hoover were elected by pluralities far more impressive than

Eisenhower's—as against Eisenhower's 10 or 11 percent, they had 28, 30, and 18 percent respectively—and until the second part of Hoover's term Congress was safely and often overwhelmingly Republican. There were few ambiguities in the election returns of those days. The country was quite certain that it preferred Republicans to Democrats.

In certain respects, this present period does resemble that one. There were sections of the Eisenhower movement—one thinks, for example, of the millionaires and would-be millionaires of the Southwest—that seemed to want little more than freedom from governmental restraint. There has indeed been an enormous growth of conservative sentiment, a renaissance of the business spirit, in this country in the past five or six-years—alongside, though not necessarily related to, a growth of out-and-out reaction. But by and large the Eisenhower movement was not based on conservatism or reaction or dreams of avarice and black gold but on fear and uncertainty about the state of the union and, further, on the belief that in General Eisenhower the country had a man who, regardless of where he stood on this foreign issue or that domestic one, was capable of providing firm and honest leadership. The fears, which centered around Communism and corruption, may in large measure have been synthetically generated, but they had, nevertheless, a genuine existence in the minds they assailed. And the hopes and promises that General Eisenhower was felt to embody were no less genuine, nor would they be if tomorrow they were proved to have been without foundation.

The search for precedents leads back not to any Republican period but to the period of Democratic power that was getting under way just twenty years ago. Although Franklin Roosevelt was, in the public mind, more closely identified with the Democratic Party than Eisenhower is with the Republican Party, and although he carried in huge congressional majorities, his election resembled Eisenhower's in that the country was not voting for a party or a program as much as it was expressing dislike of the recent past and confidence in an imposing human being. It was Roosevelt and not his program (unless his program is thought of merely as the categorical assertion of government responsibility for the general welfare, by then a rather vivid concept) that moved the voters. They replaced Hoover, a symbol of ineffectuality, with a man who, without really having said very much, somehow gave them the good feeling that he could master the situation. Eisenhower and 1952 have a great deal in common with Roosevelt and 1932.

The election of Roosevelt did not signify a mass conversion to Democratic principles, any more than Eisenhower's election signified a mass defection. It was a prelude to conversion, though. It was the months and years following the election of 1932 that saw the actual formation of the coalition that governed the country until January of this year. The coalition did not bring the Democrats to power in the first place; power was what made the building of it possible. Some of the leading elements in the coalition—organized labor, for example, and the Negro militants—had played hardly any part at all in the 1932 revolution. The trade unions were politically insignificant in those days, and the Negroes were mostly exercising the Fifteenth Amendment in favor of the party that wrote it. But Roosevelt's election gave the Democrats a chance; they used it brilliantly.

The election of Eisenhower gives the Republicans almost the same kind of chance, and there is every reason to suppose that with good management and just a small amount of luck they can build as formidable a series of political alliances as the Democrats built back in the thirties. If they are as astute as the Democrats were, they will pry loose whole sections of the Democratic coalition and incorporate them into a Republican coalition. The Democrat who voted for Eisenhower last year was not by that simple rebellious act converted into a dependable Republican. But a voter who has broken with his party once can do it again, and every disturbed Democrat is at least a potential Republican.

There are signs that the Republicans are going earnestly about the job of building their new coalition. They are presently making, for example, large efforts to complete the job of breaking the Democratic hold on racial minorities. In a discussion of the Democrats and their possible future in *Harper's* for March, John Fischer explained how this hold had been weakened over the years by the falling off of immigration and by the workings of time, which brings death and cultural assimilation; what time and the immigration laws have not done to the Democratic city machines that served the immigrant masses they have done to themselves by sloth and corruption. It is perfectly true that the minorities, by which we nowadays mean English-speaking members of second- and third-generation ethnic groups, cannot be cultivated on the old terms by the urban organizations which once served as employment brokers and helped to sustain human pride by offering kindliness and warmth. But there are other ways of cultivating the minorities. For so long as the Soviet empire holds together, the issue of "liberation," which the Republicans exploited so skillfully last year, particularly among people of Eastern European extraction, will be a valuable one. A certain risk to our diplomacy is the cost of using the issue, and "liberation" is a slogan that can backfire if it remains no more than a slogan for any considerable period of time, but for the present and the near future it is a potent political device, and the Republicans have it all to themselves. If they cannot actually be the angels of deliverance, they can at least manufacture halos for themselves by keeping alive, by means of congressional investigations, the already widespread belief that the Communist empire was built by Communists and Democrats at Teheran, Yalta, and Potsdam.

They can also awaken ancestral memories in the nearly assimilated minorities. A measure is to be introduced in the Eighty-third Congress, by Republican sponsors as yet unchosen but certain to come from states where the payoff will be large, to liberalize the McCarran-Walter Act. This act received more support from Republicans than from Democrats, and it was passed over the veto of a Democratic president, but its authors were Democrats, and it became law when the Democrats were in authority. There is some doubt as to whether the proposed Republican measure can be got through the present Congress, but if it can, credit for it will be entered in the Republican account, where it can be made to do immeasurable good.

Ethnic consciousness and xenophobia are declining in the United States, but they are a long way from being dead. There are no longer, as Mr. Fischer pointed out, friendless, penniless, ignorant newcomers to be cheered and fed and made to feel at home; they have been replaced by their children, who have been moving out of the slums for years and in many cases out of the laboring class altogether. But their movement inside American society is a form of migration, and it has its own problems, which, as it happens, the Republican Party is well equipped to deal with. Becoming established in the middle class and settling in predominately Anglo-Saxon communities, these people face some of the same difficulties their parents and grandparents faced in entering a new and strange society. Hostility is encountered among those who are already established; a new set of conventions must be learned and mastered; political representation must be fought for. In encouraging this new migration, and in helping along the new migrants, there can never be the kind of rewards the Democratic machines got for their services earlier in the century, but there are rewards all the same. So simple a thing, for instance, as making more frequent the incidence of names like Dworshak and O'Konski and Cerano and McCarthy (repeat, *names*) in lists of Republican officeholders could strengthen the party enormously. In this particular matter, moreover, it could perform a service for the entire country, for if Republicans can match Democrats at this game, then the day will be clearly in sight when this whole nonsensical business of ethnic representation will disappear from political life in this country.

In this early stage of Republican power, the party is obviously trying to unfasten every detachable and semi-detachable part of the Democratic coalition. It is bidding for the sympathy of labor, Negroes, farmers, small business, states' rights Southerners, and just about everyone else this side of Prohibitionists and Greenbackers.

In time, of course, some of the less promising of its enterprises will have to be given up in order to allow the pursuit of the more promising ones. It appears fairly certain that labor will have to be left to the Democrats. It is most unlikely that the appointment of a union steamfitter to the President's cabinet or even a relaxation of the harsher provisions of the Taft-Hartley Act will bring over from the Democratic coalition any sizable part of the class-conscious labor vote. Individual workers, great numbers of them, can be brought into the Republican camp by appeals addressed to them in their roles as consumers, taxpayers, veterans, or members of racial and religious groups; great numbers were brought over in the last election. But that part of labor which regards the voting machine as an instrument of collective bargaining is not likely to make any lasting alliance with the Republican Party—not unless the Republicans break their ties with big business, and this is as unlikely as it would be foolhardly.

It seems probable that the Negro vote, too, will in the end be left to the Democrats. There is very little in theory that argues against the re-establishment of the Negro-Republican alliance, and a lot of history argues in its favor. Although Eisenhower got very little of the Negro vote last fall, most colored communities having been more nearly solid in support of Stevenson than they had ever been in support of Roosevelt or Truman, a firm anti-segregation policy could almost certainly win back millions of Negro votes. If there is an increase of Southern power in the Democratic party, that could be handily used by the Republicans to encourage the return of Negro voters.

Winning back the Negroes, however, would mean forfeiting

much of what the Republicans gained in the South last year. An emphatic Republican espousal of the Negro cause would drive Democrats-for-Eisenhower back on their pasts in a hurry. If President Eisenhower, whose commitment to racial equality is a deeply felt one, does not appreciate this basic fact, the party managers certainly do, and when the time comes for making fundamental decisions on strategy, it will almost certainly find many of them more disposed toward strengthening their present alliance with conservative Southerners than toward reviving the old one with Northern Negroes.

By almost any appraisal of the weights and balances in American politics at the present time, this course would be mandatory. It would be agreeable for the Republicans to have the Negro vote, but it isn't essential. The 1952 election dispelled the myth that Negroes hold the balance of power in the large Northern states. It showed that a strong Republican candidate could win with both the Negro masses and the class-conscious workers against him. To be sure, it also showed that he could have won without the South. But the new Republican strength in the South holds enormous promise for the party in the future. If the party could merely hold its own in the North and achieve the status of an established minority party in a half-dozen Southern states, a status comparable, say, to that of the Democrats in Minnesota or Iowa, its prospects would be extremely bright.

There was nothing freakish about Eisenhower's 1952 vote in the South. The election was uncomplicated by the religious issue that led several Southern states to break with the Democrats in 1928. Adlai Stevenson's views were less offensive to Southern conservatives than Harry Truman's had been. Eisenhower made only the usual concessions to Southern opinion. In contrast to his victory elsewhere in the country, his victory in the South was as much a tribute to the party as to its candidate. Unlike the Northern voter, the Southern voter could not avoid an identification of Eisenhower with the Republican Party, and all the evidence now suggests that Southern voters, those at least who are susceptible to conservative appeals, suffer no anguish in casting Republican ballots. Virginia elected three Republican representatives. A few weeks ago in Georgia, where the Democratic organization stayed with the ticket last year, two young Republicans led the field in a county election. In a remarkable speech in Columbia, South Carolina, a short while after the election, Governor Byrnes urged state Democratic leaders to continue their alliance with the Republicans in "the uncertain future" and to put no faith in the word of Southern Democrats, presumably such men as Senator Russell and Representative Rayburn, who had supported Stevenson. Byrnes said that it was a matter of indifference to him whether in the long run the conservative Democrats retained their political identity or were absorbed by their traditional antagonists "either under the name of the Republican party or under a new name." All that did concern him, he said, was that cooperation continue.

The gains the Republicans have already made in the South are an example—in a sense, really, the ultimate demonstration—of what E. E. Schattschneider calls "the nationalization of American politics." This is a development closely related to the growth of federal, as opposed to state and local, authority and of American power in world affairs. It is nowadays positively bromidic to point out that the world has become smaller in the twentieth century, but a great many people who have been saying this for years have not been correspondingly aware of the shrinkage of that part of the world that is the United States and of the fact that national issues now dominate our thinking. This does not mean that we are no longer moved by a congressional candidate's appeals to local pride and local greed, but it does mean that we are tending more and more to form our judgments on the basis of issues that are not primarily sectional.

Even those who profess a principled belief in states' rights and in the decentralization of power are likely in spite of themselves to think and act primarily in terms of national policy.

Thus, a Democrat like Governor Byrnes can, in the very course of making a fervent states' rights argument before a gathering of presumably intransigent anti-federalists, plead for the putting aside of such provincial concerns as the welfare of their own party in their own state, urging them instead to serve what he regards as the cause of truth and enlightenment through a working alliance with the national leaders of the Republican Party. The matters that truly concern Governor Byrnes are matters of *national* policy; "states' rights" is merely an incantation, a phrase which suggests a particular outlook on certain national issues. One does not for a moment call the Governor's integrity into question by saying that if the values and institutions he wishes to protect could be served by federal statute and federal policy, we could be sure that he would look with favor on the federal approach. Can anyone imagine him objecting to a federal statute *upholding* segregation?

The thing we all sense, whether or not we acknowledge it, is that politically we are at last one nation. Our social cleavages have not disappeared—some have widened menacingly in recent years—but they are all national cleavages. Our minds have taken the same course that power has taken, and we now vote our views on national policy, with the consequence that it is no longer possible to detect very many regional trends in election results. None of us should have been surprised, as a great many of us were, when last year's Republican trend prevailed in a Democratic fortress like Rhode Island. We should have known that if it was to prevail anywhere it was pretty well bound to prevail everywhere, even in Rhode Island, and the difference between 1952 and previous elections was that this trend toward the uniformity of trends caught on in the South, our last stronghold of regional politics—and now a crumbling fortress.

The challenge to the Republicans, then, is to build the first truly national coalition. But even if they take advantage of all the possibilities offered by the South, by the changing status of minorities, and by the desire for stability that is a normal consequence of prosperity, they will still face the largest political problem of all—that of securing for the party as a party the popular mandate that now belongs to the President as an individual. For while the fact remains that there was a clear movement toward Republicanism last year, and one that prevailed almost everywhere, it was not a very powerful trend. The course of the current was unmistakable, but there was nothing torrential or galvanic about it. Only the President had a really safe margin.

Of all Republican opportunities, the greatest lies among those Americans responsible for the margin between the presidential and congressional votes. It is the opportunity to fulfill the hopes of the large and crucial group of voters who were happy to turn over the executive branch of the government to General Eisenhower but were manifestly reluctant to turn over the legislative branch to his party. The problem of winning them cannot be stated in terms of setting up new party organizations or of manipulating old instincts and prejudices. This is not to say that these voters are moral philosophers who have transcended habit and instinct, but it is to say that a great and apparently growing number of Americans attempt to exercise their suffrage on the basis of what they regard as a rational estimate of the needs of the Republic.

The thing that will win and hold them for the Republican coalition is a performance by the administration that will persuade them of the wisdom of the support they gave it. President Eisenhower made some large and glittering promises in his bid for their favor. Doubtless only the incorrigible dreamers among them expect early delivery on any of the promises; doubtless only a few expect that he will ever be able to deliver on all of them. Presidents Roosevelt and Truman held the confidence of independents for a great many years without redeeming anywhere near all the pledges they had made. But to hold its independent supporters, an administration must in a broad and general way live up to the standards it has set itself. If the Republicans show no signs of proving equal to their own ideals, their coalition will in time disintegrate.

Can the Republicans meet their own challenge? At times one wonders how they can possibly miss. They appear to have just about everything on their side. Money is still one of the basic raw materials in politics, and the Republicans, now that they have the wealthy Southerners with them, have just about all the big money there is. The disparity between Republican and Democratic resources—approximately two to one, according to reports on last year's campaign—is now so great that new federal legislation may be needed in order to keep political competition alive in this country. Such legislation is unlikely to come out of a Republican Congress.

Because big money is almost solidly Republican, Republicans control the mass-communications industries. Newspapers are overwhelmingly favorable to the Republican side; so are the big-circulation magazines. Recalling what the press did whenever any mischief came to light in the Truman administration, and comparing that with the almost total blackout on the early examples of Republican waywardness, one has the eerie feeling that the one-party press may shortly put an end to the two-party system. The affair of C. Wesley Roberts, the Republican National Chairman who was involved in a sharp deal to sell the state of Kansas a property already deeded to it, became known to newspaper readers only when Mr. Roberts left Washington. The impression given the public was that Republican justice was swift and even-handed. The fact that the party leadership was bitterly torn by the Roberts case, the fact that no word of disapprobation came from the White House or any of the field headquarters of the Eisenhower Crusade, the fact that Mr. Roberts had not agreed to resign until his arm had been twisted almost to the breaking point—all these were adroitly concealed.

But if we assume that political competition will somehow survive all of this, then one can foresee certain large obstacles standing in the way of Republican success. Before the administration can fulfill the hopes of those who put it in office, it will have to win the support of the Republicans in Congress and of some of its executive appointees. To date, it has had very poor luck in doing so. Far from making the way smooth for the new President, the Eighty-third Congress is giving every sign of becoming a two-year Donnybrook. Time that should be going into the implementation of his foreign policy is being spent in fighting off Senator Bricker's attempt to amend the Constitution with a view to taking foreign policy out of the President's hands. Meanwhile, House Republicans have tried to euchre him out of his discretionary authority in the field of tariffs, an authority that is essential to his effective direction of foreign policy. Senator McCarthy is conducting a brilliant campaign against the State Department and the Mutual Security Administration. In the domestic field, the Secretary of Agriculture has set himself up as the leading opponent of the farm program the President ran on. The Secretary of Commerce, by forcing the head of the National Bureau of Standards to resign because the bureau had not been sufficiently responsive to "the play of the marketplace," exposed the administration to the charge of stooging for gyp artists and of playing politics in a field that the Democrats at their worst never sought to enter, a field, in fact, which only Communists now regard as political. The Secretary of the Interior has replaced the distinguished head of the Fish and Wildlife Service with a public relations man from the paper industry. As Robert Bendiner has pointed out, the impression given is that the Republican idea of a scientist is a man who tears and compares cigarettes on television.

It is too early to assume that the confusions and frustrations of this period will characterize the administration throughout its stay. It may very well be that General Eisenhower has a plan for bringing order out of the present chaos. So far, though, his administration has shown no signs of being in control of the situation and very few signs of understanding it. But if it is not understood and mastered soon, if the Republican Party proves unequal to the job of controlling its chronic obstructionists, then it is hard to see how the Republican coalition can endure at all, much less gain reinforcements. Instead of being on the verge of a period in which the Republicans will be as clearly the majority party as the Democrats were in the thirties and forties, we may merely be going through a brief Republican interlude comparable to the interludes provided by the Cleveland administrations in the half-century of Republican hegemony that followed the Civil War.

15 Cohn and Schine

July 21, 1953

Roy M. Cohn and G. David Schine, the young men who for six disaster-strewn months have been serving as chief counsel and chief consultant, respectively, to the Permanent Subcommittee on Investigations of Senator McCarthy's Committee on Government Operations, fracture several well-established categories of human and political behavior.

Most of us are prepared by the mere experience of living to encounter paradox and contradiction in character. It surprises no one that a wolf should appear in sheep's clothing; it is in the nature of evil to masquerade, and it would be a pretty stupid wolf, outside the forest, who would show up anywhere in wolf's clothing. It is never astonishing to learn that a reformer has become a tyrant; in this century, we know very well what the road to hell is paved with. Nevertheless, there are certain laws, unwritten but intuitively acknowledged, dealing with the propriety of disguises and with the natural limits of contradiction. It is these which Cohn and Schine so spectacularly violate.

Cohn and Schine are in the inquisition game. Inquisitors dissemble in many ways. Torquemada was a monk in an order of learned mendicants. The mind does not boggle at such a fact as this. It accepts without protest the story of the poor, bookish ecclesiastic presiding over the roasting of two thousand of his fellow men. But the mind will not accept, or at least it will protest, the thought that a Grand Inquisitor might either be or pretend to be a Punchinello, say, or a common tumbler. Ridiculous!—the clown's disguise would never occur to a heresy hunter, for a heresy hunter must be a man full of earthly vanity or of spiritual pride. A Torquemada in motley—impossible! A fool turned inquisitor—absurd! Heresy hunting would never occur to a clown.

Or so, at any rate, it would seem. But now, in 1953, Cohn and Schine are on hand to prove all this wrong. Cohn and Schine are successful inquisitors who do not dissemble as such but in point of fact are buffoons. In the spring, they took a celebrated trip to Europe that was marked from beginning to end by low comedy. In the basic circumstances of the trip, there was the ready-made plot for a gorgeous farce: two young men madly, preposterously bent on the ideological purification of the greatest government on earth. Writers of fiction value such ideas so highly that they sometimes haul each other into court over them. And the journey itself, the real journey, had such familiar fixtures of farce as a female spy who had once been the toast of Vienna; a contretemps that involved a platoon of diplomats who were involved in a search for a missing pair of trousers; and an altercation, denied in toto by the principals but sworn to by reputable journalists and at all odds firmly fixed in legend, in which young Mr. Schine chased young Mr. Cohn around a hotel lobby swatting him over the head with a rolled-up magazine.

What more could anyone ask? Only, perhaps, Victor Moore as our startled, victimized minister to Graustark. Seen at close range, the performance belonged so plainly to the world of burlesque that the British correspondents immediately took to chanting "Positively, Mr. Cohn! Absolutely, Mr. Schine!" The illusion of fun and theater was fortuitously encouraged, of course, by such things as the young men's names—monosyllabic, neatly and memorably mated, advantageous for puns, rhymes, and parodies —and the fact that, like Laurel and Hardy, Rosencrantz and Guildenstern, and Abbott and Costello, Cohn and Schine are a study in contrasts: Cohn, short, dark, and jumpy; Schine, tall, fair, and sleepy.

Yet it is a register of the spoilsport quality of our age that very few of those who laughed as Cohn and Schine flew and stumbled and bumbled across Europe, visiting six countries and twelve cities in seventeen days, failed to realize that the junket was also a catastrophe of the very first order. It very nearly delivered the coup de grace to an enterprise, the International Information Administration that has been a tremendous asset to American diplomacy. And we have yet to reap the full harvest sown by these jokers. All over Europe and all over Washington there are government servants with their resignations signed, sealed, and pocketed, ready for delivery as soon as other jobs are lined up, as soon as family affairs can be set in order, as soon as enough time has elapsed to give their actions the appearance of unhurried judgment rather than of panic inspired by a pair of juvenile semi-delinquents.

To be sure, it can be argued that it was not really Cohn and Schine who did the damage but Senator McCarthy, whose agents they were. The voices in the star chambers were Cohn's and Schine's but the hand was the hand of McCarthy. Had McCarthy himself gone to Europe to terrorize American officials, there would have been nothing to laugh at. McCarthy is a man of substance, a demagogue of formidable gifts, a cause wholly adequate to the effects he produces. What is funny and pathetic and grotesque and infuriating about Cohn and Schine is their manifest inadequacy. What made the comedy they staged piquant was that two callow, shallow boys had somehow been vested with the power to stand a great republic on its ear. In their shallowness and weakness was revealed the strength of the man and the tendency they represented.

Cohn and Schine may have a future, but being only twenty-six, they have little in the way of a past. This makes them almost unique among leading McCarthyites. Before their advent, McCarthyism had been drawing for its cadres on two types: guilt-ridden ex-Communists like Louis Budenz, the Man with the Latex Memory, and careerists like Don Surine, the former F.B.I. man who in 1950 was declared unfit for Mr. Hoover's service when it was found that he had established an agreeable relationship with a Baltimore *fille de joie* he was supposed to be investigating. McCarthyites are almost all ex-something-or-others—ex-Communists, ex-cops, ex-Nazis, ex-writers—but neither Cohn nor Schine is, so far as can be discovered, an ex-anything. They have had neither the time nor the occasion to amass the fund of regrets and grudges that led so many disenchanted Bolsheviks to give themselves over to the Bolshevism of the right. And neither has been driven to McCarthyism by the spurs of necessity and failure.

Both have come, and very recently, from comfortable middle-class backgrounds. Schine's background is downright plush. Both were expensively and liberally educated. Cohn, a native New Yorker and the only son of a judge in the Appellate Division of the Supreme Court, attended the Fieldston School, which is under the management of the Ethical Culture Society, Horace Mann, Columbia College, and Columbia Law School. He is as much a child of enlightenment as a Muscovite of similar age is a child of Communism. Schine is a son of Meyer Schine of Gloversville, New York, the proprietor of a chain of hotels, the best known of which are the Roney Plaza at Miami Beach, the nearby Boca Raton, and the Ambassador on the Sunset Strip in Hollywood, and also of a chain of movie houses and radio stations. Young Schine went to the Fessenden School, Phillips Academy at Andover, and Harvard College. Those, too, are emancipated institutions.

It is difficult to relate Cohn and Schine, as specific persons with specific needs, to the McCarthy movement, but Cohn's case is on the whole easier to understand than Schine's. Cohn grew up in a political atmosphere, though one rather different from that in which he now functions. His father is a Bronx Democrat who owes his present eminence to the patronage of the late Edward J. Flynn, the tough, urbane county boss who managed Franklin Roosevelt's third campaign. Though Roy Cohn appears to have had no opportunity to develop the compulsive hatreds that lead many to adopt McCarthyism as a way of life, he is the sort of young man who takes things hard. His dark eyes are flinty, bright, and ruthless. He has a perpetual scowl and a studied toughness of manner. His voice is raspy, his manner cocksure enough to suggest vast insecurity.

He has delusions of grandeur. Last fall, when, as a Department of Justice lawyer, Cohn presented the results of a grand jury inquiry into subversion among employees of the United Nations Secretariat, he thought it fitting to advise the court that the work he had directed was "probably the most important investigation ever conducted in the entire history of the United States."

It was in the Department of Justice that Cohn acquired his knowledge of the Communist movement. Though well short of overwhelming, it is greatly superior to either McCarthy's or Schine's. He joined the attorney general's staff in New York in 1948, immediately after being admitted to the bar. It is reasonable to assume that he was not hindered by his father's high standing with the Truman administration. His first cases were routine ones—narcotics and the like—but he soon began to specialize in cases involving Communists and persons suspected of being Communists. He had a hand in the prosecution of Julius and Ethel Rosenberg and in the government's Smith Act case against thirteen Communist functionaries. He was also involved in the indictment and prosecution of William Remington. The United Nations investigation, the one he regards as the most important in American history, was almost entirely his work. On these cases, he learned a good deal, and what he learned came in handy.

Schine's McCarthyism is perplexing. Schine not only seems to lack animus; he comes very close to lacking animation. With his wavy, well-tended hair, his regular features, and his somnolent eyes, he is a good-looking youth in the style that one associates with male orchestra singers, and there is evidence that the world is not completely on the skewgee in the fact that the appearance is not altogether deceiving. He has never been an orchestra singer but he has written and published two or three songs. One is called "Please Say Yes, or It's Goodbye"—

> Haven't found a good solution,
> There is only one way out.
> My heart is in a sad confusion,
> And I've got to end this doubt.
> So I'm asking you to tell me how things stand.
> A simple "yes" or "no" is all that I demand.

Schine, who owns a Cadillac with telephone service, was also at one time a press-agent for Vaughn Monroe's orchestra. It is in character, too, that he should have sojourned briefly in Hollywood and have had a well-publicized dalliance with a starlet named Piper Laurie. "He was kind of strange," Miss Laurie is reported to have said. Schine's hobby is cigar collecting. His Gloversville home houses what is said to be the world's largest cigar collection.

When Schine is asked about his competence as Chief Consultant to the McCarthy Committee, he refers to a curious work called "Definition of Communism," of which he is the author of record. This is a six-page pamphlet bearing the colophon of the Schine Hotels ("Finest Under the Sun"). It is quite remarkable. It puts the Russian Revolution, the founding of the Communist Party, and the start of the First Five Year Plan in years when these things did not happen. It gives Lenin the wrong first name.

It confuses Stalin with Trotsky. It confuses Marx with Lenin. It confuses Alexander Kerensky with Prince Lvov. It confuses fifteenth-century Utopianism with twentieth-century Marxism. Schine is said to have prepared this anthology of wrong dates and mistaken identities as a class assignment at Harvard. He had copies of it put on every bureau in every one of the Schine Hotels, of which his father had two or three years earlier appointed him President and General Manager. Why he felt called upon to undertake the indoctrination of his guests with this compendium of ignorance is a matter for conjecture, though perhaps not a great deal of conjecture. In any event the pamphlet is reported to have been the instrument that brought together Schine, Cohn, and McCarthy. The story goes that last fall a certain Rabbi Benjamin Schultz, who runs an organization called the American Jewish League against Communism, sought out the hospitality of a Schine hotel in Florida, found "Definition of Communism" alongside the room service menu in his suite, and was so dazzled by its depth of understanding that he sought out the author and introduced him to George Sokolsky, a journalist, who introduced him to Roy Cohn, who was then preparing to go to work for McCarthy and introduced Schine to the Senator, who promptly hired him. That's the story. It is reasonable to assume that Schine was not hindered by having a fortune or by the fact that part of the fortune was in hotels located in warm, attractive places. It is doubtful if his experience with investigations was of much help, though this was not a wholly inconsiderable part of the innkeeper phase of his history. In August 1950, the Kefauver Committee disclosed the fact that the Roney Plaza and the Boca Raton, two of the "Finest Under the Sun," had for $67,000 sold gambling concessions to Frank Erickson, who until his recent imprisonment was the most celebrated bookie of our epoch, and to the S & G Syndicate of Chicago, which certain knowledgeable people assert is the legitimate successor to the House of Capone. In his first appearance on the stand, Meyer Schine denied the truth of all this but he confirmed it in the course of a second appearance. No mention was made of G. David Schine as a party to these transactions, and evidently he was not one, though they were in force during his brief career as a boniface.

Immediately on joining the committee staff, Cohn and Schine were placed in full charge of the first big McCarthy production for 1953, the campaign against the Voice of America and its parent agency, the International Information Administration.

Cohn and Schine arrived in New York, where the main operating force of the Voice of America works, with nothing to go on but a few bits and pieces collected by members of a group of employees, some twenty-five or thirty in number, self-styled the "Loyal American Underground." This "underground" appeared to consist—as perhaps most "undergrounds" do—of out-and-out zanies, the professionally disgruntled, and the politically mischievous, one category being approximately as numerous as another. The screwballs, the grudge holders, and the troublemakers had gathered scraps of this-and-that (so-and-so's wife had once been a Communist's wife, Mr. Mister didn't like a book that all good anti-Communists were supposed to like, Miss Miss had been heard to say that the administration was being rather tactless in its approach to the Papuan question), and they gladly presented them to Cohn and Schine. For their part, Cohn and Schine cheerfully acknowledged that they had made no particular study of conditions at the Voice, but they saw this as anything but a disqualifying admission. They were right. The magic of McCarthyism lies largely in its Luther Burbank touch with humble and unpromising materials; working with nothing but a mass of trifling, unrelated, and as a rule purely negative facts (or positive unfacts) it can produce whole fields of Shasta daisies. By the time Cohn and Schine and McCarthy and the television cameras were through, they had toppled most of the Voice leadership, forced the leaders of the administration to disown the agency, and sown despair and confusion everywhere in the middle and lower ranks.

It is impossible to escape the conclusion that ruin was what they had sought from the start. One of the extraordinary things about McCarthyism is that it is a point of view—and for some people, indeed, a way of life—that can only be described in terms of itself. Most movements, whether angelic or infernal in character, have some sort of end in view; they seek either to reconstruct or to modify men or institutions. This is true of Communism, Fascism, Moral Rearmament, Social Credit, Technocracy, Democracy, Anarchism, Cooperativism, Greenbackism, Existentialism, even, perhaps, Mau Mauism. McCarthyism, however, seeks nothing; it has no positive goals; it doesn't seem to want to do anything at all to the social order except kick it around; and those who take it up as Cohn and Schine have done come very close to being the purest sort of nihilists. When, during the Voice investigations, officials who had been accused of nothing at all and were merely eager to preserve their own good reputations or that of their offices against the testimony of wounded or embittered or nutty subordinates sought to explain what they had been trying to do, they found Cohn and Schine supremely uninterested. Causes and reasons and explanations and extenuations simply bored them. They were frank to say that all they sought was circumstantial evidence of malfeasance; surrounding circumstances were none of their business, and they didn't care to be told about them.

Many Voice executives learned this. One after another, while the investigation was on, they would go to Cohn and Schine to argue that the information the investigators had, while not necessarily inaccurate, was misleading. They would appeal to the good sense and discrimination of the investigators and petition them that no judgment be made on the basis of this or that piece of testimony standing by itself. Numerous interviews were pretty much along the following lines, which are those recalled by a Voice executive who swears he was party to such a dialogue:

Cohn-Schine: So what you're after is a chance to clear your department. Are you here to tell us no mistakes have been made?

Petitioner: Of course I'm not. I admit there have been mistakes. More than a few, I suppose. But there ought to be some way of showing that by and large we're doing what we're supposed to do. I just felt that there ought to be a little sense of proportion in all of this. You fellows are giving the impression we never do anything right.

Cohn-Schine: Well, this committee isn't set up to show that agencies are doing what they're supposed to do. Our job is to find the weak spots. We'd waste money if we did it the other way around.

Petitioner: I understand that. I'm just saying you give the impression we have nothing but failures.

Cohn-Schine: We're not concerned with what you do ninety percent of the time. It's the ten percent, the mistakes you yourself admit you make, that interest us.

Petitioner: I never said we made mistakes ten percent of the time. My God, if I thought that, I'd be agreeing with you. I'd say it's less than one percent of the time.

Cohn-Schine: Have it your own way—ten percent, one percent—whatever it is, that's what we're after.

Petitioner: Then I guess what you're telling me is that the committee doesn't want to hear my side of this. Is that it?

Cohn-Schine: No, we're not saying that. We're not the committee. We only work for it. All we're saying is that we don't think the committee would be interested in this kind of testimony. We're not going to recommend that the committee hear you. But if you want to write out your answers to all this, that's your privilege. Give it to us, we'll give it to the committee, and maybe they'll want to hear you. We wouldn't know. We just don't think so.

Petitioner: I see.

Cohn-Schine: Of course, if the committee does hear you, we'll have to go into the *whole* record. We can't just put your story on. We'll have to subpoena a lot of other people in your office. You understand that, don't you?

As an instance of moral nihilism, nothing excels, nothing quite matches the behavior of McCarthy and Cohn during the interrogation of Reed Harris, the former State Department official who headed the International Information Administration during a kind of interregnum last winter and who was driven from the government by McCarthy after it was revealed that twenty years ago Harris had written a book, *King Football,* in which he had had some harsh things to say about college athletics and about higher education in general. In Harris's testimony, it came out that in 1932 he had been suspended from classes at Columbia College because some of his editorials in the *Spectator,* the campus daily, had struck the college authorities as being in poor taste. McCarthy asked Harris if he had at the time been provided with an attorney by the American Civil Liberties Union. This exchange took place:

Harris: I had many offers of attorneys and one of those was from the American Civil Liberties Union, yes.

The Chairman: The question is: Did the Civil Liberties Union supply you with an attorney?

Harris: They did supply me with an attorney.

The Chairman: The answer is "Yes"?

Harris: The answer is "Yes."

The Chairman: You know that the American Civil Liberties Union has been listed as a front of the Communist Party.

Harris: Mr. Chairman, this was 1932.

The Chairman: I know this was 1932. Do you know that they since have been listed as a front doing the work of the Communist Party?

Harris: I do not know that they have been listed so. I have heard that mentioned, or read that mentioned.

Now what is wrong here, what is in fact altogether monstrous, is not simply that the American Civil Liberties Union was not in 1932 or at any time before or after that a Communist front; or that it has never been so listed by the Attorney-General or the F.B.I. or any committee of Congress; or that the only charge of this nature ever to be publicly made came from the Tenney Committee of the California Legislature, a source of such monumental disreputability that even the House Committee on Un-American Activities will not give credence to its findings. All these objections to McCarthy's behavior are serious enough, but they do not suggest the spectacular cynicism of this perform-ance. The really breathtaking thing about the Harris incident was not the gall and amorality required to pursue the line of questioning McCarthy pursued but, first, the fact that it was done on March 3, 1953 and, second, the fact that Roy M. Cohn was in the counsel's chair when it was done.

Those of us who watched this particular exchange observed that McCarthy, just before asking Harris if he knew about the political coloration of the Civil Liberties Union, paused and looked hesitantly, inquiringly at his chief counsel, clearly asking Cohn's approval of what he was about to do. Cohn responded with a lack of response, a silence that was McCarthy's cue to press forward, to lay on, and with that silence new ground in political morality was broken. For the fact of the matter was that less than three weeks earlier—on Abraham Lincoln's birthday, to be precise—Roy Cohn, chief counsel, had attended and ad-dressed and by his remarkable little presence endorsed an Amer-ican Civil Liberties Union conference at the Henry Hudson Hotel in New York City.

The Voice of America investigation came to an end in late March. It merely came to an end; it was not completed. It is characteristic of McCarthyism never to complete anything. This show just trailed off into nothingness. Then, suddenly, Cohn and Schine turned up in Paris—on Easter Sunday, April 4 and were off on their European tour. They spent forty hours in Paris, six-teen in Bonn, twenty in Berlin, nineteen in Frankfurt, sixty in Munich, forty in Vienna, twenty-three in Belgrade, twenty-four in Athens, twenty in Rome, and six in London. The trip cost the government $8500, a large part of it in counterpart funds.

This expedition appears to have been set up only a few days in advance, and the purpose of it was so obscure that every-

where the travelers touched down they gave a different account
of why they were traveling. In Paris, they said they were looking for inefficiency in government offices overseas. In Bonn they
said they were looking for subversives. Asked in Munich which
it was, Cohn explained that it was both. "Efficiency," he said,
"includes complete political reliability. If anyone is interested
in the Communists, then he cannot be efficient." Back home on
"Meet the Press," he said he didn't consider himself competent
to judge performances abroad and had gone only to look into
"certain things."

In Rome, a new angle came to light. McCarthy, back in
Washington, had told the press that they had been sent abroad
to bring back a report on the amount of money that had been
spent "in putting across the Truman administration" in Europe.
This was news to Cohn, but he was equal to it. "We haven't
heard about that," he said, "but anything the chairman of our
committee says, if he said it, goes with us."

The truth is they had no purpose beyond McCarthy's continuing one of free-style, catch-as-catch-can harassment. For this
the trip was unncessary; its victories could have been enjoyed
without any traveling at all. The book burning was not a consequence of the trip; the State Department had begun to pulp,
ignite, and donate to charity the offending volumes the moment
it learned that McCarthy had developed bibliographic interests.
By the time Cohn and Schine got to the libraries, most of them
had been thoroughly bowdlerized; what remained to be done
scarcely required their attentions. In terms of McCarthyism's
own economy, the trip was wholly unnecessary.

Nevertheless, it was richly productive of mischief. Cohn and
Schine were a pair to be laughed at, but they made a bitter jest,
for they moved about under a crazy-quilted panoply that unmistakably bore, among other devices, the Great Seal of the
United States.

Merely by their well-publicized presence in Europe, Cohn
and Schine robbed this Republic of some of its dignity. Their

statements made matters worse, and some of their actions were very nearly unspeakable. Nothing, perhaps, was worse than their use of European informants to test the loyalty of American personnel.

Once, when Cohn and Schine were teen-agers, an F.B.I. man called on a British subject working in Washington and asked his opinion of the loyalty of an American the Englishman chanced to know. The Englishman drew himself up and said, "Am I to presume, sir, that you mean loyalty to the Crown? In this regard, I would suppose Mr. A. to be most deficient."

Among men of principle engaged in the sort of work Cohn and Schine were supposed to be doing, the use of foreign informants is thought to be indefensible except in the most extreme of circumstances. Yet it was mainly foreign informants that Cohn and Schine relied upon. Lacking cohorts who could help them pull an inside job, they quickly made contact with dubious outsiders. One of their principal informants was a man named Hermann Aumer, a former Bundestag representative who lost his seat in October, 1950, when it was revealed that his vote for a raise in gasoline prices had been purchased by an oil company for a fee of 22,000 marks. As a bribetaker he was expelled from the ranks of the party he represented, the Bayernpartei. Yet he was requested by Cohn and Schine to brief them on the activities of employees of the United States government in Germany.

Cohn and Schine not only accorded their peculiar informants the privilege of being heard; some they actually deputized for further services. Thus, Herr Aumer informed Americans he met after the departure of Cohn and Schine that he had been assigned by them to report to the McCarthy committee on any anti-McCarthy articles that appeared in German newspapers that were even partly financed by American funds.

In somewhat similar fashion, Mrs. Hede Massing, the former toast of Vienna, became an authorized representative of the Congress of the United States. Mrs. Massing was, in one post-toast stage, the wife of Gerhart Eisler, the Cominform agent who jumped bail in this country to become one of the leaders of the Grotewohl government in East Germany, and she was herself, so she said, the leader of a Communist spy ring in Washington in the 1930's. Regenerate or not, she was the companion of Cohn and Schine during their two tours of inspection in Munich and was made by them a member of the committee staff.

As a naturalized American, Mrs. Massing had a perfect right to that sort of employment provided she could do the work, and of that there was little doubt. Her association with Cohn and Schine, though, provided an interesting example of the power of good connections with McCarthy. For some six months before the arrival of Cohn and Schine, Mrs. Massing had been trying to carve out a career for herself as a field officer in the Cold War. She had had the thought that it would be a fine dramatic stunt if the American High Commission would authorize her to broadcast through the Iron Curtain appeals addressed to her former husband, Herr Eisler, and she had also thought it would be helpful if she lectured in Germany, under American auspices, on the subject of "Communist Infiltration of the United States Government." As a sometime journalist, she also wished the High Commission to give her access to classified political information within its possession.

The High Commission considered her various requests and decided that the national interest would not be served by granting any of them. This continued to be the High Commission's view even after Mrs. Massing appeared with a letter from Cohn and Schine vouching for her good character and requesting the extension of courtesies. The High Commission, however, is an agency of the Department of State, and when Mrs. Massing protested to Cohn and Schine, and Cohn and Schine protested to McCarthy, and McCarthy protested to Dulles, instructions were promptly transmitted from Washington that Mrs. Massing would henceforth be recognized as a representative of the legislative branch and that she was immediately to be given access to the classified information she regarded as necessary to her work.

Cohn's and Schine's dealings with persons such as Aumer and Hede Massing were for the most part conducted in private. What made the trip a sensation was the public behavior of the travelers, which was observed and recorded for posterity by as many journalists as are normally assigned to such eminences as kings, presidents, and Rita Hayworth.

Even their exchanges with hotel clerks were taken down. They had a standard and characteristically tasteless joke for hotel registrations. Asking for adjoining rooms but insisting that the accommodations be separate, one or the other would explain to the generally uncomprehending room clerk, "You see, we don't work for the State Department."

When Cohn and Schine repaired to their hotels, the reporters covered the building like cops preparing to close in on a jewel thief. They did not always learn the identity of visitors—many were skittish about revealing it—but they at least made an accurate count on those using the front stairs and those using the back stairs and they were able on occasion to put certain statements made on the run by Cohn and Schine into a proper historical perspective. In Bonn on April 6, for example, the travelers told the press that they had been conferring with "representatives of the German community." As background for this, one reporter cabled his office: "Since they arrived on the night of April fifth, and since all of their meetings and movements then and today are known, it is probable that the 'representatives' referred to are taxi drivers and restaurant waiters, these being the only Germans they have met so far."

Vienna was a typical way station for the investigators. They arrived there by plane from Munich on Friday evening, April 10. (Hede Massing had been at the airport to see them off and as Cohn and Schine went up the ramp, Cohn shouted down, "So long, Hede. If anything goes wrong, get in touch with Joe!") They stayed in Vienna all day Saturday and into Sunday afternoon. The total elapsed time was forty-one hours, which was slightly above the par of thirty-eight.

Three and a half of the forty-one hours were devoted to the labor of inspections, surveys, and talks with government officials which they explained was their principal business. This was one hour more than they devoted to press conferences. They held their first press conference immediately upon alighting from their plane. At it, Cohn denied the *Abendpost* story about Schine having hit him on the head. It was, he said, "a pack of lies." He did not try to pretend that he and Schine always saw eye to eye. "We are not always in constant agreement," he said, "but then I am not always in agreement with Senator McCarthy." He did not choose to elaborate on this intriguing assertion. The report that he and Schine had come to blows was, he said, "so fantastic it is really amusing." He then went on to give the routine talk about the purposes of their inquiry, pointing out that the visit to Austria was unique in that they had had no reports of subversion in government agencies there. "Nobody in the State Department projects in Austria has been named before our committee as a possible Communist sympathizer," he said. "We are not trying to get after anybody here. We only want to check on mismanagement and fix any responsibility for it."

After the press conference, Cohn and Schine repaired to their hotel and did not emerge until noon the next day. They had left instructions not to be disturbed on Saturday morning. The newspapermen were hard by in the corridors and noted that their only caller was the Vienna correspondent for Hearst's International News Service, a German. At noon, they paid a twenty-minute call on the American ambassador, who had them given a twenty-minute briefing on the work of the embassy and the information services. Since our information services in Austria are about as elaborate as they are any place in the world—they include the management of Austria's biggest daily newspaper and its leading radio network, as well as the conduct of intensive film, pamphlet, lecturing, and book-publishing programs that reach far into the Soviet occupation zone—time must have imposed a rigorous economy on the briefing officials.

Informed and enlightened, *au courant* with diplomacy and psychological warfare on that particular frontier, Cohn and Schine went shopping. Schine visited a tobacconist and picked out some unusual cigars for his cigar museum. This, if the correspondents' timing was correct, took an hour and was followed by a latish lunch with two American officials, the editor of the subsidized newspaper and the officer in charge of the subsidized radio network. The conversation was general, according to subsequent interviews with these men, and could not greatly have augmented Cohn's and Schine's store of information.

They next went back to their hotel, leaving it in mid-afternoon for a tour of the spacious Soviet Information Center. Here, their interest, which reporters say had been noticeably lagging, perked up. According to one American reporter's account, Cohn and Schine, "speeding through the cards, discovered that the authors Agnes Smedley and Theodore Dreiser, among others, were represented in the Soviet Information Center's collection. A U.S. escorting officer, pointing out other books in the open shelves, showed them that Mark Twain was also represented. Then the party headed for the U.S. Information Center three blocks away. Cohn and Schine took only a cursory glance at the bookshelves and the lines of customers in front of the circulation desk. As usual they shielded their search from the prying newsmen, but it was clear that they were studying the files for the presence of such authors as had been spotted in the Soviet's card catalogue down the street.

They went briefly into the periodical room, determined that neither *The Freeman* nor the *American Legion Magazine* was available, and complained of these lacks. The man in charge confessed a regrettable ignorance of the existence of *The Freeman* as he scribbled down the name of it; as for the *American Legion Magazine*, he said his view of the matter was that the number of American Legionnaires in Vienna wasn't quite great enough to justify a library subscription.

The full inspection of books and periodicals lasted just a bit less than thirty minutes. Right after it Cohn and Schine held their second Vienna press conference. It was like all the others. The reporters asked, politely, how a combination of ignorance of the subject and half-hour inspections could possibly enable them to form reasonable judgments of our government operations in Vienna. They airily explained that they were supplementing what they had seen and learned with information gathered from reliable "Austrian sources." The press was unable to learn the identity of the Austrian sources; some of its members wondered by what feats of magic they had managed to see any Austrians, since their only known visitor was a German newspaper writer and they had visited no one. They are still wondering.

On Sunday morning, nothing was accomplished. Schine stayed in his room—possibly sorting out cigars—and Cohn went for less than half an hour to the Information Center to read some interoffice memos. Right after that, the travelers went out to the airport and said farewell to lovely Vienna.

That was the grand tour. It ended with a visit to London, where the reception was icy. Deeply hurt by the jeering of the British press and by the angry, challenging questions about them in Parliament, they did not look deeply into the workings of the BBC, though it would have been entirely legitimate and possibly most beneficial for them to have done so. They talked for twenty minutes or so with one BBC official, Hugh Carleton Greene; conferred briefly with our Ambassador, Winthrop Aldrich, and gave the world one last belly-laugh by announcing that in Aldrich "President Eisenhower has chosen wisely. He impressed us as being right on top of his job." They got out of London fast, returned to Paris, and flew back to McCarthy.

16 Truce

July 31, 1953

As the Korean war ends, the mood of most Americans is downcast and self-commiserating. The armistice has been welcomed, but it has not been celebrated. There have been no demonstrations, no wild embracing in the streets. Sales of confetti and party-horns were no better than normal. For the average American, while he may not regard the Korean settlement as a defeat, is unwilling to accept it as a victory. It is clear that the whole affair has filled him with shame and a sense of guilt.

Are the shame and guilt rational? They don't seem to be. It is a fact, of course, that we have failed to destroy or subdue our enemy. But that was not what we set out to do. We undertook, hesitantly at first, to help stop a particular violation of a particular boundary. Then, following our contribution of air and naval support with a commitment of ground forces, we took full responsibility for driving back the invaders, which is what we have done.

Nowhere in any declaration of the United States or the United Nations is there a definition of victory that is not fulfilled in the present settlement. Unification was never one of our military aims; indeed, we have always opposed forceful unification of any country, Korea most specifically and explicitly included. Years before the fighting started there, we advised Syngman Rhee that we would withdraw military aid if he attempted to unite the split peninsula by force of arms.

Thus, in the purely technical and military sense, the victory is ours. But a Korean victory that was purely military would not be worth very much, for the reason that Korea has relatively little military significance for us. Senator McCarthy may say that dark, dishonorable motives led Dean Acheson to announce, early in 1950, that Korea lay outside our defensive perimeter, but the fact is that Acheson was merely announcing a decision in which all our military leaders—including General MacArthur, who had twice said exactly the same thing—at one time concurred. Strategically, Korea was expendable; after all, we did ourselves quite proudly when not only Korea but very nearly all of Asia was in the hands of a hostile power, Japan.

More than a military victory was needed to justify Korea; more than a military victory has been won there.

No one able to recall the faraway world of June 1950 can doubt that a failure to have intervened in Korea would have encouraged the Communists to have attacked elsewhere. It was not the territory on which we fought that was strategically important but the time at which we chose to fight. Aggression had at that moment to be resisted, no matter where it took place; had we failed to respond, the slave world would have been greatly emboldened, the free world greatly dispirited.

In the three years before we undertook the Korean resistance, Communist power in the world very nearly doubled; in the three years since then, it has made no gains. On balance, it is probably a good deal less formidable. In Korea, the United States proved that its word was as good as its bond—and even better, since no bond had been given. History will cite Korea as the proving ground of collective security, up to this time no more than a plausible theory. It will cite it as the turning point of the world struggle against Communism and as the scene of a great victory for American arms, one the future will celebrate even though the present does not.

17   The Unmentionable Victory

Letter from Washington

July 31, 1953

Only Mr. Dulles among government officials has expressed any pride or satisfaction in the terms of the Korean armistice, and only the information services of his department, which speak nowadays in soft and barely audible voices, are disputing the Communist claim that Communism won the war. Hardly anyone here is saying that we won; in fact, hardly anyone here is saying anything about either the war or the peace. The general mood was most accurately reflected in the remarks broadcast by the President immediately after the signing of the truce, when he said he could find consolation only in the fact that a bloody business was over at last and in the hope that someday Americans would be able to extricate themselves from the tangle of events on the remote and uncongenial peninsula that has been the scene of so much American grief. The President's talk was short, and his Wednesday news conference, at which he might have amplified his remarks, was, for unstated reasons, cancelled. The lack of comment from the President's office since last Sunday night has put the White House in speechless accord with the rest of Washington; thus far, the most conspicuous reaction to the truce has been silence. This may or may not be the only American war that has ended short of conquering the enemy (it all depends on definitions and on whether one chooses to overlook the War of 1812, which ended in a settlement that the enemy considered anything but a defeat and many Americans regarded as a pretty bad deal for our side), but it is certainly the only war that has not ended in speeches. Congress greeted the armistice with a torrent of talk about immigration policies, shipping problems, and a proposed investigation—it would be the second in less than a year—of tax-exempt foundations. A few congressmen, badgered by reporters and unable to resist, have given out statements to the press, but none of them have been notable for firmness, boldness, or imagination. Representative Dewey Short, of Missouri, spoke for many when he said, "I hope for the best."

The silence conceals—or, rather, fails to conceal—an almost universal pessimism. It afflicts both those who, like Mr. Dulles, feel that the truce itself will be a considerable victory if the Communists, who accused us of eight violations of it the first day, abide by its terms and those who regard it as a first-class defeat. "If we had won the war," an editorial in the *Times-Herald* said, "our flags would be flying along the Yalu River, the Chinese Communists would have been driven out of the peninsula, Korea would be reunited, and Syngman Rhee would be the happiest man in Asia." Since none of these things happened, or is likely to happen, the *Times-Herald* and the many congressmen who share its views in this matter are sunk in gloom. But their gloom is not much darker or deeper than the gloom of those who are, on the whole, glad that the war ended when and where it did and who are reluctant to elevate Syngman Rhee's happiness to a principle of American foreign policy. The despair, or near despair, of these people is based on their professed inability to see how we can conceivably get any of the things we hope for out of the political conference that will take place three months from now. They feel that we would have a hard enough time of it if we faced only the problem of trying to talk the Communists into seeing and doing things our way, but they also realize that the Communists are far from being the only hazard on the course. Even if we enjoy unexpected success in dickering with the Communists, we shall have to sell our success to Mr. Rhee, who plainly doesn't want to buy it if he can possibly avoid doing

so. By having committed himself in advance to the failure of
the conference, he has committed us to abandoning the conference if it doesn't progress satisfactorily. "We and the whole
world will come to fully realize the futility of a peaceful means
in settling our problems," he said three days ago, which was
two days after the truce had been signed, and he went on to say
that when this realization has dawned, "we will be able to pursue our own method of achieving unification." Stuck with these
words, Mr. Rhee is in a position where any success of the conference will turn into a disaster for him, and he is not the sort
to let the tide of events roll over him. He has already taken care
of the possibility of Communist agreement to unification and the
holding of Korean elections by saying that he will tolerate only
an election to fill the twenty-three seats his Parliament has held
open over the years for representatives of Koreans living north
of the thirty-eighth parallel. In other words, he will accept only
elections that could not result in the retirement of his government. (His government was very nearly retired by South Korean
voters in 1950, shortly before the war began.) We, of course,
are not bound to any such program as this, but we are bound
to Mr. Rhee in any number of ways, and it is hard to see how
we can make a success of a conference he is determined must
not succeed. From the standpoint of domestic politics, the truce
has come at a fairly auspicious time. Congress is on the point of
adjourning which means that during the period in which the
most delicate negotiations are taking place, no one will be able
to turn the House and Senate floors into platforms of dissent.
Some administration leaders are hopeful that when the congressmen go out and mingle with their constituents for several
months, they will learn that most voters approve of the truce,
even though their approval may be in contradiction to their
views about the wisdom of the settlement being contemplated,
and that, in fact, the country will accept the ending of the
Korean war as the first major accomplishment of the Republican
administration. Up to now, the administration has not tried to

link the signing of the truce to its campaign promises to bring about an end to the war, for its spokesmen are painfully aware that this isn't quite the kind of end that the Republican leaders, who in their platform had criticized the Truman administration for lacking "the will to victory," were talking about. They are also aware, though, that in the public mind the central fact is that the shooting has stopped. To be sure, it has taken quite a while to stop it, and its end has apparently come as the result of negotiations begun by President Truman (whose terms, however, were harsher and who, as Senator Douglas, of Illinois, recently pointed out, would have been flayed from one end of Washington to the other if he had accepted the present agreement), but in the perspective of 1954 and 1956 the truce will appear as one of the early developments in the history of the Eisenhower administration, and if we are not re-engaged in Korea or on some other battlefield by that time, Republican candidates will surely wish to take credit for the event. It is unquestionably the administration's present hope that Republican members of the Eighty-third Congress will see the possibilities for taking this credit in the course of their visits home this summer, and that there will therefore be less tension between the Republican executive and Republican legislators when Congress meets again.

But hopes of this nature are expressed only when there is a psychological need for relief from the apprehensions of the moment. It may be that most people in Washington are exaggerating the darkness of the outlook, but if they are taking exceedingly black views, they have good authority for doing so. "Judging from the statements of Secretary Dulles," the Washington *Post* said yesterday morning, "the truce at Panmunjom has merely opened a Pandora's box of new troubles." The Dulles statements the *Post* was talking about are the ones he made in his press conference, following his relatively hopeful broadcast Sunday night, when he pointed out that aggression had been turned back and the principle of collective security vindicated in the Korean war. Perhaps these two achievements vastly outweigh in importance all the diplomatic difficulties now confronting us.

18 Robert A. Taft: 1889–1953

Letter from Washington
August 1, 1953

T. V. Smith, the academic philosopher who served briefly as a Democratic congressman from Illinois, once described Robert A. Taft as a man "full of character." It was a splendid tribute and just the right one for Taft. It is more to the point to speak of Taft as a man of character than as a man of integrity, courage, and rectitude. He had these estimable qualities, but they were complicated and sometimes compromised by other traits. About his being "full of character" there can be no question or dispute. It was the despair of his political managers that he lacked a politically marketable personality; he could never develop one because his character kept getting in the way. The words that would have made him seem a good fellow always stuck in his throat. Words that made him seem a bad fellow kept springing forth—as when, for example, he gave his classic formula for meeting the challenge of high food prices: "Eat less." (Charles Luckman, who was in the personality-marketing business and who had quite a snazzy little item in himself, was asked the same question, and he advised "economy in the use of certain foods through personal restraint." For this, he was adjudged a good fellow, while Taft, for his direct and precise use of language, was put down as a flint-hearted Bourbon.) Taft was an odd, improbable combination of sweet reasonableness and ungovernable passion. The public thought of him as a dogmatist, and the public wasn't entirely wrong, but behind Taft's tough and self-assured rhetoric was a questioning mind and one at least as familiar with doubt as with certitude. The chilliness the public sensed in him was an illusion. He liked people very much and was shy and careful in all his relationships. Sometimes his self-control wasn't all it might be, and the spectacle could be unlovely. But T. V. Smith had it right: Taft was unique, identifiable, typical only of himself. Few Americans saw their own image in him, or their father's, or their brother's, and that is probably why he died a Senator. It is also why he died a Senator who will be remembered.

19   Policies, Problems

Letter from Washington

September 23, 1953

Braced and freshened, possibly even surfeited, by mountain air, the President has returned to the White House and for the first time since he took office is sampling the quality of life in the Washington that presidents like most: Washington sans Congress. He will not be here all the time that Congress is away. In mid-October, he goes to Hershey, Pennsylvania, where some admirers will give him a birthday party under a circus tent, and from there he travels cross-country to speak in several Western and Southern cities, the list of which is still growing. Then, in November, he expects to get in a good bit of golf at Augusta National, on the edge of which a new winter White House is being rushed to completion. But at least there will be two periods of a few weeks each in which he will be continuously in Washington and free whenever the spirit moves him to devote himself to questions of policy and administration. It is said that he has been looking forward to this ever since early last summer when, without abandoning his belief in the need for a humane approach to congressmen, he began to see a certain wisdom in Artemus Ward's famous program for the legislative branch—"Go home, you miserable devils—go home!" His staff members welcome the coming period with at least as much enthusiasm as he is said to. They confidently assert that the coming months will one day be seen in retrospect as the period in which the Eisenhower administration, having been in office long enough to check theory and principle against practice and experience, finally settled upon its major strategies and forthrightly explained them to the American people.

This is perhaps too bold an assertion. There are many things the administration won't be able to decide this year. When Adlai Stevenson said a while back that the Republicans appear to be going in for "government by postponement," he was only pointing to a condition that administration leaders have frequently acknowledged, some of them in rueful terms. (Procrastination has always been on a firm bi-partisan footing. Soon after Stevenson spoke, his party decided to lay aside for a year the settling of its leading dispute, the one involving "loyalty pledges" for convention delegates.) The President's fondness for commissions of inquiry and for the conference method in general has led him to put a large number of issues, some of them close to burning, into the cool hands of committees that will not be reporting to him for quite a while. Thus, for instance, it is unlikely that the administration will hammer out its trade and tariff policies this fall, for it is pledged to wait upon the advice given in by the Commission on Foreign Economic Policy, headed by Clarence Randall of the Inland Steel Company. (It has already had some advice on the subject from a group headed by Lewis Douglas, the insurance man and diplomat, but Mr. Douglas's views, which are on the anti-protectionist side, have merely become data for the Randall commission, which has a larger frame of reference.) Wide areas of domestic policy are being examined by the Commission on Intergovernmental Relations, headed by Dr. Clarence Manion, formerly of Notre Dame University, and empowered to re-examine the balance of responsibility between the federal government on the one hand and the lesser units—state, county, municipal—on the other. Last month, Herbert Hoover's Commission on Organization of the Executive Branch of the Government was revived and given a much broader mandate than it had under President Truman. This time it will report not simply on methods of improving on operations authorized by law but on the wisdom of the laws that authorize the operations. Mr. Hoover's views on many things being well known, his commission is expected to find unwisdom rampant. There is a National Agricultural Advisory Commission, an Advisory Committee on Government Housing Policies and Programs, and committees and commissions on social security, health and education, universal military training, and the postal service. The government is not bound to accept the recommendations of any of these groups, or even to defer its decisions until their views have been presented, but the moral and political obligations to do so are quite heavy, and it would be destructive of morale in all commissions—which is, really, to say in the administration itself, since practically every member of the administration is a member of one or more of these advisory boards—if major policies in their fields were to be formulated in advance of the appropriate reports.

If there are some areas in which policy will necessarily continue to be a matter of conjecture and debate, there are others in which the administration has little choice but to figure things out in a hurry. The budget, which is the mirror of a hundred policies, must be prepared this fall, and before the year is out it will be imperative for the President and his advisers to come to some basic conclusions about taxation and defense. In a speech last week, the Secretary of the Treasury, trying to take the sting out of some of the protests that have arisen over the suggestion of a national sales tax, said a sales tax is only one of some forty possible means of gathering new revenue that his department is considering at the present time. The implication was that there was only about one chance in forty of its being adopted. But a further implication was that there would be a need for new sources of revenue, and this, in turn, implied increased expenditures. (There could be a need for new taxes simply to replace the ones due to expire next year, but up until recently it has been assumed that cuts in the budget would offset those losses.) The possibility of expenditures running above the levels anticipated earlier in the year has been a recurrent note in the public addresses and private conversations of government spokesmen during the past few weeks, and it has led many people to believe that the administration will shortly abandon some of its plans for cutting back defense expenditures. There is no doubt that the announcement of the Soviet Union's success in developing the hydrogen bomb has jolted administration people severely, and there is no doubt that the jolting has been followed by prolonged and not always even-tempered disputes between those in the government, led by George M. Humphrey, who wish to make budget-cutting the first principle and those who think the news from the Soviet Union demands an immediate enlargement of our military establishment, with particular emphasis on air defenses.

The dispute can be settled only by the President. His Boston speech a few evenings ago stressed the point that no cost would be "too hard for us to bear to support a logical and necessary defense of our freedom" and was seen here as a clue to the way his thoughts are tending, but no one took it as a certain sign of the course he will pursue. The speech did not go into the question of what a "logical and necessary" program would be and the omission was regarded as significant in view of the fact that he was known to have discarded another speech, written by his own staff upon his request, that went into it at some length. This was to have been a kind of preface to a series of talks on the world situation that he has been urged to make by those of his advisers who are the most alarmed by the present situation. That he rejected it and chose instead to talk about the glories of past Republican administrations is regarded here as an indication of the great pressures he is under. Those who would have him give his first thought to the domestic economy point out that even if we keep defense expenditures at their present levels and cut all other government operations by ten percent, we will face a certain deficit of five or six billions during the fiscal year of 1955, which starts next July. To increase the budget by some of the amounts now being discussed—they go as high as twenty billion dollars—would give the present Republican administration the distinction of presenting the country with the highest peacetime deficit in history. To the political spokesmen, it would be a perfectly hideous distinction. Of course, new taxes could reduce the deficit or even eliminate it, but it would be no easy job to get Congress to vote new taxes in an election year—especially since the taxes that would be needed to balance a budget increased by anything like twenty billion would be the largest in peacetime history and would earn for the Congress that levied them a distinction fully as hideous as that of a deficit in like amount.

Yet the pressure for proceeding without reference to deficits and unwanted distinctions is also quite heavy. The military establishment is full of experts who can turn spines to ice with descriptions of what is likely to happen if appropriations are not increased, and the State Department is full of men who say that the cuts we have already made have put us in a most awkward position in dealing with those allies whom we have been beseeching for years to make great outlays for armaments. What greets such pleadings these days, they say, is horse laughs.

The decision on defense policy is clearly the most important one the President has to make, and it will have a powerful bearing on many other decisions. But there are also large questions awaiting him that are not closely related to the budget and that are outside the scope of his many commissions: whether, for example, to yield to the pressure for talks with the Russians and what kind of action to take in the face of what appears to be a considerable rise in unemployment and an ominous decline in farm prices. All in all, he should have quite an autumn. He begins it, however, with certain immense advantages. He has the indulgence of just about the entire American press and of nearly all the Americans who voted for him last November, as well as that of a good many who didn't. Resentment is building up against certain other administration leaders—notably Secretary Benson and Secretary Dulles—but none of it seems to rub off on him and there is scarcely a shred of evidence that he has met any public disfavor except in places where he didn't have much favor to begin with. The only poll that has shown any decline in his popularity is one taken recently at the Minnesota State Fair, in which a majority held that he was doing a poor job. Whatever this vote may have reflected, it was not the sentiment that political observers have found in most parts of the country. The reaction generally noted is not one of enthusiasm for specific policies but of general approval of the President as a national leader, coupled with the feeling that in the interests of fair play nothing that he does in this period should be judged harshly. Naturally, if the decisions he takes now lead to an end that the public disapproves of, they will later be recalled and charged against his account. But right now, he is free in a way that chiefs of state seldom are. He can think in terms of end results rather than of immediate political consequences; for the time being, there will not be any political consequences.

20 Three Heads of Government

Letter from Bermuda
December 9, 1953

Though it is only a matter of hours since the conference
between the heads of government of the United States, the
United Kingdom, and the French Republic came to a close, one
somehow has the feeling that the conference never took place at
all, or at least that it took place somewhere else at some remote
period. Even with Sir Winston Churchill and the convalescent
M. Laniel still on the island, it requires a considerable effort of
mind to convince oneself that only a few hours ago this elegant
reef was the scene of deliberations so momentous and so secret
that it was judged necessary to string barbed wire around the
conference sector, to guard every approach to it with troops
and bayonets, and to station offshore what is reported to have
been a veritable armada of ships. There are several reasons that
the conference has so quickly taken on this dim aspect. For
one thing, President Eisenhower's speech on the horrors and
hopes of atomic energy before the United Nations General
Assembly, merely by embodying a real proposal or two, completely eclipsed it. Whether the President's speech was a master-
stroke of diplomacy or not, it was certainly a far showier thing
than the conference communiqué issued here in the small hours
of yesterday afternoon. Actually, the communiqué was read as
an account of what did not take place; it was a document intended to put the best possible face on the fact that no decisions
of importance were reached during the four days of talk. It will
be said that a conference cannot be adjudged a bust merely be-

cause the conferees didn't produce much, and no doubt this is
true. It does not, however, alter the fact that everything about
this conference has seemed insubstantial and difficult to credit.
The information policy of the three governments contributed to
the air of ghostliness. No one would say anything about the nothing that was being done. Governments have a way of increasing
concealment when there is nothing to conceal. If big things are
in the wind, the press will be told about them; if nothing is stirring, the press attachés seek to hide the void. Aside from its
purely ceremonial features, this conference was characterized
principally by its negations, its omissions, its silences. All this
hiding of nothing, combined with one's knowledge that nothing
was there to be hidden, has made the Bermuda conference
ephemeral, phantasmal even in short memory. Was there really
a convention of the mighty in the fortified golf club? Were matters of global significance really being discussed by men of
global distinction behind all that barbed wire, which struck so
silly and jarring a note in this community of unlatched doors
and high-priced but not altogether false hospitality?

Of course, the Big Three were here—and two Bigs, British and
French, are here right now. They did meet, or at least two of
them, British and American, met and were joined by a deputy,
M. Bidault, who sat in for the indisposed Gaul. They foregathered often in the lounge of the Mid-Ocean Club, and when all
the jokes about men at sea have been made, one knows very
well that an international conference is always something more
than the observable emptiness and baloney of the communiqués.
Even if nothing happens, something has happened, and besides,
things can happen without seeming to. There are things that
aren't on the agenda but are terribly important. It was never
formally announced, for example, that the subject of the atomic
bomb ever came up at the Potsdam Conference in 1945. Yet we
now know that it did, and we know from Sir Winston's latest
volume of memoirs that the deadly business was discussed long
and earnestly by him and President Truman, and that Stalin was

informed of the existence of a new type of bomb in a studiedly offhand way by the President. While it would surely be impossible for anyone to appraise the exact importance of Bermuda now, there is no denying that it may have been an important conference and that its very indecisions may someday be shown to have had a profound effect on the course of events.

It was in any case part of history, and it had a history of its own. To the observer who could accept his fate and realize that he would never, in Bermuda, be advised of even the most harmless and banal things that were said, there was available a certain amount of diversion—and even, at times, of elevation—merely in sitting back and regarding it all as a piece of theater. Once the conference had got under way, one could not see the playhouse, much less the stage, but during the preliminaries and the aftermath, as well as at various moments during the sessions, it was possible to perceive a performance that offered a little tragedy, a little comedy, and some patently sound showmanship. The critical verdict rendered by those who viewed last weekend as a show is, happily enough, that the honors must be divided about evenly among the three principal players. Indeed, the weekend arranged itself rather tidily into a three-act play, with each of the leading men having an act to himself.

The first act was Sir Winston's. He was the host and the moving spirit, and he played the opening scenes to the full. Arriving here two days before the sessions were scheduled to begin, he promptly captivated the waiting correspondents by the simple rightness, the good humor, and, when occasion demanded, the splendor of his bearing at the elaborate public ceremonies that welcomed him and, later, his fellow-conferees to the island. His visibly enfeebled figure, housing a visibly unenfeebled spirit, was at each of the ceremonies the center of all attention. True, he had the advantage of a setting that was as appropriate for him as a forest is for a dryad. The Royal Welch Fusiliers, who were out in formation at each arrival, constitute a military organization that is in fact a parading museum of British history. It tenderly preserves the archaic, even to the point of spelling "Welch" with a "c" instead of the "s" that is nowadays always used, and among its accoutrements are symbolic picks and axes, a mascot goat with gilded horns, and the "flash"—a broad ribbon down the Fusilier's back that originally served to keep the grease on his regulation pigtail from soiling his uniform. Delightful as the Fusiliers were, though, no one would have wanted to see them three days in a row if it had not been for the presence with them of the Queen's First Minister, the great antagonist of contemporary tyrants, and the latest winner of the Nobel Prize for Literature, who quite thrillingly invested with a sense of continuity and urgent modernity a display that by the third time would otherwise have appeared tedious, silly, and antiquarian. It was not only because of the part Sir Winston played in this ritualistic prologue that he seemed the central figure here at the outset. It was in everyone's mind that the underlying purpose of this conference was to give the Prime Minister an opportunity to talk with the two other heads of government, and particularly with President Eisenhower, with whom he has for some time wished to exchange words. Thus—at least up through the first day of the conference—the question everyone most wanted an answer to was whether the Prime Minister had met privately with the President to talk him into the idea of a "parley at the summit." Then, as it quickly became apparent that there was no possible way of getting an authoritative answer, speculation was all but abandoned.

At just this point, the President of the Council of Ministers of the French Republic moved to the center of the invisible stage. His role was mute but formidable. In a way, it was formidable *because* it was mute. M. Laniel, it was announced on Friday evening, had attended the first gathering of the heads of government but at that presumably crucial session had elected not to utter a single word. Instead, France had been spoken for by M. Bidault, the Foreign Minister. Had M. Laniel delivered himself of volumes of lucid, mellifluous French prose, had he outshone Sir Winston himself as a controversionalist, he would not have provoked half the breathless discussion he did by saying nothing whatever. For one thing, if he had spoken volumes, no one would have known anything about it, since up to the time the communiqué was released, the briefing officers were forbidden not only to relate the content of the talks but even to say who had done the talking. Such a mild question as which of the participants had opened a particular discussion was greeted with exactly the kind of rebuff that should greet a request for the hydrogen-bomb recipe. But no one had thought to make it a violation of the rules to reveal who had *not* spoken, and so the first real sensation of Bermuda was the announcement that M. Laniel had made diplomatic history, had opened up broad new horizons in negotiation, by the simple expedient of letting the cat get his tongue. It was a great sensation, though it lasted only a day.

It has not yet been satisfactorily explained whether M. Laniel's silence on the first day was part of a crafty and well-planned strategy or whether it was occasioned by the first symptoms of the ailment that confined him to his room and his bed for the rest of the conference. The latter explanation would seem reasonable if it were not known that just prior to the first session the French Premier had gone on a sight-seeing tour and had spoken quite volubly to the people who guided him through the parish church of St. George and to his companions on the jaunt. Anyway, he continued to be the center of interest and speculation for at least another day and a half—though less, at the end, because of his seemingly novel approach to world affairs than because of the sympathy he aroused by being so unfortunately stricken at so unfortunate a distance from France. The Laniel portion of the program lasted through Sunday morning, when the welcome word went round that his fever had subsided, thanks to British wonder drugs administered by Lord Moran, the Prime Minister's personal physician. (Lord Moran and his drugs helped somewhat to restore the wounded pride of the

colonials here, who took it very hard that the decade's most publicized rheum should have made its appearance in a community
that insists before the world that such things just don't happen
in it.) Once it was known that M. Laniel's health was improving, the medical bulletins, though still the most specific and informative ones, were no longer the most eagerly awaited, and
observers once more tried to direct their attention to the diplomatic business theoretically being transacted around the cedar
table in the Mid-Ocean Club. M. Laniel's name did not return
to the forefront of consciousness until—and then rather briefly—
the day after the conference ended. It cropped up then only because an enterprising representative of the United Press had
submitted to the Premier a series of written questions that were
intended to bring out his estimate of the proceedings. The Premier did not answer these questions, but he obliged the news
agency by dictating some questions of his own and then an-
swering them in detail. The burden of these answers was that,
despite his malady and despite any suppositions to the contrary,
he had kept abreast of all the discussions and had, indeed,
played a major role in the conference. Though confined to his
bed, he said, he had sent out instructions to the French delegation whenever instructions were needed, and he had seen to
it that the final result of the conference reflected his thoughts
and French national interests. *"La rédaction du communiqué,
bien entendu,"* he declared in his written statement, *"a été faite
en liaison constante avec moi."* It was well that he issued this
statement, for the French briefing officer had not conveyed the
notion that M. Laniel was an active participant.

In the closing act of the conference, President Eisenhower had
his day, or day and a half. His press secretary, Mr. Hagerty, announced at a briefing session on Sunday that the President, instead of returning to Washington on schedule, planned to fly directly to New York and address the General Assembly on the
subject of atomic energy and its perils for mankind. This would
have been only a moderately piquant bit of news—in fact, a poor

substitute for details about the conference—if Mr. Hagerty had not, intentionally or otherwise, given the impression that the speech was in some way an outgrowth of the Bermuda conference. He was to deny this within a few minutes, but not before he had said that Lord Cherwell, Sir Winston's friend, confidant, and adviser on nuclear matters, had "worked on" the speech the President was planning to deliver. He also gave his auditors the distinct idea that the speech had been enthusiastically endorsed by the British and French delegations. Then, when questioned rather closely about the authorship of the speech and about the nature of the endorsement, he began moving in the other direction and seemed to be seeking to give the whole business a strictly American coloration. This, he said, was a speech the President had for a long time contemplated making; Lord Cherwell and others in Bermuda had read it only because of the wholly coincidental fact that the President happened to be working on it in his off hours here. Here was conflict, and it provided material for thought and inquiry at a time when there was a conspicuous shortage of such material. It may also have brought about certain changes in the speech itself, for—if gossip now in circulation among the remaining members of the British delegation is to be credited—when word reached Sir Winston that people were wondering to what degree he had approved the speech and to what degree he and his aides were responsible for its composition, he decided that the world would hold him responsible in any case, and that he had better take a close look at what he would be held responsible for. It is said that he thereupon called for a text of the speech, read it for style and content, and then respectfully suggested to the President the alteration of a few thoughts and phrases. If the Prime Minister actually did do this, his revision must have been the fortieth or fiftieth, for it has been definitely established that the speech— part of what has for some time been known to newspaper readers as Operation Candor—had already gone through endless revisions before the President brought it down here.

It could easily be that the Bermuda conference, in spite of the evasions and ambiguities so clearly revealed in the official communiqué—or, quite possibly, because of them—will some day be looked back on as a turning point in international relations. For all anyone knows, Sir Winston talked President Eisenhower into agreeing to a parley "at the summit of the nations" and into working toward a new American policy in the Far East; for all anyone knows, President Eisenhower and Secretary Dulles talked the British into seeing things the way they see them. Either conversion would be of enormous significance, of course, as would any one of a hundred other things that *might* have happened without the knowledge of more than a few in the galaxy of statesmen that convened on this island. It does not follow that the conference was a dud because it looked like one, as it most certainly did. Nor, on the other hand, does it necessarily follow that history will not reckon it a disaster merely because it now appears to have been no worse than innocuous. Whatever judgment history may finally stamp on the conference, it will be possible to describe it as one of the first attempts made by the West to work out a policy for what may be regarded as the third stage of the cold war. The first stage lasted, roughly, from 1946 or 1947 to 1950. It was characterized principally by the fear that Western Europe would suffer internal collapse; that is to say, that Communism would conquer the free nations because their social fabrics were not tough enough to resist the assaults of the native Communist parties. The Marshall Plan and the Truman Doctrine were fabric stiffeners. By 1950, a new stage had begun. It was characterized by a fear not that the West would succumb to revolution but that it would succumb to aggression by Soviet and satellite armies moving from East to West. In the late nineteen-forties, the Communist parties inside the democracies had been the main enemy; in 1950, it was the totalitarian armies. Two things appear to have brought about this change. First, the Marshall Plan and the Truman Doctrine did what was expected of them; second, on

June 25, 1950, the North Koreans crossed the thirty-eighth parallel, making it altogether plain that world Communism was capable of military aggression. To be sure, the North Atlantic Treaty had been signed the year before, so one cannot really say that aggression did not seem a menace until 1950. But in 1950 an event in space and time confirmed the fear of aggression and Western policies underwent a perceptible change. During the next three years, the rich and vital and generally admirable portion of the globe known as Western Europe was seen as an open, undefended plain inviting speedy, brutal conquest by the Communist armies poised along its eastern frontiers. Aggression was the menace, rearmament and military assistance the slogans. American economic aid was quickly transformed into military aid. Troops were dispatched to the continent, either to replace the political and economic missionaries or to supplement their activities. Congress was persuaded that aggression was an imminent prospect and voted military assistance by the billions. The sense of urgency was greater in the United States than in Western Europe, but Western Europe felt it, too, and the leading statesmen of that region today are the ones who felt it most keenly and who best succeeded in dramatizing their feelings.

Lately, the sense of urgency has all but vanished. Exactly why this is so no one seems able to explain. And whether the danger really is less great no one, of course, knows. Our European allies give indications of having a greater feeling of safety than we do, but one had only to recall the American defense cuts earlier in the year to feel certain that Americans also no longer live with the dreadful apprehension that war may be just a week or two away. Even the Bermuda communiqué, which did not take note of many realities, took note of this one. It acknowledged that "the danger of aggression now appears less imminent." It is true that at West Point last week, Admiral Radford, the Chairman of the Joint Chiefs of Staff, said, "The threat of war has not diminished," but the opinion of this notable expert seemed to derive so obviously from his responsibility to prevent complacency that newspaper editors across the nation buried his statement in the back pages. Admiral Radford may very well have stated the truth. If so, it is a truth that not many people at present perceive.

In any event, most people in most places no longer think the danger of war is very great. Therefore, fear—the motive power of so many things in life and most certainly the motive power of Western rearmament and solidarity—can no longer be successfully appealed to. The French, who originated the idea of a European Defense Community, are dragging their feet because none of their major parties now believe that aggression is likely. The Germans are bidding up the price of their participation not only because their bargaining position improves with every passing day but because they, too, feel there is no special hurry. Indeed, there is no better measure of the change that has occurred than the fact that in millions of European minds Germany has come very close to replacing the Soviet Union as the chief potential disturber of amity and general contentment. One of the most effective arguments for E.D.C. now available to its European supporters is the argument that it is absolutely essential as a device for checkmating not Russia but Germany.

If the delegates to this conference took the rifts in Western unity to be the consequence of the virtual disappearance of fear of war and conquest—the only known cement for uniting peoples—then it is reasonable to suppose that they spent at least some of their time casting about for a new basis for the policies most of them have long been associated with. The American answer, it would appear, is the rekindling of fear by calling attention once more to the horrors of atomic warfare, combined with the attempted kindling of hope by describing the blessings of nuclear fission peacefully employed. It may be that talk of atomic horrors will do the trick, if there is enough of it, but it is hard to find anyone who seems to think so. That the horrors are real is beyond dispute, but the feeling seems to be that most people have become immune to lectures on them. Moreover, the conviction that the Soviet Union is not of a mind to provoke a war right now makes the lectures seem irrelevant to the present situation. They certainly don't have much bearing on the problems that will arise at the forthcoming Berlin Conference of Foreign Ministers. It is quite apparent that the Russians will come to it carrying crowbars to be stuck into each of the cracks now evident in the West. They will make proposals calculated to convince the West Germans that German unity can be had without any sacrifice of German sovereignty, and proposals calculated to make the E.D.C. even less attractive to the French than it is now, which isn't very attractive. The only piece of real information in the Bermuda communiqué was the statement that "The French Minister of Foreign Affairs explained the problems facing his government in regard to the European Defense Community." (In the first version of the communiqué, the word "facing" was misprinted as "forcing," which struck everyone as a very fitting typographical error.) Since it is well known that raging mobs demanding the ratification of E.D.C. do not constitute one of the problems facing, or forcing, M. Bidault's government, it was assumed on every hand that the story he had to tell was a melancholy one.

Bermuda was to be the setting in which the Western allies would decide on a common stand for future dealings with the Russians. It was a setting, all right, and a common stand was announced. It is, however, the stand the West has been making all along. The communiqué describes the extent of Western unity, which, all things considered, remains impressive. But nothing the communiqué says could not have been said weeks and even months before this, and what it fails to say about the contribution of this meeting is a great deal. If a contribution was made here, either no one knew what it was or no one knew how to describe it.

21   Four Foreign Ministers

Letter from East Berlin

February 4, 1954

For the time being, and perhaps for whatever time remains to it, the conference of Foreign Ministers has taken on the aspect of hopeless, irreconcilable conflict that has characterized all East-West meetings since the end of the war. The Western powers cannot do business of any sort with Mr. Molotov while he persists in demanding that they sponsor a forced union of the Adenauer and Grotewohl governments. Politically and morally unacceptable for reasons eloquently set forth by Messrs. Bidault, Eden, and Dulles, this fire-and-ice solution is also, as Molotov has every reason to know, chemically impossible. There is, of course, no doubt that Moscow could use its good offices to persuade the Grotewohl government to sit down in a parliament with what the East German *Tägliche Rundschau* calls "the Bonn revengists" and "Adenauer's seedy jackals." Molotov himself once explained, in the course of a memorable deal he was making with Joachim von Ribbentrop, that there are times when it is prudent to overlook differences between political systems. Asked in 1939 how he could align himself with Nazis, Molotov shrugged and said that in matters of this sort he was inclined to favor the rule of *"chacun à son goût."* What was good enough for Old Stony Bottom (this is reputedly the sobriquet given Molotov by colleagues in the Foreign Ministry) would surely be good enough for Otto Grotewohl and Wilhelm Pieck. The West, however, could not hope to make the present Bonn government see things in that light. Chancellor Adenauer today speaks for a Germany that, though clobbered, truncated, and still technically subject to military occupation, in fact exercises a formidable sovereignty. Even if the Western nations saw any good in the Molotov proposal, they would lack the power to make the Adenauer government submit to it. The Molotov plan for Germany—in essence a coalition government—could become effective only through the capitulation of a successor government that had been abandoned to its fate by the West, and neither a successor government nor Western abandonment is at this stage conceivable. The most isolationist of American politicians and the most neutralist of French and British politicians adhere to the general proposition that a defense of Europe conducted east of the Rhine is to be preferred to one conducted west of the Rhine; no substantial body of opinion in any Western country could approve the Soviet proposals. Indeed, French spokesmen here were saying last night and this morning that nothing would improve the currently dim prospects for ratification of the European Defense Community by the National Assembly as much as a few more speeches along the lines of the one Molotov delivered yesterday.

If Molotov will not give ground on Germany, at least to the extent of passing on from it to the somewhat less thorny Austrian question, the conference here will soon be finished. Just now, as the sessions grind on in the Soviet Embassy—an incredibly bourgeois olio of fancy stonework, stained glass, and light-opera staircases on Unter den Linden—there is nothing to suggest that Molotov intends to give ground on anything. But then neither was there anything to suggest, at the time the conference got under way, that he had brought the authority to make Soviet policy here in Berlin or that he would be flexible enough to reverse his field on two or three occasions. That, however, is exactly what happened during the meetings in the West sector, and it gives the Western delegations some faint hope that similar wonders may come to pass when the conference moves back to Western ground next Monday. Though Molotov opened the formal proceedings with a snarling attack on the United States and the Adenauer government, it was his only tirade of the week, and it was both preceded and followed by sweet talk. Much of the time, his politeness seemed to know no bounds. Before the first meeting, he begged the privilege of conferring with Mr. Dulles, and at this tête-à-tête laid before the Secretary of State what seemed a perfectly reasonable suggestion. He pointed out that although the conference was a quadripartite meeting, convened by equals and without prejudice to any single power, all the world knew, and surely Mr. Dulles would acknowledge, that it was really a three-against-one deal, and that before very long, Eden, Bidault, and Dulles would be ganging up on him, Molotov. Dulles replied that this did seem to be a plausible forecast, and when Molotov asked if the American Secretary, who was to be chairman of the first session, didn't think it would be only fair to allow him a little more speaking time than the others on opening day, Dulles said he thought that Molotov had asked no more than was his due.

Molotov got his time and used it to belabor the republic represented by the obliging chairman, but for the rest of the week he was uncommonly obliging himself. He let himself be persuaded to set aside his proposal for a five-power conference, and then he agreed to set aside his astonishing proposal for a conference of all the powers on the face of the earth—including, presumably, two Germanies, two Chinas, and two Koreas. Finally, he acquiesced in a violation of the very agenda that he himself had drawn up and sold to the conference; where once he had said that all logic and reason demanded a settling of the problems at issue by proceeding from the general to the specific—by drawing up a German settlement only after having first reduced "tension in international relations"—he now consented to an immediate concentration on the German situation. This was one of the two things about Molotov's behavior that made the deepest impression on the Western delegates. Just a week ago tonight, most of them were willing to wager a month's foreign-office pay that Molotov would never consent to starting a discussion of Germany while the meetings were being held in the West sector. It simply wasn't in the books, they said; it couldn't possibly happen. He would wait until he got over into Communist territory, richly festooned with banners reading "All Germans at One Table," and then, perhaps, he would show up at the conference table flanked by Pieck and Grotewohl and bearing stacks of petitions signed by twelve million East Germans demanding immediate unity. (These petitions, though they have not yet been introduced in evidence, are known to exist. Dozens of them are to be seen Scotch-taped to walls in Stalin-allee restaurants, shops, and apartment building lobbies. While it is thought improbable that two-thirds of the East German population have signed them, this is the claim the East German press makes.) But although two days of discussions in the West sector remained and although, by all rights, he should have been smarting under the rebuffs administered him in the preceding days, Molotov graciously agreed to a consideration of the German question, and there were two days of civil and sometimes sensible talk.

Molotov's acceptance of the revised agenda, his temporary withdrawal of proposals for talks with other powers, and his recurrent changes of pitch were made, so far as anyone could tell, without any instructions from Moscow. Generally at gatherings of this sort, the Russians delegates call a halt in the proceedings every time something new comes up and refer the matter to headquarters. Under the last Soviet administration, the basic principle seemed to be "When in doubt, ask Stalin"—or, as someone said here the other day, "Don't talk, telegraph." Molotov has unquestionably been in close and frequent touch with Moscow, but there have been times when it was plain to all the Western delegates in the room (who promptly made it plain to all the Western correspondents not in the room) that Molotov was meeting a new British, French, or American argument by the simple and admirable device of listening to it, taking notes on it, and then preparing his own speech. According to certain members of the American delegation, some of whom must be advanced practitioners of the art of reading upside down, he is a most assiduous note-taker, a man who breaks things down in a-b-c style and makes heavy use of arrows, asterisks, and the like. To be sure, his freedom to improvise and formulate policy can exist only within narrow limits (no foreign minister of any state has complete freedom in this field), but the important and interesting fact is that for the first time in many years a representative of the Soviet has been, if not his own master, at least his own technician. This could indicate a change in the nature of Soviet power or a change in the nature of the relationship between Molotov and his boss. (Or, though many facts argue against this, it could be read as evidence that Molotov *is* boss.) For the moment, most people here are content merely to observe the events of the day and let the future provide the interpretation. The most favored interim thesis is that nothing at all has changed but that Malenkov has found it advisable to relieve himself of some problems he is ill prepared to cope with by delegating a measure of his authority in the diplomatic field. No one is in a position to say whether Molotov's apparent free-wheeling is something the West should welcome or something it should regret, but if the show he has been putting on since the conference moved to the East sector is the kind of show he is going to continue putting on, there is no cause for rejoicing in London, Paris, or Washington.

If it should develop that Monday's Molotov, who rejected out of hand the Eden plan for German elections, is the final 1954 model, observers here will find themselves hard put to it to explain the atmosphere of welcome and cordiality that Molotov's and Malenkov's subordinates have plainly been ordered to create for this conference. If Molotov is to remain as churlish as he is now, why have other Communists in East Berlin made such great and often ludicrous efforts to win favor with Westerners whose favor would do them precious little good if they could win it, which they can't? It is easy enough to understand the Communists' eagerness to lure visitors on inspection tours of Stalinallee, the Marxist Parkchester; the East Berlin bureaucracy is itself wowed by this creation and spends enormous sums celebrating it in books and pamphlets whose psychological basis is quite evidently narcissistic, and it would doubtless be pleased to see pictures of it in the Western press. But there is no such easy explanation why the rulers of East Berlin have been going to tremendous lengths to please Western newspapermen with cocktail parties, elaborate cuisine, and dazzling bargains in cameras, typewriters, and objets d'art. It is true that satisfying the grosser appetites of newspapermen is the first principle of public relations as practiced from Miami Beach to Madison Avenue, but according to the Communist ideology, which is eternally right in this instance, the Miami Beach and Madison Avenue approach is unavailing when applied by revolutionaries to newspapermen representing a vigorous capitalist economy—or, for that matter, to anyone else representing such an economy. Yet the fact remains that from the start of the conference right down to the present impasse, the Communists here in East Berlin have been under instructions to extend all manner of privileges to what they must regard as agents of the enemy powers. It is not only unprecedented but downright fantastic that the past ten or twelve days have seen the development of a situation in which an American passport opens all doors and makes all things possible, hyperbolically speaking, in an Iron Curtain country. With this invaluable green document, an American can walk into any of the H.O. stores, the state-controlled agencies of distribution, and with East German marks bought in the West at a most favorable rate of exchange (eighteen or nineteen to the dollar), purchase commodities so staggeringly expensive in the East German economic scheme that they are far beyond the aspirations of even those on the upper rungs of the financial ladder. Openhandedness of this sort has never been seen before and may never be seen again, but it is in full swing at this moment, and many people here are wondering why. This kind of thing, as word of it gets around, will certainly do nothing to strengthen the Communists' already tenuous hold on the East German population.

In the view of many Westerners here, the answer to this and certain other riddles is that Soviet power actually has been striving for some sort of accommodation with the West. The Malenkov regime may be unsure as to what kind of accommodation is feasible, and signs multiply that it does not want a relaxation of tensions badly enough to meet the West's minimum terms, but for all that, there is a feeling that Molotov, however shabbily he may behave during the rest of the conference, did come to Berlin in search of amelioration. No other explanation, it is pointed out, accounts for his being here at all. (He remarked in a talk with M. Bidault, incidentally, that it was his first visit to the city since the days when he and Ribbentrop were doing business. "The air is much better here now," he said. M. Bidault did not find this attempt at pleasantry very pleasant.) It cannot be argued that the Russians have much to gain—as the West certainly has—from the mere fact that an attempt at negotiation has been made. From the Western point of view, it is a useful thing to remind the world every so often that the democracies stand ready to discuss their differences with Moscow amicably and without sabre-rattling. It was five years since the last such attempt, and another was due. But an East-West dialogue yields no propaganda dividends to Moscow unless it results in some specific gains. On the contrary, it holds a certain potential of danger. Molotov's friends in Peking, for example, are not interested in moral bona fides; they are interested in getting trade and recognition and a seat in the United Nations, and Molotov's failure to win these things is likely to reinforce whatever tendencies toward diplomatic independence may now exist in Communist China. The general view here is that Molotov came to Berlin because the power complex he speaks for wants the heat taken off. If, in spite of his increase in flexibility, he

nonetheless proves too rigid to accomplish this, it does not necessarily signify that another meaning must be read into his purposes. It can mean merely that he and his government are incapable of satisfying their own needs and desires, which is a
common and tragic failing of men and governments.

Molotov has been the principal object of interest and speculation here, but he has not been the whole show. Mr. Eden
and Mr. Dulles have been pretty close to the top of their form.
Eden has generally taken the honors for eloquence and wit, and
Dulles has displayed a maneuverability that will require his
critics to make some modifications in their appraisals of him. But
the star performer for the West has been, in the judgment of
almost everyone, M. Bidault. For weeks before the conference,
and especially in the dismal period of the electoral crisis at Versailles, it was widely held that M. Bidault, if he ever got to
Berlin, would be pushed all over the lot and would be forced by
the situation at home to find almost any deal that Molotov offered France irresistible. It was known, of course, that he himself was wholly in agreement with Eden and Dulles, but it was
felt that his isolation in French politics, his lack of a solid base
in public opinion, would drive him into representing a point
of view he has little use for. Nothing of the kind has happened.
At times, Bidault has even seemed to exceed his British and
American friends in militancy. He has listened courteously as
Molotov has attempted to win him over, but he has made a
close and brilliant examination of the substance of each Russian
proposal and has found them all lacking. (At a private dinner,
which Bidault reported on to his Anglo-American friends, the
Soviet foreign minister broached the subject of Indo-China in
a curious way. Molotov said that he understood the French
were much troubled by the course of a certain war in that quarter of the world, and that the Kremlin, despite its regrettable ignorance of what, exactly, was at issue in the war, would like to
be of some assistance to France. He himself, Molotov said, was
not familiar enough with the situation to know whether any as-

sistance could be given or what its nature might be, but he would investigate the matter immediately upon his return to Russia and, if M. Bidault wished, would inquire whether any of his associates had contacts down that way who might make themselves available for purposes of mediation. Bidault did not report his reply to this suggestion.) Seeking light on why the rock of the Western alliance should be a statesman who represents so thin a vein of public sentiment in his own country, some people have propounded the theory that political responsibility can be a by-product of political insecurity. Representing, to all intents and purposes, no one in France but himself, Bidault, unlike anyone else at this conference, is in a position to handle himself exactly as he sees fit. Because he speaks for the shakiest member of the anti-Communist alliance and the one most torn by dissension, he can—for the moment, at any rate— be the firmest of speakers.

After the ministers themselves, the most interesting and possibly the most important people here are the delegation briefing officers, who after each session vie with one another for the attentions of the press. Because the Western powers have always regarded this conference as valuable chiefly from the propaganda point of view, and because Moscow is, of course, eager to make propaganda of any grist at all, nothing whatever that goes on around the conference table can be kept within the conference room. What one delegation tries to conceal another will be anxious to report to anyone it can get to listen. The attempts to get listeners are ingenious and sometimes almost frantic. The French run buses to their briefing sessions. The Russians try to start theirs ahead of anyone else's. The British offer two consecutive briefings—a very short one for those who want the news in a hurry and a longer one for the reflective types. The Americans sell speed and—thanks to Mr. Henry Suydam, a highly cultivated gentleman who until a few months ago was chief editorial writer of the Newark *News*—the most literate and amusing summaries and paraphrases. Paraphrase is used only when verbatim texts are unavailable; whenever possible direct quotation is the rule. There are private meetings and dinners, of course, and semi-formal ones at which stenographic transcripts are not made, but no discussion of any sort takes place without the presence of someone whose chief interest is telling the world about it. Whether this garrulity contributes to the welfare of the nations involved is an open question. It is, in any event, unstoppable. There will be no secret covenants secretly arrived at in Berlin; indeed, from the appearance of things at present, there will be no covenants.

Not very much light has been thrown by the Berlin press or by the Berliners themselves on what the people of the host city have been thinking and feeling about the proceedings. The press of the East sector is, naturally, nothing but a daily exegesis of Molotov's speeches and a reiteration of the general thought that they are as pearls cast before swine. The press of the West sector presents more stimulating material, but it is still not especially helpful on Berlin reactions; it runs less to the reporting of sentiment than to polemics derived from fixed political positions. And one cannot learn a great deal from the Berliners, for their talk with strangers and foreigners is seldom casual; in fact, it is very often guarded, cryptic, or deliberately misleading. This is true even in the free area, where the man next to you is not likely to be a member of the secret police but is very likely—particularly if he adopts a casual air—to be a masquerading officer from one of the dozen or so intelligence agencies, mostly American, that compete with one another for every scrap of information, however trivial, that can be picked up here. Nevertheless, certain things have been reasonably clear. In the early days of the conference, as in the days immediately preceding it, the prevailing mood of the Berliners was one of apprehension and fear that the Western Ministers, having yielded to Communist wiles to the extent of agreeing to meet and talk with Molotov, would have no choice but to go farther along the road to appeasement, possibly even agreeing to surrender Berlin and West Germany within a matter of weeks. The conviction that the Western occupiers were on the verge of decamping was so strong that it affected the real-estate market in some areas. One woman who owns a home in the Dahlem district, where the American High Commission has its Berlin office, received half a dozen unsolicited bids on her property—all the bids and all the suggested prices being contingent upon early American evacuation. It seems plain, too, that the apprehension was widespread. On the opening day of the conference, a great many West Berliners took part in a three-minute demonstration of silence. The Freedom Bell tolled clear and brassily at nine-thirty in the morning, and all observable activity—on streets and sidewalks, in stores and hotel lobbies—ceased until nine-thirty-three. In the East sector, according to reporters who had stationed themselves in Stalinallee and on the Potsdamer Platz, people tended to go about their business a bit more briskly and self-consciously during the appointed minutes, of which they made themselves aware by frequent consultation of timepieces.

The exact aim of the demonstration, which had been organized and encouraged by municipal authorities in the West sector, was never satisfactorily explained, but since bell tolling and voluntary silence are generally associated with prayer and meditation, it seems reasonable to suppose that Berliners East and West, except for that sizable minority that has understandably become thoroughly defeatist and cynical, were attempting to communicate a hope that Molotov would meet with resistance from the Western Ministers—and no doubt, too, a hope that someone would have the foresight, the opportunity, and the courage to set banana peels wherever they would do the most good along Old Stony Bottom's path. (As always, the Communists were on to such hopes. On the day of Molotov's arrival, pilot train after pilot train, each followed by an imposing collection of de luxe Communist rolling stock, highballed into the Soviet sector from the east. Then the dignitaries that one of these trains had been presumed to be carrying arrived in East Berlin by plane.) But to what degree Berliners have been surprised, disappointed, or gratified by later developments is hard to say. There have been no subsequent demonstrations, silent or brassy.

One thing that Berliners will discuss with anyone is their city. They do so, for the most part, in terms that reveal more about the human mind than about politics or war or the specific Berlin tragedy. The single fact that impresses people visiting Berlin for the first time since the war, and also people who have seen it only at widely spaced intervals since the war, is the staggering thoroughness of the destruction. The postwar rebuilding, especially in the West, is impressive, too, but because the sight of construction is too common in most of the civilized world to give one any particular pause, the eyes focus immediately on the gutted buildings, which somehow look all the more completely gutted when they stand—filthy and unwanted and inviting only further destruction by sledge hammer and bulldozer —next to some new and almost glistening edifice of clean brick or stucco, and the mind becomes absorbed with thoughts of how many and whose bodies may be concealed in the heap of rubble alongside the shiny hotel or camera emporium.

This response of the eyes and the mind of the newcomer seems not morbid but normal—it seems, in fact, so reasonable that it is the only possible one under the circumstances. But it is by no means the only possible one, because the average Berliner—and even the average Englishman, Frenchman, or American who has been in Berlin any length of time—sees and feels something almost totally different. The Berliners have lived with their ruins for so long now that they are almost incapable of seeing them or of thinking about them as anything but unimproved land. "Haven't we done a remarkable job here?" a West Berliner will say, pointing to a scene in which a few new or rebuilt buildings merely call attention to the surrounding devastation. "We never thought we'd get the place cleaned up at all. Did you know that more bombs fell on Berlin than all of England?" The conviction in the voice restrains one from observing that the place *hasn't* been cleaned up at all—or, rather, that the imagination reels at the thought of what remains to be done, although notable things have been accomplished, and some of the new buildings in the West sector are quite stunning. If, choosing one's words carefully, one should make approximately this observation, one would be confronted with the challenge of the Kurfurstendamm, West Berlin's broad and handsome street of shops, hotels, night clubs, and good restaurants. The Kurfurstendamm is the showpiece of the reconstruction, and it does, in all truth, make quite a showpiece. At night, with its good-looking curbside display cases brilliantly lighted to show off arrays of goods as tastefully arranged as anything in Paris, it has a glitter unexcelled by any similar street anywhere. But the illumination only makes the total effect stranger, for eyes that have not been conditioned to blot out all signs of destruction are bound to look up and around at the buildings that house the elegant shops and restaurants, and the panorama that greets them there is the eeriest kind of façading. The Kurfurstendamm has not been rebuilt, as the Chamber of Commerce literature insists that it has; it has merely undergone a partial transformation that momentarily deceives the eye. Quite as often as not, the elegance is merely at ground level; from the second story up, there are mostly husks. And if one tries to take in the whole sweep of the Kurfurstendamm, what really sticks in the mind is not the symbol of rebirth supposedly provided by the lighted showcases but the symbol of war and political horror provided by the famous Gedachtniskirche, the church whose ugly, blasted shell still dominates the Kurfurstendamm and will continue to do so no matter how many more kilowatts are made to flow into the street's lighting system. Indeed, the more light there is, the more one's attention is called to the ghostly presence of this structure, whose steeple was knocked galley-west and whose tower was cut off halfway from the top, so that it now resembles some ungainly cooking vessel. But Berliners—to their credit, perhaps, since it is doubtless better to accentuate the positive than to brood over ruins—are unable to see the church as a disfiguring or disconcerting element in the picture. In fact, most of the come-on literature of the business groups features the Gedachtniskirche as the centerpiece of Kurfurstendamm pictures, whose captions explain how the street far surpasses Fifth Avenue, Regent Street, the Via Veneto, and the Place Vendôme. By the same token, the come-on literature exploits the wretched little saplings in the Tiergarten—bought and planted with Marshall Plan funds, and none of them much more than five or six feet tall—as evidence that Berlin's parks are all that they were of old.

In the East sector, the self-deception that is a private enterprise in the West has been collectivized, rationalized, and managed by the state. Possibly what the Russian masters ordered for East Berlin—the concentration of almost all rebuilding in a single, planned area—was rather smart, for at least it is possible to stand in the center of Stalinallee and see no outward signs of destruction, unless one counts it as destructive of certain higher values that the new buildings should be as dreary and conventional as they are, that nowhere can one see a single evidence of taste or the modern spirit, that a community with a chance to rebuild should do nothing more than imitate the apartment-house style instituted in another city, Moscow, twenty years ago and copied by that city from still another, the New York of thirty years ago. Stalinallee, a housing project and shopping center for bureaucrats and trained-seal workers, is something that no life insurance company in its senses would nowadays finance. The most backward of municipal housing authorities would be offended by the architects' failure to take advantage of the new methods and materials that have for years been available to builders at no extra cost, or very little. Nevertheless, the sheer massiveness of the thing, the fact that it is one continuous stretch of unscarred human habitat, does make it stand out in the surrounding desolation and does give it a kind of impressiveness, which the pitifully scattered, though demonstrably more extensive, reconstruction in West Berlin lacks. In the end, though, it may be that the Stalinallee fraud has no power to deceive or mislead those who see it all the time, for the Stalinallee project, unlike the construction projects in the West, cannot in all probability be thought of by the East Berliners as solely an essay in masonry. It must also stand in their minds as the symbol of the bureaucracy that takes over its one achievement in reconstruction as its dormitory and playground. The Berlin seen by those who live off Stalinallee, even a block off it, is not desolation relieved by an occasional new building or façade but the real McCoy—desolation unrelieved. It is, or in any case should be, impossible for anyone to be fooled by that.

22 Who Promoted McCarthy?

Letter from Washington
March 4, 1954

Nothing, not even the lunatic carnage in the House of Representatives early this week has diverted Washington's attention from the latest McCarthy case—that of Dr. Irving Peress, the Fifth Amendment dentist who, according to McCarthy, should never have been let into the Army and should certainly never have been let out. Now that the President seems to have defined an attitude, however, one element of suspense has been removed, and it may be that people will be able to turn their minds back to other affairs, many of which are pending and many of which are pressing. Thanks largely to McCarthy and his dentist, very little attention has thus far been paid to the approaching conference at Geneva, to the troubled meetings currently taking place at Caracas, and to the difficulties confronting

Western policy in France, Indo-China, England, Italy, India, and an appalling number of places in the Middle East. The President's legislative program has receded so far from the center of consciousness here that it is doubtful whether one person in five recalls any longer what it is. It is possible, now that Mr. Eisenhower has told what he thinks, or part of what it is commonly hoped and believed he thinks, and McCarthy has replied, that the next few days will see a return to something like the normal rhythms and preoccupations of Washington life, but it would be imprudent flatly to forecast such a development. Senator McCarthy is a man of large abilities; the depths of his imagination have never been plumbed, and if his strategic resourcefulness knows any limits, they have not thus far been measured. Washington is now waiting for *his* next move, pretty much as in other times and circumstances it has waited for Hitler's next move, or Tojo's, or Stalin's. There is less doubt about what sort of move it will be than there was while the President's words were being awaited, for McCarthy, to the surprise of no one, has insouciantly brushed aside the President's statement and announced that he plans to resume the offensive right away. The remaining uncertainty concerns not his strategy, which he has explained in detail, but his tactics, and these will be on display next week, when he reopens his controversy with Secretary of the Army Stevens.

The general feeling here now is that the President, in yesterday's statement, made a slight advance in what can only be regarded as the war being waged on him and his office by Senator McCarthy. While this first hesitant assertion of leadership leaves McCarthy about where he was, it is believed that it may embolden the Republican press throughout the country to handle the issue with less equivocation, and it may, though this is more doubtful, prompt some Republican leaders out in the provinces to conclude that McCarthyism is not a necessary item in the credo of party regularity. Hope for this development received mild encouragement from the statement issued a couple of days ago by Leonard Hall, the party's National Chairman, who, plainly the bearer of instructions from the President, said he didn't think McCarthy was always right. But nothing the President said apropos of McCarthy was as useful, as welcome, as badly in need of saying as his declaration—apropos of Mr. Dulles's demotion of Scott McLeod, the F.B.I. man who last year became the State Department's arbiter of morals and philosophy —that the responsibility for anything that happens inside any of the executive departments belongs to the heads of those departments and to no one else. What was distressing and destructive about the Zwicker case was not simply McCarthy's brutal handling of the officer but the fact that General Ralph Zwicker was called to account in the first place and the fact that it was McCarthy's plan to call others, both above and below General Zwicker in the chain of command, to account for their roles in the granting of an honorable discharge to Major Peress. As Secretary Stevens implied in the celebrated statement of defiance that he composed last week but never got around to delivering, the only man truly accountable to the legislative branch in such a case is the civilian head of the department. Under any other arrangement, chaos and madness would prevail, for if an officer or administrator who is subject to departmental discipline when he fails to carry out orders is to be subject to congressional discipline when he *does* carry them out, then all government is bound to find itself in a state of catalepsy.

By endorsing the first principle of sane administration, the President has undoubtedly gratified his subordinates all through the executive branch, and if the principle is adhered to—if, that is, Cabinet members and agency heads insist at every opportunity on being held personally accountable for what happens in their departments, if they instruct their aides to pass every buck along to them—some of the damage done in recent years may be repaired. The assault on the executive branch is, however, only one aspect of McCarthyism; the largest, most important aspect is the Senator's existence as a sovereign force in American political life. The administration has come to take a less amicable view of McCarthy than it did in the past, but the measure of his force and the measure of the administration's fear of it is the President's unwillingness to lend a hand in attempting to reduce it. The administration is resting what hopes it has in this regard on a reform of the rules and procedures governing congressional investigations. White House pressure has been brought to bear on the Senate Republican Policy Committee, whose chairman is Senator Ferguson, of Michigan, and the committee, to whose past indulgence McCarthy owes much that he will never acknowledge or repay, has announced that it will sponsor a study, with a view to possible change, of current codes and practices. Eminent lawyers and political-science professors will be called in as consultants, and proposals will be welcomed from all quarters. Of suggestions for change, there will be no lack. A spate of proposals, some of them tarnished by years of exposure, has already been made: that hearings be held only when authorized by committee and subcommittee majorities; that testimony be taken only in the presence of a majority; that all witnesses be accompanied and advised by counsel; that the witnesses or the witnesses' counsel be permitted to cross-examine accusers; that testimony taken in closed sessions be made public only after a majority has approved the release. It has also been suggested that Congress relinquish altogether the investigation of subversion and that the job be turned over to a nonpartisan commission drawn wholly or in part from outside the government.

Senator Ferguson has given it as his opinion that if and when new rules are worked out, it should be left up to the chairman of each committee to decide whether or not they ought to be applied; he expressed this open-minded, democratic view of the situation immediately after yesterday's meeting of the Policy Committee, in which Senator McCarthy was an interested and attentive participant. Still, with a certain amount of pressure from the White House and the public, it is possible that changes will be forthcoming in this or the next session of Congress and that in theory, at least, they will be binding on all congressmen. It would be hard, though, to find anyone here who has any confidence that the problems posed by McCarthy can be solved or appreciably diminished by any mere tinkering with the rules. For one thing, McCarthy has never given a fig for the rules that already exist; there is no reason to believe that new ones would impress him more favorably than the old ones. He has broken Senate rule after Senate rule, violated convention after convention, forgotten promise after promise; for his vast accumulation of infractions there have been few in the Senate to censure him and none to discipline him. The very committee that has now, under prodding from the White House, undertaken a reconsideration of the rules refuses to acknowledge that its action is in any way related to McCarthy's bullying of General Zwicker, despite the fact that the alterations that are being suggested make little sense except as a means, dubious or otherwise, of curbing McCarthy. Most of them would actually, in the view of many people here, be positively detrimental to useful congressional investigations. The abolition of one-man hearings, for example, would hamstring a number of committees that are doing valuable work, particularly in fields where the sources of information are likely to be far from Washington. Moreover, the average witness before the average congressional committee would be encumbered rather than aided by a legal adviser; in many cases, witnesses would be better served by a consulting economist or accountant than by an attorney. What would happen, it is being asked here, if McCarthy declined to be bound by the rules intended to restrain him? In view of the fact that only a few weeks ago the Senate voted eighty-five to one to give him the full appropriation he sought this year, it is impossible to believe that anything at all would happen.

Nor can it be assumed that McCarthy would be much affected if his subcommittee was put entirely out of business. It has been a long time, in the opinion of many here, since McCarthy's power has rested on any institution not of his own making. Indeed, it is doubtful whether there ever was such a time. His fellow-senators developed their mortal, paralyzing fear of him not after he became a committee chairman but in the Eighty-first and Eighty-second Congresses, when the Democrats were in control and his committee assignments were of no importance. His role in the Tydings investigation was merely that of a witness, but he played it effectively enough to drive the chairman out of public life. He had earlier, while still an obscure figure to the public, driven Senator Raymond Baldwin, of Connecticut, out of the Senate by a skillful disruption of the work of another subcommittee to which he did not belong—a subcommittee that was investigating the Malmédy war atrocities. Nearly all the triumphs that make him so formidable and so dread a figure in the Senate today date from a period in which he held no conspicuous office and was possessed only of what power he was able to generate on his own. He could subpoena no witnesses, deprive no brigadier generals of the right to counsel, release no closed-hearing testimony, send no disagreeable young men abroad to ride herd on American diplomats; he managed, nevertheless, to win a following that seemed to number in the millions, to become an issue in a presidential campaign, to determine the outcome of several campaigns for lesser offices, and to make his name an eponym for a doctrine known and discussed around the world. During the past fifteen months, McCarthy has neglected none of the opportunities for political mischief offered by his position as chairman of the Committee on Government Operations—and as self-appointed chairman of its Permanent Subcommittee on Investigations. But the melancholy feeling here is that it is idle to suppose that he would be seriously handicapped if subversion became the province of an impartial commission and he found himself stripped of his authority to conduct what he calls his investigation of Communism. In all probability, he would make fat political capital of the loss. It requires no great gift of prophecy to foretell the kind of language he would use before the first American Legion gathering he was asked to address following such an event.

In other words, if the prevailing view here is sound, the country has in McCarthy no ordinary demogogue but a political figure of the first rank, a man cast in a large, unique mold, quite possibly an authentic genius, and, at the very least, the most daring and original political innovator since Franklin D. Roosevelt. His following is large and fanatical; an awareness of its existence and a belief that it occupies a pivotal position in hundreds of American communities have led many public men to keep their opinions of him to themselves and to vote as he would have them vote. It may be that the lead given by the President, the one man in the country able to match his prestige against McCarthy with confidence as to the results, and the one man who can get the ear of the people any time he wishes, will encourage others to resistance. But the lead was pretty feeble, and it was a very long time coming. The expectation of most people here is that it will have to be beefed up and given time and again if it is to achieve the results the President evidently desires.

23   Unrestricted

Letter from Washington

March 6, 1954

On December 15 of last year, the White House, in a move welcomed on almost every hand, promulgated Executive Order 10501, a document intended to make government information easier to get at. The order abolished the "Restricted" category for papers in the possession of federal departments, thereby reducing from four to three the number of rubrics under which information could be classified and withheld from circulation. At the same time, it reduced from forty-five to seventeen the number of agencies authorized to use any of the remaining categories—they are, from least to most arcane, "Confidential," "Secret," and "Top Secret"—and placed the responsibility for ordering classification on the head men of the seventeen agencies still empowered to sequester. "This is one of the things the President feels most strongly about," a White House spokesman explained to a representative of the Washington *Daily News.* "He believes the taxpayer has a right to know all he can be told safely." The explanation itself had a ring of bureaucratic arrogance, but it was hoped that the new policy would, as the President so clearly hoped, liberate some information and relieve some of the congestion in government files.

No one has conducted a systematic inquiry on the workings of the new order, but, according to reports circulating here, its consequences appear to have been rather different from those that were intended. Most government security officers, when asked what has become of the information for which no category of classification exists, have said that they upgraded the "Restricted" documents to the category of "Confidential." In some other cases, they have stamped the legend "For Government Use Only" on documents formerly marked "Restricted," which means that they have simply replaced the forbidden word with its official definition. In no known case has a document unavailable to the public under the old rules become available under the new ones. To be sure, some have been declassified and not placed in any new categories, but according to a recent account in the Washington *Daily News,* the word "declassified" has taken on a new meaning. The *News* quoted a Navy Department directive as saying, "The declassification of information does not constitute authority for its public release." The text of this odd directive was obtained by the *News* from the trade journal *Aviation Week,* which, in turn, obtained it from a manufacturer of equipment for Navy airplanes. Both the magazine and the *News* pointed out that its publication was probably illegal, since the manufacturer received it in an envelope marked "Unclassified." According to the *News*, the effects of the declassification have been all but disastrous to some manufacturers. One Navy contractor was almost driven out of business in the aftermath of Executive Order 10501, because he was instructed to upgrade the security rating of all his products, including those that went to buyers other than the Navy. He suddenly found, the *News* reported, that "everything he had to sell was classified."

Executive Order 10501 has unclogged few files. Before it, information that was marked "Restricted" could be kept in desk drawers, closets, or just about anywhere else. Information marked "Confidential" had to be, and still must be, kept under lock and key in steel cabinets. So large is the amount of information that was supposed to be made available to a wider public but was actually made available to a narrower public that one firm has found it necessary to spend three hundred thousand dollars for new safes and cabinets and strongboxes to hold all the unclassified material in its possession.

24 Indo-China

Letter from Washington

April 8, 1954

Indo-China has become the most pressing of all problems here, exceeding in urgency even the question of what to do with our rapidly multiplying megatons. As the President pointed out in his clarifying remarks a few evenings ago, Malenkov and his colleagues appear to be human at least to the extent of not relishing the idea of being vaporized. In Washington—as in London, and perhaps even in Moscow—it is felt that a global anti-vaporization policy has to be worked out, but, rightly or wrongly, it is also felt here that time is not absolutely of the essence. Indeed, there is something to be said in favor of a leisurely, reflective approach to the thermonuclear problem. No one advocates such an approach to Indo-China. The bomb deepens the world's quandary but does not confront it with a steadily deepening crisis, as Indo-China does. There are varying estimates of how much time we can afford to spend in deciding what we are and are not prepared to do there, but agreement is general that by April 26, when the Geneva conference opens, Mr. Dulles must be armed not only with a policy but with a mandate.

No doubt exists as to what sort of mandate Mr. Dulles thinks he ought to be given. He plainly believes that we should not flinch at doing anything that is needed to prevent a Communist victory in the Associated States; if increased American support fails to better the French and Vietnamese position, or if it betters it but still does not overcome the French desire to withdraw, then we ought to commit our own forces to the conflict. He would favor doing this even if we have to do it alone—even, that is, if he fails, as he almost surely will, in his current effort to persuade European and Asiatic powers to join us in "united action." And although he has recently given the impression in his speeches, press conferences, and congressional testimony that American intervention, if it comes, will be a response to further Chinese intervention, it is patent that in his mind it is not the action or inaction of the Chinese Communists that really matters but the success of Communist armies of any national or ethnic composition. In making these public statements, he has been trying to restrain the Chinese from giving further aid to the rebel forces by causing them to associate his earlier words about "massive retaliation" with their policy in Indo-China. It all makes an interesting essay in diplomacy, and it may prove to be an instructive test of the theory that aggressive powers respect firmness. The statements, though, are to be read not as an expression of the true substance of American policy but as the expression of Mr. Dulles's hope that he can frighten the Peking government into abandoning its Vietminh allies, or at least giving them no more assistance than they are being given now. (It is said in the State Department that whatever hope Mr. Dulles has for the success of this attempt at intimidation rests largely upon a recent speech by Chen Yun, a Peking bureaucrat, who suggested that China's government might soon find itself faced with a choice between cutting off its aid to General Ho's armies and precipitating a bigger war, and that the first alternative might be more desirable than the second.) But Mr. Dulles's intense concern with Indo-China would not, it seems, be conspicuously lessened if Peking did heed his warnings and refrain from stepping up its aid to the Vietminh, for the French are manifestly unable—and now apparently unwilling, as well—to deal decisively with the strictly native Communist forces; it is not the threat of Chinese intervention that makes the French eager for an early settlement but their profound distaste for continuing a stalemated war in Oriental swamps and jungles. Regardless of where the opposing troops happen to hail from, the French would like to bring the whole disagreeable business to an end.

Mr. Dulles believes that no compromise settlement is even theoretically possible in Indo-China. The facts of geography and politics are all against it. The war has been a strategist's nightmare, in which each side surrounds the other and the battle lines are everywhere and nowhere; no hope exists for establishing even the most nebulous line of demarcation. This being so, a settlement that allowed the Communists anything would result, he feels sure, in their eventually getting everything, and this, in Mr. Dulles's opinion, would be a calamity of the very first order—a disaster greater than the Communist conquest of all Korea would have been. Therefore, the commitment of American ground forces and the sacrifice of American lives to prevent it would be fully justified. Realizing that public opinion has not up to now shared this view of the matter—in fact, the view seems to be of fairly recent origin in Mr. Dulles's own mind, and is certainly so in the mind of the President, who as late as February 10 told a news conference that he could scarcely imagine a tragedy greater than American intervention—the Secretary in the past couple of weeks has been conducting what must undoubtedly be one of the boldest campaigns of political suasion ever undertaken by an American statesman. Congressmen, political leaders of all shadings of opinion, newspapermen, and radio and television personalities have been rounded up in droves and escorted to lectures and briefings on what the State Department regards as the American stake in Indo-China. The somber word-portraits of the diplomats show Communist influence radiating in a semicircle from Indo-China to Burma, Malaya, and Thailand, and then across the South China Sea to the islands of Indonesia. They show Soviet Russia and Communist China economically and militarily strengthened by the strategic raw materials available to them in that region, and the United States and other anti-Communist powers correspondingly weakened by the loss of those materials. They show Nehru's India impressed more deeply than ever by Communist power and no longer offering any sort of resistance to Communist infiltration, and they concurrently show Pakistan, the Philippine Republic, South Korea, Formosa, and Japan disheartened and discouraged by an American failure to succor a threatened Asiatic people. Even Australia, Mr. Dulles's lieutenants argue, would find its security threatened by a Vietminh victory. Hearing this analysis, one gets the impression that they have grave doubts whether the United States could survive the establishment of Communist power in Indo-China.

How successful Mr. Dulles has been in conveying his own alarm to others here was made plain in the discussion of Indo-China on the floor of the Senate two days ago. Of the several men who spoke, only Senator Dirksen, of Illinois, took an unequivocal stand against American intervention. The majority leader, Senator Knowland, of California, supported Mr. Dulles but urged that we should employ our own troops in Indo-China only after we have received assurances from England and France that their troops will march with ours—rather an odd stand for Senator Knowland to be taking, since he formerly held, along with General MacArthur, that allies are more trouble than they're worth. Senator Kennedy, of Massachusetts, thought that the only way to win the war, even with American participation, would be by forcing the French to grant complete freedom and sovereignty to Laos, Cambodia, Vietnam. But no one who took the floor, except Senator Dirksen, disputed the Secretary of State's appraisals. The debate revealed that an extraordinary shift of opinion has occurred in the last few weeks; a month or so ago, no member of the Senate would have even entered into a discussion of Indo-China without asserting his unalterable opposition to direct American involvement. In spite of the trend in Mr. Dulles's favor, however, it is still anything but certain that he will get the clear mandate that he wants and will need if he is to persuade the French to reject any proposals for negotiation that may be made at Geneva. (It has yet to be established, of course, that the Chinese or Russians will bring any settlement plans to the conference. Past performance suggests that they may offer nothing except a demand for outright surrender or something tantamount to it. Still, the only safe assumption, the administration feels, is that they will be shrewd enough to advance some proposal that would not—in appearance, at least—entail a complete loss of face for the French.) For one thing, only a small minority of congressmen has thus far taken part in the discussion of American policy, and that minority, naturally, was heavily weighted by those who have the clearest sense of urgency. For another, there has been as yet no true sounding of the views of the public. It will take another week or ten days for the first waves of public reaction to break on Washington.

Unless some sharp change of feeling has taken place unnoticed in the country at large, the public reaction will be a long way from enthusiastic. The Korean war was the most unpopular war we have ever fought. Its purpose was understood by fewer people than that of any other war in our history, and not all those who understood approved of it. There was almost universal relief and thanksgiving when it ended, even though it ended short of what is normally accounted to be military victory. And despite the cogency of Mr. Dulles's pleadings for support, intervention in Indo-China would be harder to justify to the people as a whole than the intervention in Korea was. Korea was a republic—or at least a state that presumably had aspirations to become a republic—which the United States and the United Nations had helped to establish. It had been garrisoned with American troops, who clearly had a direct concern in its survival and independence. Its proximity to Japan gave a certain graphic plausibility to its importance in American strategy. None of this can be said about Indo-China. It is much farther than Korea from the American mainland and from all areas of American responsibility. The appeal of independence does not exist there, since Indo-China is not in fact independent; although its civil affairs were belatedly put into the hands of native retainers of the French, it remains to all intents and purposes a colony, and therefore a responsibility, of France, which appears determined to shed the responsibility but is nevertheless unwilling to free the colony. These and other objections are certain to be raised as the debate continues, and they will be echoed in Washington. No matter how astutely Mr. Dulles and his staff go about the job of seeking support for their view, they will find it difficult, and probably increasingly difficult, to win the kind of support they are going to need.

So far, to be sure, no one has challenged Mr. Dulles's appraisal of the consequences of a Vietminh victory in Southeast

Asia, and no one—even among those congressmen who will certainly resist our going to war there—has suggested that the situation is any less serious than he says it is. There are, however, a few people who believe that Mr. Dulles's remedy would not be quite as effective as he seems to think. They contend that although the Secretary is perfectly correct in saying that a Communist victory in the Associated States would enhance Communist prestige throughout Asia, he is mistaken in his belief that a defeat of the Vietminh at the hands of a coalition dominated by Western powers would greatly weaken Communism or reinforce anti-Communism. In most of Asia, they point out, the Vietminh already have public opinion (or at any rate the view of the tiny literate and articulate minority that passes for public opinion in that section of the world) and a good share of official opinion on their side. Sympathy for the rebels would only be increased and intensified if American troops took the field against them; indeed, this move might actually strengthen them militarily by causing some fence sitters in Indo-China itself to jump off the fence onto the Communist side. And even if we should achieve a decisive military defeat of the Vietminh—an achievement, incidentally, that may very well be outside our present powers—they would be honored for what most of their fellow-Asiatics would persist in regarding as a heroic struggle against colonialism. While American intervention would contribute nothing toward the destruction of Communist influence in Asia, these people feel, it would contribute handsomely toward the destruction of American influence in Asia, which is thought by many to be so low at present that at the next decline it will drop out of sight altogether.

Moreover, in this view of the problem, so different from Mr. Dulles's, the most compelling argument against intervention is its probable effect on our European strategy. Nothing we could do, it is held, would contribute more to the destruction of our plans and hopes for European unity than prodding the French into staying on in a hopeless cause. The reluctance of the French to bring the European Defense Community into being is a consequence of French weakness, and French weakness is a consequence of the war in Indo-China. Freed of the burdens of that war, France would also be freed of its besetting fear of German power, which would appear less menacing to a French Army that was no longer called upon to consign the cream of its officer corps to certain death in Indo-China. (In France itself there are some advocates of European unity who think the Communists will want to avoid negotiation at Geneva simply because they regard the war as an excellent device for stalling the European Defense Community. Jean-Jacques Servan-Schreiber, the highly respected French publicist, recently appealed to Americans, on Edward R. Murrow's television program, to promote E.D.C. by urging the Quai d'Orsay to speed its plans for withdrawal from Indo-China.) It is also held that peace in Indo-China would end the present paralysis in French political life by depriving both the Communists and the Gaullists of the issue they have had the most success in exploiting. As Pierre Mendes-France, the Radical Socialist deputy from the Eure, wrote the other day, "The continuation of the Indo-China war, with the human and material sacrifices it entails, does much less to bar the road to Communism in Asia than to open it in France." Those people here who think that M. Mendes-France is speaking what is essentially the truth point out that even if his view is wrong, it is so prevalent among the French that either he or someone who thinks as he does is likely to become premier at an early date, and then the war would be called off whether or not the United States was engaged in it; that is to say, we might find ourselves fighting in the defense of a French colony without even the French as allies.

Mr. Dulles, who is an experienced diplomat and is served by an able staff of advisers, has unquestionably considered the case against intervention and found it less impressive than the case in its favor. He has not made any detailed public refutation of the arguments advanced by those who oppose intervention on other than purely isolationist grounds, but he must surely have refuted them to his private satisfaction. In the last week or so, it has frequently been remarked here that Mr. Dulles's and the President's conviction of the need for action must be even deeper than their public statements would indicate, for in risking American involvement in another, Asiatic war they may be depriving the administration they head of its greatest single political asset—the fact that under its leadership an armistice was negotiated in Korea. In every congressional district in the country, Republican aspirants have been looking forward to the opportunity of taunting their Democratic opponents with the accusation that a Democratic administration led us into war in Asia and with the boast that a Republican administration led us out. With the Eighty-third Congress drawing to an undistinguished close, there are not many other boasts a candidate can make. But if November finds American troops engaged in combat in such places as Caobang, Fansipan, and Baolac, the political going will not be any too easy for Republicans. Beyond that, another war would end whatever frail hopes remain of keeping expeditures below the level set up by the Truman administration, of balancing the federal budget, and of reducing the national debt. Consequently, it is felt here that whether or not the course Mr. Dulles is advocating, with full support from the President, is the course of the highest wisdom, it is one that reveals disinterestedness, a high sense of responsibility, and a good measure of political courage.

One clear accomplishment of the debates on Indo-China and the hydrogen bomb has been to put an end to the debate on the so-called "new look" in military strategy. As one elucidation of policy has followed another since Secretary Dulles sprang the phrase "massive retaliation" on January 12, it has become increasingly evident that what we have is merely a new verbal packaging of the strategy we have followed over the last seven or eight years. The Eisenhower administration may not find it possible to save the situation in Indo-China, but its reaction to that situation is very much of a piece with the Truman administration's reaction to Korea. Yesterday, in a speech before a Republican women's gathering here, Secretary Dulles explained that all he had meant by "massive retaliation" was "retaliation in kind." He also said we would never use thermonuclear weapons until they had been used against us. He did not explain why, if the policy is to be tit for tat, it was necessary to suggest that it would invariably be "massive," a term that the world took to mean atomic. The answer seems to be that it was not necessary at all but that the psychological-warfare commanders thought it was a pretty good idea. In any case, if we are merely to retaliate in kind, then we are merely following precedents established long before the Truman administration.

And, as Dean Acheson pointed out in a magazine article a while back, if "retaliation"—massive or feeble or simply in kind —is our policy, then it is a contradition in terms to say that our policy gives us the "initiative"; retaliation is not initiative but a response to someone else's initiative. About all that seems to be left of the "new look" now is a budget that strengthens the Air Force at the expense of the ground forces. But if the worst happens in Indo-China, where atomic bombs would be as useless as crossbows, the ground forces will have to be restored to their former strength—and then some.

25   I've Got a Paper Here

April 10, 1954

(*Note: I did not report the Army-McCarthy hearings. Thanks to television, everyone in the United States was his own correspondent at that Senate investigation, and there seemed little point in writing about it. The event, however, moved me to a reminiscence.*)

I never see a picture of McCarthy flourishing a document without thinking of a meeting I had with him in May, 1949, about a year before he went to Wheeling, West Virginia, and held aloft the piece of paper that made him famous. (He said it was a list of Communists in the State Department. It turned out to be a letter from James F. Byrnes to Adolph Sabath, and had no list of Communists or of anything else in it.) I was in Washington, and I dropped in at a Senate hearing at which testimony was being taken on the alleged mistreatment by Americans of some German S.S. men, members of an outfit called the Blowtorch Battalion, who had been accused of massacring a hundred and fifty United States troops and a hundred Belgian civilians at a crossroads named Malmédy, in December, 1944. I had been in the hearing room only a few minutes when McCarthy became involved in an altercation with Senator Raymond E. Baldwin, of Connecticut, a fellow-Republican who has since become a judge of the Supreme Court of Errors, in Hartford.

It was an angry exchange. McCarthy took the view that the Americans had in fact been guilty of brutal conduct. In this first brush with the Army, he claimed that it was coddling not Communists but sadists and crooked lawyers. He said that he had documentary proof of this but that Baldwin, intent for some unexplained reason on protecting the accused men, wouldn't pay any attention to it. Baldwin insisted he wasn't trying to protect anyone. After a while, McCarthy rose from his seat, stuffed a lot of papers into his briefcase, and left the room, saying he would no longer be a party to a shameful farce, a "deliberate and clever attempt to whitewash the American military."

Curious about the dispute and at that time ignorant of its background, I followed McCarthy into the corridor and asked him if he would be kind enough to tell me what he was in such a stew about. He said he would be glad to, and suggested that I go with him to his office. "It's time the American people knew about this," he said. "These documents will speak for themselves." He hefted up the bulging briefcase to give me some idea of the sheer bulk of them. "When you've looked at a few of my documents, you'll agree with me that this is one of the most outrageous things the country has ever known." I said that if this was the case, I'd certainly feel privileged to be allowed to inspect them. "You'll see them, all right," he said. "I'm not holding anything back. I'm through with this investigation, and I'm taking my case to the public."

He struck me as being a bit overwrought, but on the whole he seemed an earnest and plausible young senator. Though he used extravagant language, his tone was restrained, his manner almost gentle. As we walked along through the wide, echoing corridors of the Senate Office Building, he kept talking of the magnitude of his revelations, and although I had wanted—for a starter, at least—just a brief résumé of his side of the story, he succeeded in whetting my appetite for the contents of the briefcase.

We reached his office at last and sat down at his desk. He emptied the briefcase and piled the papers up in front of him. "Let's see, now," he said as he thumbed his way down toward the middle of the pile. "I know just the thing I want you to see first. I've got one thing here that's a real eye-opener. Oh, yes, here we are now." He pulled out several pages of photostat paper and handed them to me. "I think the facts will mean more to you than anything I could say. Once you've looked this over, you'll see that Baldwin has been playing a pretty sinister role in trying to whitewash the administration."

I read rapidly through what he gave me. Then I read it a second time, more carefully. When I'd finished the second reading, I was certain that the Senator had selected the wrong document. I no longer recall just what was in it, but it was a letter from one Army officer or government official to another, and although it had, as I recall, some bearing on the Malmédy affair, it didn't seem to me to prove anything about anything. I told McCarthy that as far as I could see, it was a pretty routine piece of correspondence.

"You're certainly right about that," he said. "Don't get me wrong, now. I didn't mean you'd find the *whole* story there. Standing alone, it doesn't mean much—I know that just as well as you do. But it's a link in a chain. It's one piece in a jigsaw puzzle. When you've seen some of the other documents, you'll know what I mean."

This was reassuring. In fact, I felt a bit ashamed of myself for expecting to master a complex situation in a few minutes. I began to read the next document McCarthy handed me. "Now, when you put these two together," he said, "you get a picture." The second document was mainly a listing of names. None of them meant anything to me. I tried to think what connection they might have with the letter I'd just read or with Senator Baldwin. I tried to "put them together," as McCarthy had advised, and "get a picture." No picture came. I confessed this to the Senator.

"Exactly," he said. "That's exactly my point. Those names mean nothing to you. They didn't mean anything to me, either, when I began to look into this conspiracy. But they're going to mean something to you before long, I can guarantee you that. I wanted you to have a look at them, because when you've seen some of the other things I've got here, you'll see how this jigsaw puzzle fits together. Now just bear those names in mind."

I tried to bear the names in mind and found it was impossible. Nothing unsticks faster than names you can't associate with real people. But although it was, I thought, curious that the Senator hadn't shown me the documents explaining the significance of the names before showing me the names themselves, I continued to be impressed by his manner. And the papers themselves were impressive—not by virtue of their contents but by virtue of their existence. Photostats and carbon copies and well-kept newspaper clippings have, I think, an authority of their own for most people; we assume that no one would go to the bother of assembling them if they didn't prove something.

As McCarthy sat at his desk sorting out the papers, putting some in a stack to his right and some in a stack to his left and consigning others to a filing cabinet behind him, he seemed knowledgeable and efficient. "I'm just trying to put this picture together for you," he kept saying. Two or three times in the course of our interview, which must have lasted about an hour and a half, he called in a secretary and asked her to fetch him some document that wasn't among those he had taken to the hearing. I wondered as I watched him what had become of the promise to provide a blinding illumination with a single document, but for quite a while I assumed it was my fault, not his, that I wasn't grasping the details very well.

McCarthy kept handing papers across the desk to me. "Here are a few more links in the chain," he would say as he handed me more correspondence, more lists, and a good many pictures of the Germans who had accused the American of brutality, of the accused Americans, of Malmédy farmhouses, and of Army barracks in Occupied Germany. None of them seemed to advance his argument by very much—by anything at all, in fact— but then he was no longer claiming very much for them.

"You don't get to the bottom of these things in a few minutes," he said. "Especially when so many powerful people are trying to hide the truth. Believe me, it wasn't easy for me to put this story together."

At one point he handed me a rather thick document. "I don't want you to leave without seeing this," he said. "Here we have the facts in the Army's own records. This is a transcript of the first hearing on this affair. This is what Baldwin and the administration are trying to cover up. Remember, now, this is from the records the Army itself kept."

I read here and there in the record the Army itself kept, and told McCarthy that, perhaps because of my ignorance, I was unable to see any holes in the Army's case.

"Of course you don't," he said. "Naturally, they're going to make out the best case they can for themselves. You wouldn't expect them to spill the beans in their own records, would you? The whole thing is a pack of lies."

I was beginning to get a bit impatient, though I tried not to show it. I said that as I understood the situation, he, McCarthy, was persuaded that the Malmédy massacre was a fiction of our own military authorities, that Germans had been tortured into confessing acts that had never been committed, and that a Republican senator, a man with a considerable reputation for probity, was trying to protect the torturers. I was about to go on to say that thus far nothing he had shown me established the truth of all this. But McCarthy interrupted me.

"That's right," he said, in a manner that suggested appreciation of my insight and my gift of summation. "You're beginning to get the picture now. I think the next thing I'll do is show you some of the affidavits we've gathered on this case."

He handed over a stack of affidavits. They were the sworn statements of the S.S. men held as war criminals, and they alleged the most hideous mistreatment by the Americans. It was because these statements were being published in newspapers throughout Germany and, the government had been advised, were being believed by large numbers of Germans that the Senate Armed Services Committee had decided to conduct its own hearings, assigning the job to a subcommittee led by Senator Baldwin and including, besides Baldwin, Senator Kefauver, of Tennessee, and Senator Lester Hunt, of Wyoming. Although McCarthy had given the impression of resigning from this group, the fact, as I later learned, was that he couldn't resign, because he hadn't been a member to begin with. He had merely exercised the senatorial privilege of sitting with the committee during the hearings, at which, from most newspaper accounts, he had done most of the talking. He was able to do this, incidentally, only after he had won a long fight to get from Senator Baldwin the right, which isn't normally regarded as part of the privilege, to cross-examine all the witnesses. Senator Baldwin later said it was McCarthy's bullyragging of him in the Malmédy affair that finally led him to give up politics.

After scanning some of the affidavits, I said that while it was entirely conceivable that a Nazi under sentence of death or imprisonment could be telling the truth about his own past behavior, it was at least equally conceivable that he would falsify. I wondered, I said, what McCarthy had in the way of evidence that it was not the convicted Nazis but the Americans who were lying.

"You've put your finger on it," he said. "Those are precisely the facts that Baldwin and the administration don't want me to bring out. That's why I walked out of that hearing. They're concealing all the evidence. I've shown you some of the pieces in this jigsaw puzzle, and believe me, when I take this story before the American people, the truth will be forced to come out."

I asked McCarthy if he had anything else he wanted to show me. "Well, I've got the affidavits of the Army people here," he said. "But I guess you can imagine what's in them. Lies from start to finish. Naturally, they're trying to protect themselves. I've got them here if you want to see what's in them."

I said I thought I'd skip them. I thanked the Senator for his courtesy and left.

26 The Amendment Fever

Letter from Washington

June 10, 1954

Herbert Block, the *Post & Times-Herald* * cartoonist, recently published a sketch of two statesmen, presumably senators, seated dejectedly before an untidy heap of papers representing that part of the administration's legislative program which isn't getting legislated; the pair would have looked the very soul of ennui even if Mr. Block had not caused one of them to be flying a paper airplane presumably made from a doomed bill and the other to be saying, "This bores me, Let's amend the Constitution today." As usual, Mr. Block, whose name graces the latest list of Pulitzer Prize winners, has spotted a trend. Indeed, on this occasion he has spotted a brace of trends—one toward bored statesmen, the other toward Constitution-amending as a diversion, like Scrabble. The present session, which has dragged its feet on most administration bills and has shown a notable lack of interest in getting on with such essential public business as authorization and appropriation, has displayed an enormous zest for framing, debating, and recommending alterations in the basic charter of the Republic. Since the opening of this Congress, there have been brought to the floor of the Senate, which seems to be the kicking-off place for constitutional amendments nowadays, no fewer than six proposed amendments, all of which have been supported by simple majorities and four of which have been supported by the two-

* On March 17, the Washington *Post* acquired the Washingon *Times-Herald* and two papers of very different tendencies were consolidated.

thirds majority that is necessary to refer the proposals to the House of Representatives and, after that, to the state legislatures. The debate on one of these—the Bricker amendment, which evolved gradually and against the will of its author into the George amendment—compared favorably in length and wordage, if not in eloquence, with the original debate, at the State House in Philadelphia in 1787, on the document it would very likely have modified if it had not fallen one vote short of the majority needed. The other amendment that was brought to the floor and rejected was one to have the federal government extend the franchise to citizens between the ages of eighteen and twenty-one. Introduced by Senator Langer, of North Dakota, and endorsed by the President, it failed of passage by five votes. Of the four amendments that have cleared the Senate, one would fix the number of Supreme Court justices at nine and make retirement at seventy-five compulsory for all federal judges except those appointed for a stipulated number of years; one would prevent presidential seizure of property except on congressional authorization; another, the so-called Equal Rights amendment, is intended to end discrimination based on sex; and the fourth, introduced by Senator Knowland, would provide a means whereby the state governors might fill "vacancies" in the House of Representatives in the event that this city was made the target of an atomic or hydrogen bomb. Senator Knowland's amendment won approval less than a week ago, by a vote of seventy to one. The solitary naysayer was Senator Stennis, of Mississippi; he is of the opinion that there is altogether too much amending going on here, and he opposed this amendment not so much to express dissatisfaction with its provisions as to register his disapproval of what he regards as a frivolous approach to the Constitution of the United States.

The amendments the Senate has thus far discussed are a selection from one hundred and seven that have been introduced in this Congress and referred to committee. Some, like the one that passed last week, are merely procedural in nature; some are quaint; some are bizarre; and some are almost revolutionary. There are several proposals for outright repeal of the income tax; several that embody formulas for limiting non-military expenditures to a fixed percentage of the national income (five, ten, fourteen, and twenty being among the percentages suggested); one to forbid the expenditure of a single dollar of federal funds for any purpose covered by the term "general welfare"; one prohibiting conscripts from serving in any foreign country except in time of war; one prohibiting any American troops from serving in any foreign country except on the soil of the country we are fighting against; one to deprive new states of representation in the Senate or to limit the representation to one senator (this being proposed despite the fact that the Constitution stipulates that, as the single respect in which it is never to be amended, no state "without its consent, shall be deprived of its equal suffrage in the Senate"); one to prevent "interference with or limitation upon the power of any state to regulate health, morals, education, marriage, and good order in the state"; one to redefine treason to include the activities not only of persons working for the overthrow of the government but of those working for the "weakening" of it, "whether or not by force or violence"; one to give Congress control over trademarks; one to provide for the holding in perpetuity of patents and copyrights; and one to add to the Constitution the assertion that "this nation devoutly recognizes the authority and law of Jesus Christ, Saviour and Ruler of Nations through whom are bestowed the blessings of Almighty God" and at the same time to provide a new oath or affirmation for "citizens whose religious scruples prevent them from giving unqualified allegiance to the Constitution as herein amended."

There is nothing out of the ordinary in either the number or the character of the proposed amendments now in committee; there have been times in the past when the House and Senate Committees on the Judiciary, which get all the resolutions for constitutional changes, have had many more than a hundred amendments on their calendars, a good proportion of them at least as curious as some of those now pending. Over the years, it has become customary for congressmen to cast the drollest and most dubious schemes submitted to them by friends and supporters in the form of constitutional amendments; they have done this secure in the knowledge that the proposals would be allowed to gather dust until the sitting Congress was succeeded by another. What is decidedly new about the present situation is that as many as six amendments have been reported out of committee and that as many as four have carried in one house of Congress. Since 1879, when the first ten amendments were ratified *en bloc*, only fifteen have passed both houses of Congress. Of these, fifteen, twelve were ratified in the state legislatures. If the Eighteenth and Twentieth Amendments—prohibition and repeal of prohibition—are excluded from consideration, on the ground that they cancel one another out and leave the basic law unamended, the Constitution has been altered on an average of once in sixteen and a half years. And the Congress has recommended amendment only once in fifteen years.

A number of observers see behind the current speedup what they regard as a significant change in the attitude of many Senators toward their responsibilities. The traditional view of Senate responsibility is the one expressed by George Washington, who, when asked by Jefferson why he favored having a Senate, countered by asking of Jefferson why he poured some of his coffee into a saucer. When Jefferson replied that he wanted his coffee cooler, Washington said, "Even so. We pour legislation into the senatorial saucer to cool it." In what appears to be the new and spreading view here, it is the Senate's job to give the most important kind of legislation no chance at all to cool but to pass it, piping hot, directly to the states. (Oddly, the amendment fever has not taken hold in the House, which is generally thought to be the less responsible of the two chambers. There are seventy-five amendments on the calendar of the House Judiciary Committee, but not one has been reported on the floor, and no hearings have been scheduled for any of the sixteen on subcommittee dockets.)

This view was given vivid and forceful expression in the course of the recent discussion over Senate Joint Resolution 53 —the amendment extending suffrage to eighteen-year-olds. Senators Dirksen and Knowland, two of the most influential leaders of the Eighty-third Congress, argued that it is less the duty of the Senate to pass upon the wisdom of a proposal for constitutional change than to give the forty-eight legislatures and, through them, the people of the states an opportunity to express themselves in regard to it. Senator Dirksen freely conceded that there were two possible views on the amendment—for and against—and that he had not decided which view he would choose for himself. He felt, however, that there was no need to tax his mind and conscience with the arguments, since it would be up to the legislatures to make the final determination and since a beneficial discussion would be bound to ensue.

> I want the country to think about it [Senator Dirksen said]. The best way to have the country think about it is to pass this proposal, send it to the House, send it to the state legislatures, and let the people of the country discuss it. . . . It will be a moot question [unless] the Congress takes action and exercises its prerogative under the Constitution of the United States by saying to the States of the Union, "It is your baby now. Call in the people and hear from them, and then determine what, in your judgment, should be done."

He indicated that, for his part, he would be able to view the outcome with benign detachment "If the legislatures say 'No,' that will be all right with the junior Senator from Illinois; if they say 'Yes,' it will also be all right with me."

The majority leader, Senator Knowland, took substantially the same mellow, tolerant view. Although the amendment would obviously have diminished the authority of the states, since under the Constitution the states determine the qualifications of voters and under this plan they would be forced to accept a uniform standard with respect to age, Senator Knowland defended it not on its particular merits but, rather, as a device for according the states a rare chance to settle a broad and fundamental question of policy. He felt that, quite apart from whether or not it would be a good thing to allow eighteen-year-olds to vote, passage of the resolution would have "great value," because it would give "the people of the United States . . . an opportunity to express themselves on this very basic issue." Senator Hennings several times asked Senator Knowland to examine the implications of this position. "Is the Senate," he inquired, "to be merely a conduit, so to speak, or a channel through which various attempts to amend the Constitution of the United States are to be funneled so that they may be submitted to the states?" The majority leader made no direct reply to this question, but he asked some of his own that revealed a good deal about his point of view. "What in the world," he said, "are those who are opposing the amendment afraid of in submitting the matter to the forty-eight states of the union? Why not let the states express themselves? I am willing to rely on the judgment of the states."

The present attitude in the Senate suggests that the views expressed by Senators Dirksen and Knowland are shared by a formidable number of their colleagues. The Senate was well attended when they spoke, but objection was made to the doctrine they set forth only by a handful of states' rights Southerners, and by Senator John Kennedy, of Massachusetts, who said that "reluctance to amend the Constitution is one of our most valuable safeguards and bulwarks of stability." There are more than a score of senators, preponderantly from the administration party but numbering among them perhaps a half-dozen members of the opposition, who have supported every one of the amendments thus far brought to the floor, and many of them have signified support for several of the proposed amendments still in committee. If a group this size persists in the belief that the role of Congress should be essentially a permissive one, it would seem to follow that our political institutions are in for quite a round of overhauling. For it is well known that there is less independence of judgment and a lower resistance to mobocracy in the state legislatures than in the Congress, and especially in the Senate. If any proposal that flatters a minority without offending a majority or has the surface aspect of exalting the flag, the home, the church, or strict economy leaves Washington with the blessing of the Senate and the House, it is sure to have clear sailing in most of the provincial assemblies. Had the Bricker amendment passed both houses, either in its original form or in the form of Senator George's substitute, no amount of pleading by the President and the Secretary of State would have prevented it from becoming the Twenty-third Amendment before the end of this year. If the national legislature, which determines the expenditures that are to be met with the revenue from federal income taxes, were to leave the question of repealing the Sixteenth Amendment up to the state legislatures, there could scarcely be any doubt of the outcome. Nor could there be much doubt, in the present atmosphere in this country, of what would happen if the Congress recommended that the states cooperate in broadening the definition of treason just a little, or in establishing a ceiling for federal expenditures, or in praising Christianity; the state legislatures would collaborate eagerly, for their members would immediately sense the dangers of taking a position that exposed them to charges of coddling traitors, of favoring reckless and unlimited spending, or of being hostile to religion.

It is ironic that most of the recent attempts to alter the Constitution by means of amendment have been made by conservative leaders—men like Senators Knowland and Dirksen, who have so often detected conspiracies on the part of others to flout, subvert, or evade the principles laid down in 1787. Nothing could be more out of keeping with the language and the spirit of the Constitution than Senator Dirksen's it's-your-baby-now doctrine. Article V, which describes the amendment procedure, provides that an amendment may originate in the Congress "whenever two-thirds of both houses shall deem it necessary." (Article V also provides an alternate means for amendment— a convention to be called by Congress upon a request from two-thirds of the states. No such request has ever been made, and those who admire the Constitution pretty much as it stands have uttered fervent prayers that no such request ever will be made. Conventions have a way of gathering a momentum of their own. The convention of 1787 was called to amend the Articles of Confederation, and ended by throwing out the articles entirely and starting from scratch. It has always been feared that this is what would happen in the event of another convention, and that the laws of chance would run heavily against our getting a new constitution as good as the old.) The requirement that a sense of necessity, or urgency, exist—as it clearly did not in the minds of Senators Dirksen and Knowland when they urged the passage of Senate Joint Resolution 53—has frequently been cited in judicial decisions and opinions. In a celebrated test of the Eighteenth Amendment, the question was raised as to whether those in Congress who voted for national prohibition were earnestly convinced that there was a need for it, and the Supreme Court held that the mere passage of the enabling resolution "sufficiently shows that the proposal was deemed necessary by all who voted for it. An express declaration that they regarded it as necessary is not essential." As far as anyone here knows, there has never been a time in the past when congressmen supported alterations in the Constitution with lighthearted assertions of indifference to the proposal itself and confidence in its value as a conversation piece.

As Senator Kennedy observed, this represents a profound change of temper in the Congress. But it has been pointed out here that the Dirksen-Knowland doctrine is only one aspect of what appears to be a rapidly developing impatience and dissatisfaction not only with the Constitution as a written document but with the institutions that have either grown out of it or grown up alongside it. The plain fact of the matter is that a great many more Americans than even Senator McCarthy would proscribe have somewhere along the line lost their faith in what the sloganeers call the American Way, or Our Form of Government. In such a forum as the Army-McCarthy hearings, for example, the introduction of so basic a constitutional concept as checks and balances or separation of powers produces either exasperation or boredom. The feeling seems to be that if there is something in the Constitution that requires the President of the United States to protect the confidence of his advisers, then whatever it is ought to be changed, provided it cannot simply be overlooked. There is an evident feeling on the part of many that if there is some law or custom that makes it improper for Senator McCarthy to be in possession of a document prepared for executive use, then the law or custom ought to be swept aside; clearly, the prevailing sentiment seems to be that it is more important for McCarthy to be in on the doings of the executive branch than for the nation to preserve some archaic notion about the rights and privileges of one branch of government vis-a-vis another. Senator Mundt has announced that he is working up a law to take care of that annoying situation. Similarly, the Fifth Amendment, which was regarded for over a century and a half as a guarantee of justice equivalent in importance to the right of habeas corpus, has fallen into terrible disrepute; its misuse by Communists has led to a spate of proposals for circumventing it and to some demands for outright repeal of it. No one speaks up in its defense or points out that it was always intended that it should be misused by some people. Many other first principles are being strenuously challenged. In the past few weeks, a movement to combine a declaration of religiosity with the pledge of allegiance to the flag has made great headway; if this would not in itself destroy secularism and the separation of church and state, the proposal to amend the Constitution by making Christianity the official state religion would greatly fur-

ther the job. The Senate sponsor of this last amendment, which
has been introduced in identical form in the House, is Senator
Flanders, of Vermont, a man whose colleagues regard him as
a rugged constitutionalist. Civilian control of the military is also
looked upon with suspicion. When President Truman relieved
General Douglas MacArthur in 1951, his contention was that he
was acting in accordance with the role prescribed for him by
the Constitution and with the elementary doctrine that a President proposes and a general disposes, whether he likes it or not.
While it was conceded that this was the custom, it was widely
agreed that it was a most undesirable one and ought to be
abolished.

The signs of impatience, of discontent and irritation, multiply
on every hand. Sooner or later, such dissatisfaction expresses
itself in changes in the structure of law and government. If the
Dirksen doctrine prevails, the changes may be numerous and far-
reaching.

27 Some Fun

Letter from Washington

August 19, 1954

For sheer chaos, irony, and grim comedy, nothing in recent years has matched the situation that has developed here
over the outlawing of the Communist Party. It is not yet known
whether the President will sign, veto, or pocket-veto the bill that
has passed the Senate 79–0 and the House 265–2. As he remarked, a couple of days ago, he couldn't say what he was going
to do about the bill because he didn't know what was in it. In
this respect, he was like everyone else, including the authors,

whoever they were. It is being said that the bill was "written on the floor," which in a manner of speaking was true, since it wasn't the work of any committee. Actually, it wasn't "written" at all but was improvised, like a kindergarten play, and it is only now, when everything that was said is in print in the *Congressional Record*, that it is possible for anybody to know what it contains. It contains something less than at first it did (no longer, for example, making Communist membership in and of itself felonious, a provision that would have wrecked the McCarran Internal Security Act, a companion measure, since it would have made the act of registration a piece of self-incriminating testimony and therefore avoidable under the Fifth Amendment) but it is nevertheless a stew of all the anti-Communist measures ever suggested over the past twenty-five or thirty years. It probably violates the Constitution at a half-dozen points, and, as the Department of Justice has pointed out, it appears to nullify, even as it apes, many of the internal-security laws already on the books.

If the President signs it, or if a presidential veto is overridden, it will be law that came into being by almost unanimous consent when in point of fact there was no one at all who really wanted it. The President didn't want it. The Republicans in Congress were committed to handling the problem in a different way. So far as is known, Senator McCarthy wasn't for it. Senator Pat McCarran was not enthusiastic. J. Edgar Hoover and the Federal Bureau of Investigation thought it ill-advised. The Attorney General, though he likes to put Communists in jail, was appalled. It came up because a handful of Democrats—men who strike the loftiest moral attitudes—led by Senator Hubert Humphrey, a pharmacist with preaching blood in his veins and a fatal weakness for all the pieties of contemporary liberalism, thought it would be at once an excellent joke and a political master-stroke to put the Republicans in the position of publicly opposing a measure that would appear to the unenlightened to strike a powerful blow at Communism. The Republicans, as might easily have been predicted in any August preceding an election November, weren't in a joking mood and weren't ready to be put. They not only accepted the Democratic proposals but started stuffing in ideas of their own. There was a country-auction atmosphere about the whole business. All participants were sure that somewhere there was someone who would get them off the hook. But now, unless the President wants to be the sucker, there is no one who will break up what today's Washington *Post & Times-Herald* describes as "this emotional and political stampede." The President probably won't play sucker, and Senator McCarthy is said to be laughing his head off.

28 The Board of Governors

Letter from Washington

September 10, 1954

Whenever Senator Arthur V. Watkins, the Mormon elder from Orem, Utah, who is presiding over the current investigation of Senator McCarthy, announces that he is speaking in the name of the select committee of which he is chairman, his dry, sharp voice makes the most of the dry, sharp word "select." The point is not lost on his colleagues, on Senator McCarthy, or on anyone else regularly in attendance in Room 318 of the Senate Office Building, the marble-paneled, chandeliered caucus room that was earlier the scene of another inquiry into McCarthy's affairs, and that, earlier still, was also the scene of many of the actions for which McCarthy is now being called to account. This particular adjective, it turns out, has not been debased in Congress as it has been in the world of merchandising. "Select" eggs are just plain eggs, but a "select" committee of the Senate consists of good eggs, deliberately chosen for the purpose at hand —or *ad hoc,* as committee buffs put it. This makes for a difference in outlook. A senator has only to be alive in order to find himself on one of the standing committees; he rises to a position of influence by the mere act of survival. If it falls to his lot to perform some distasteful duty, such as sitting in judgment on Senator McCarthy, he can attribute his misfortune to the workings of a cruel, undiscriminating fate, and thereby justify himself in following the line of least resistance. The members of the Watkins committee may regard themselves as unlucky and ill-used—not that there is any present evidence that they do— but they cannot ascribe their predicament to the blindness of fate. They were chosen, culled, winnowed, tapped, and selected by officers of the Senate—the Vice-President and the majority and minority leaders—presumably on the ground that they were, as individuals, well qualified for the job. When sitting, they are expected to represent not the people of their state or the policies of their party, or even the national interest, but a force that to many senators has greater luster and majesty than any of these— the United States Senate itself.

All this is clear enough now, after more than a week of hearings, in which McCarthy has twice been gaveled into silence, once over a point that he described as "the most unheard-of thing I ever heard of," and in which Walter Winchell has been treated as a mortal being and the immortality of J. Edgar Hoover has not once been mentioned. It was not clear beforehand, for it has been a long time since a select committee had performed anything but ceremonial duties, such as attending funerals and glad-handing itinerant kings. Besides, recent events had led many people to doubt whether there were any senators left who truly venerated the Senate. Nobody doubts it any longer. Symbolically, the Watkins committee does not seat Republicans to the right of the chairman and Democrats to the left but mingles the parties on both sides of the table. "By way of comment," Senator Watkins said in his opening statement, "let me say that the inquiry we are engaged in is of a special character that differentiates it from the usual legislative inquiry. It involves the internal affairs of the Senate itself in the exercise of a high constitutional function." The select commitee's job is not to determine whether McCarthy is a good man or a bad one, a dedicated man or a faker, honest or crooked, useful or useless. Its job is simply to report to the parent body its findings with respect to Senate Resolution 301:

> "*Resolved,* that the conduct of the Senator from Wisconsin, Mr. McCarthy, is unbecoming a Member of the United States Senate, is contrary to senatorial traditions, and tends to bring the Senate into disrepute."

To a member of a select committee that is genuinely select, it is far more serious, it would appear, for a man to be accused of contravening senatorial tradition than it is for him to be accused of lying, demagogy, or even blackmailing the United States Army. It is, indeed, so grave a matter that steps must be taken to maintain the purity of the very air in which evidence is being given and received. "In general," Senator Watkins announced at the outset, "the committee wishes it understood that the regulations adopted are for the purpose of insuring a judicial hearing and a judicial atmosphere, as befits the importance of the issues raised. For that reason, and in accordance with the order the committee believes to be the sentiment of the Senate, all activities which are not permitted in the Senate itself will not be permitted in this hearing." This was Senator Watkins' way of saying that while it may be all right to foul the atmosphere of regular committees—those, for instance, considering the defense of this republic, its relations with other sovereign powers, and the future of its economy—with the sooty gases given off by cigarettes, cigars, and pipes, the rule of a committee weighing alleged affronts to the dignity of the Senate should be NO SMOKING.

By the close of the first session, it could be seen that McCarthy was up against something very formidable and totally unlike anything he had ever known in all his wide experience with Senate committees. "It could not be more different if a spectacle once staged by Cecil B. DeMille had been transferred to the drafty reaches of a town hall," Mary McGrory, a correspondent for the Washington *Star*, observed in a report that contrasted these hearings with those held under the chairmanship of Senator Mundt. This was written after Senator Watkins' gavel had come smashing down "with the force of a headman's axe," as the *Star* put it. Two hours earlier, when the committee members first seated themselves at the unsegregated table, observers were about evenly divided between those who were certain that a man as pale and seemingly frail as Senator Watkins would be bound to give way to the bull-throated McCarthy sooner or later and those who thought that the hearings would, for a change, be decorous throughout but would be a whitewash nevertheless. Both groups began revising their views within ten or fifteen minutes. Upon finishing his opening statement, Senator Watkins announced that the committee would "permit" Senator McCarthy to read into the record some remarks in his own defense. It was made unmistakably plain, however, that this was altogether an act of charity—a concession to McCarthy, not an acknowledgment of any "rights" of his. Senator Watkins said that he and his colleagues had looked over what McCarthy intended to read and had found it for the most part "not material and relevant to the issues in this hearing." No precedent was being established by the introduction of this material, he said.

Here, right at the beginning, was a case of *lese-majesté* that would certainly have shocked Stuart Symington, and perhaps Joseph Welch also. For what the chairman was describing as immaterial and irrelevant, and even, in a later comment, "incompetent," was nothing less than an assertion of the view that "this country and its institutions [are] in imminent peril of destruction by international Communism." Beyond that, it was an apologia in which McCarthy made his first known attempt at greatness of spirit, a characteristic of which is moderateness of expression:

"This is a serious matter to me and I think to the country. It weighs heavily on me, and I would like my feelings known, in broad outline at least. . . . I was late, Mr. Chairman—we all were late, although I daresay some of us were earlier than others. . . . I have carried on my part in the fight as best I know how. . . . It has been said that I am the cause of disunity in the country and in my party. There is disunity, and perhaps my activities have been part of the cause. . . . But now it is urged that I be censured. I would be untruthful if I agreed that my accusers were not affected by ulterior political consideration."

This noble-Roman rhetoric, said to be the work of L. Brent Bozell, a young Yale man of flagrant gentility who once wrote that "McCarthyism . . . is a movement around which men of good will and stern morality can close ranks" and who is now one of McCarthy's lawyers, was clearly an effort to place McCarthy in the company of Socrates, Bruno, Saint Ignatius of Antioch, and others who have been mocked and persecuted for their devotion to truth as illuminated by conscience, and it was as successful as it could possibly be in the circumstances. The Watkins committee, though, showed a limited appreciation of martyrdom. It listened courteously but with no discernible manifestation of sympathy as McCarthy struggled with the alien tempo and the sometimes startling vocabulary of his unfamiliar script. Once he read "spacious" for "specious," paused, aware that something was wrong, shrugged an authentic McCarthy shrug, and went on gamely. The instant he had finished, Senator Watkins, who could have said something complimentary about this brave try at eloquence, made a crisp announcement: "Now we proceed to a consideration of the matters which the committee deemed of first importance in connection with these hearings."

The committee proceeded. The man appointed to spread the first of several wet blankets was E. Wallace Chadwick, the special counsel. He read into the record some items from a correspondence of three years ago in which McCarthy had, time after time, and with interesting variations of language, told the members of an earlier investigating committee to go to hell. ("Frankly, Guy [Senator Gillette, of Iowa], I have not and do not intend to even read, much less answer, Benton's smear attack.") Mr. Chadwick, who is from Chester, Pennsylvania, is a man with a bent, benign, bookish appearance and a vaguely disappointed look— the look, perhaps, of a retired classics professor who, after giving the best years of his life to teaching college students Latin and Greek, is in serious doubt about the results. He read from the McCarthy anthology he had compiled with just the manifest discomfort that such a professor might exhibit if he were punished for his sins by being compelled to give a recital from the works of Nick Kenny. He had as much difficulty in adhering to the McCarthy text as McCarthy had had in adhering to the Bozell text. Once, where McCarthy, employing a well-known mannerism, had written of "Democrat senators," Mr. Chadwick paused after "Democrat," coughed a polite little cough, and said "ick senators."

This very practice of making an official record by endlessly reading from other official records revealed the style and the aims of the Watkins committee. When Mr. Chadwick began, McCarthy's counsel, Edward Bennett Williams, who is one of the most capable trial lawyers in Washington and an extremely personable young man, said that he and his client would agree to stipulate the authenticity of most of the documents that Mr. Chadwick thought relevant. Why not save time, he asked by simply entering them, with the consent of the principals, instead of plodding through them. Most of the legal minds around thought that this would be a sound procedure, but Senators Watkins said no. His rejection of the proposal, however, was based on something other than juridical propriety, for he said that if the need for "economy measures" should arise, he would reconsider Mr. Williams' idea. Mr. Chadwick was instructed to get along with his reading. Two possible explanations of the chair's ruling offered themselves. One was that Senator Watkins saw some positive, and perhaps purgative, value in assaulting the ears of the committeemen with McCarthy's repertoire of impudence and defiance; the other was that this stern critic of the practice of turning the solemn deliberations of Senators into public entertainment was intent on making the open hearings as boring as persistence and ingenuity could make them. The first explanation may be valid, and the second certainly is. "Let us get off the front page and back among the obituaries," Senator Watkins subsequently told reporters. "That would suit us fine." The reporters were unable to accommodate him, but there was agreement among them that some aspects of the proceedings would not be altogether out of place among the obituaries.

Other aspects, however, had the vital glow. It was after Mr. Chadwick had exhausted his voice and that of his assistant, Guy de Furia, by reading McCarthy's insouciant communications that Senator Watkins decided to recess. But then Senator Johnson, of Colorado, asked to be given a few minutes in which to read a statement. Senator Watkins obliged. The statement dealt, rather inconclusively, with the question, publicly raised by McCarthy the day before, of whether Senator Johnson should disqualify himself, or be disqualified, because of his personal feelings about McCarthy, which were reported to be unfriendly. Senator Johnson said that he felt fully qualified to serve, but he failed to cast any light on whether his dislike for McCarthy was powerful, average, or nonexistent. McCarthy's lawyer called attention to this notable omission. He would like to learn the truth, he said. Senator Watkins regarded this as legitimate curiosity and recommended that Mr. Williams satisfy it by addressing the question to Senator Johnson during the recess. Like Communism, Senator Johnson's attitude was, he said, outside the scope of the select committee's inquiry. This was too much for McCarthy. "Mr. Chairman," he began, and the words and the leaden tones were a magic carpet back to the spring of the year. Whammo! The gavel. Senator Watkins was no longer pale. He reminded McCarthy and Williams that under the rules either one or the other of them, but never both at the same time, could raise a point of order. "Mr. Chairman—" Again, whammo! "We are going straight down the line," Senator Watkins said. He announced that the hearings would resume at 10 A.M. the next day.

It was significant that when Senator Watkins refused to discuss the qualifications of Senator Johnson, a Democrat, his decision was promptly endorsed by Senator Case, of South Dakota, and Senator Carlson, of Kansas, both Republicans. It was obvious that this early show of what seemed like simple bi-partisanship but was actually something more complicated was made according to some pre-arranged plan. It was another key—perhaps the master key—to the character of the select committee. The display was really one of senatorial solidarity rather than of good will toward Democrats in general or Senator Johnson in particular. Senator Watkins was defending his associate not on the ground that his associate was unprejudiced but on the ground that he was a United States senator—one in whom the entire Senate had placed its confidence—and was therefore, by definition, a man who could rise above his personal feelings. If senators did not have this capacity, he pointed out, then it would be impossible for the Senate to carry out the job, assigned it by the Constitution, of judging and disciplining its own members.

Whether or not this is arrogant doctrine, it is doctrine of a sort that most people here had not encountered for quite some time. Before the first public session of the select committee, it was in no way appreciated that its members were the sort of men they have turned out to be. Not much of anything, in fact, was known about the six senators, and it was precisely this circumstance that led many people to suspect that the whole thing was a put-up job. It was felt that a search had been made for the six most obscure men in the Senate, and that the searchers, ably led by Vice-President Nixon, had exhibited in their choices a sure instinct for obscurity. Except for the controversial Senator Johnson, whose concern over anti-militarist movements and the morals of motion-picture performers had won him a dim celebrity in certain quarters, the members of the Watkins committee were all conspicuous for their inconspicuousness. Because in politics obscurity is commonly associated with lack of strength and talent, it was hastily concluded that the committee was one McCarthy could intimidate with fair ease. The lion, it appeared, was to be thrown into a den of lambs. A little investigation might have revealed, in advance of Senator Watkins' iron-handed rulings, that the obscurity of these six men is of a very special sort. Some men are without renown because nothing they do is of any interest to anyone, and others lack it simply because they have never troubled to seek it. The Senate has always contained both kinds of men, but it has been noteworthy—in the past, anyway—for having in it a sizable number of men with no national reputation who nevertheless wield great influence in the chamber itself. Mostly they are men who prefer it that way. They find life in the Senate, which is often compared to life in an exclusive and well-managed men's club, so full of satisfactions that they have no desire for any sort of activity outside it—apart, of course, from the activities in their home states that are essential to their continued enjoyment of club facilities and privileges. They like the leisurely ways of the Senate, its tradition of unlimited debate, its tolerance of eccentricities and crotchets. Though they sometimes speak of themselves as congressmen and bear a massive ill will toward the executive branch, they look, as a group, with horror upon the jungle they know as the House of Representatives. They prefer the company and esteem of their fellow-members to the praise of crowds, holding with Daniel Webster that the Senate "is a hall for mutual consultation and discussion; not an arena for the exhibition of champions." Some of them have a truly Roman piety in regard to their function as lawmakers. Beyond all question now, it is such a group of men that McCarthy confronts.

Each of the six obscure committeemen has spoken for the record, and at least five of them have shown themselves indisputable examples of the classic breed. The one possible exception is Senator Samuel J. Ervin, of North Carolina, who is a new-comer to the Senate, having been appointed in June to the seat left vacant by the death of Clyde Hoey. Senator Ervin, a former judge, is a rather bubbly character, a jollifier and storyteller in the tradition of Alben Barkley, and it is conceivable that his obscurity will be short-lived. But five, at any rate, are as one in their basic outlook. "McCarthy has run smack into the club's board of governors," someone said the other day. This, it is felt, bodes ill for McCarthy, because what he must be conceded to have done—even by those who maintain that he has served the country well—is a violation of the Websterian canon. He has made the Senate less a hall for mutual consultation and discussion and more an arena for the exhibition of champions, or any-way a champion. He is pre-eminently an enemy of club spirit. He has made the Senate a less comfortable place. He has upset the potted palms, defaced the woodwork, placed thumbtacks in the upholstered chairs, embarrassed the members by insulting their guests, and put the house committee to no end of trouble. It may or may not be found that his conduct has, as Senators Flanders, Morse, and Fulbright charge, brought the Senate into disrepute, but it is clear from his behavior as a respondent in this case, as well as from the uncontested record, that he has brought disrepute into the Senate, in unabashed violation of Rule XIX, Section 2, of the Standing Rules of the Senate, in which it is set forth that "no senator in debate shall, directly or indirectly, by any form of words impute to another senator or to other senators any conduct or motive unworthy or unbecom-ing a senator." Because of him, it is the Senate now that many people think of as a jungle. And largely because of his cultiva-tion of the mob and the rabble, many people here found them-selves unable to believe that a committee of six quiet, inconspicu-ous men could deal with the challenge he presented. Strength of character has insidiously become equated with extent of fame and volume of publicity; it was felt that because Senator Watkins and his colleagues were peaceful, uncommunicative men who had given to their views no forceful expression, they must either be without views or secretly approve of McCarthy. McCarthy and his followers, indeed, made it all but impossible to believe in the existence of Senator Watkins, a two-hundred-proof Republican who only yesterday, in the course of questioning McCarthy, ventured the opinion that there might be something wrong in describing a man as a Communist simply because he availed himself of the Fifth Amendment to the Constitution—a heresy no one ever dreamed would be voiced by a member of the Eighty-third Congress.

"The hearings," Senator Watkins said on the opening day, "are not to be adversary in character." Yet that is what they have been—in substance, if not in form. During the first week, Mr. Chadwick and Mr. de Furia assembled a record no part of which reflected credit on McCarthy. Most observers felt there was merit in Mr. Williams' claim that the committee counsel was sounding more and more like a prosecutor, but there were few who were able to see how the counsel could avoid it, considering the nature of the material he had to work with. The committee's questioning of witnesses, including McCarthy, has not been hostile, but it has inevitably been tendentious. McCarthy is an adversary type, and the mind boggles at trying to picture him being involved in a non-adversary proceeding. Despite the committee's evident lack of sympathy for him, however, it is far from certain that it will report favorably on the Flanders resolution. McCarthy and his counsel have conceived a bristling and in some respects an impressive line of defense. Noting that what the committee is considering is a series of instances of purported misconduct, they are making little effort to defend McCarthy's record as a whole, or even to offer it for examination. Instead, they are taking up the allegations one by one and seeking to establish either that each specific act was justified by circumstances or, failing that, that nothing McCarthy has done in the Senate has been without precedent. Thus General Zwicker's "arrogance" provoked a natural human response in McCarthy, who, as it happened, had had to sit up all the night before with his injured wife. Moreover, if McCarthy is to be censured for his rough handling of General Zwicker, why should not Senator Bush, of Connecticut, also be censured, for allegedly similar discourtesies in a one-man hearing on housing profits held just the other day? Mr. Williams does not deny that McCarthy spoke unkindly of Senator Flanders. He simply points out that Senator Flanders had earlier compared McCarthy with Adolf Hitler. Which is worse—to be senile or to be a Hitler? McCarthy and Mr. Williams know that Rule XIX, Section 2, and the elaborate respect that senators show each other on the floor are strictly hot air. (Former Senator Tom Connally, of Texas, had a way of crouching down in debate and holding the palm of his right hand about six inches above the floor as he addressed himself to "the great, the truly distinguished Senator from—.") There is no doubt at all that McCarthy, over the years, has given no better than he has got. He has just given more of it.

There will probably be a defense of some sort for everything he has done. Other senators have made secret information public. Only a few years ago, one of McCarthy's present judges, Senator Johnson, was widely criticized for giving out, on a television program, information that dealt with our progress on the hydrogen bomb and that was said to be classified. Senator Jenner, of Indiana, once called General Marshall a "living lie," which was a little farther than McCarthy went in his celebrated speech. Besides—and this may well impress the members of the select committee—to censure a man for extravagance of language on the Senate floor might be to inhibit senators in the exercise of the free and unlimited debate they set such store by. Senator Watkins himself recently signed a committee report that urged "employees in the executive branch of the government. . . . to turn over to committees of Congress any information which would help the committees in their fight against subversion." Other senators, plenty of them, have made questionable deals with private enterprises. And for none of these things has any senator ever been censured. Senator Watkins, it is true, is limiting Mc-Carthy's use of the *tu quoque,* or "you're another," defense—allowing him to cite the actions of other senators in arguments on the law but, on at least some counts, disallowing these precedents as evidence. Even so, it may be hard for the senators to ignore the precedents when they vote.

The feeling here is that it will be difficult to sustain any case against McCarthy that is not based on the whole course and meaning of his career—and that would be a sticky problem for a committee, though perhaps not for this select and tough-minded one. But the feeling also is that it does not matter very much what is done, for the career is almost over; the spell, as the hearings themselves show, has been broken. One senses this not only in the behavior of the committee but in the meager interest of the public. The caucus room has been filled each day, but it has been barely filled. Even when the American Legion came to town, one hundred thousand strong, McCarthy drew no crowds. There has never been a time when more than five people were waiting outside for seats and never a time when any of them had to wait more than five minutes. Not much of the audience appears to be sympathetic. When McCarthy goes outside the caucus room, as he frequently does, to address "the great American jury" by way of television, a handful of the faithful leave at the same time and pick their way toward him over the scattered boxes and the tangled wires that Senator Watkins keeps on the wrong side of the floor. They are an odd assortment—small children seeking a handshake, teen-agers seeking autographs, gamy-looking men and women seeking a wink or a smile in exchange for their "Give 'em hell, Joe." They are never more than a handful. Everything about the scene here suggests that Senator Watkins was right in his choice of the proper newspaper page for the record of these proceedings.

29 Elections

Letter from Washington

November 4, 1954

"The administration," according to this morning's *Post & Times Herald*, "has experienced neither victory nor overwhelming defeat at the polls." This is about as conclusive a statement on the broad meaning or non-meaning of the elections as anyone here has been able to make, and, as a matter of fact, practically everyone here has made it. However, to say that the Eisenhower administration is neither much better off nor much worse off than it was when this memorable week began is not to say that its opponents, the happy Democrats, failed to improve their lot. In any kind of contest, it violates logic to claim that while one side has not lost, the other has won, but nevertheless that seems to be the state of affairs at the moment, at least in the view most commonly encountered here. The thing that has struck Washington as having the greatest significance is the Democrats' success in picking up governorships. The state governments may have lost power and precious rights to the federal authority in the course of the last twenty years, but they have tended to gain in political importance during this time. Control of federal patronage doesn't do a party much good any more, as the Republicans have learned to their sorrow and surprise, and this gives state patronage a value it never had in the days when a village postmastership was a thing worth having and militant and high-minded civil-service rooters had not yet swept all before them. The party that controls the machinery of government in a populous state like New York or Pennsylvania counts itself far more blessed than the party that elects all its congressional candidates but misses its chance at the state house. Party control of the most powerful and well-intentioned congressional delegation is no match at all, in terms of political effectiveness, for party control of a state highway department or tax commission. Congressmen merely pass laws and put their nieces on the payroll, but the men and women who give out hunting licenses, direct the affairs of penitentiaries, and order textbooks by the carload—in every case unhampered by such restraints on individual liberty as the federal Corrupt Practices Act—can work wonders for the ticket. With the sovereign people as evenly divided in their political preferences as this election shows them to be, the new managements that appear to have been installed in New York, Pennsylvania, Connecticut, Minnesota, and a few other states could provide the Democrats with precisely the energy, booster spirit, free labor, and folding money they seem to have lacked in 1952. It is being said on every hand here that while nothing that happened on Tuesday can be read as a repudiation of President Eisenhower, the changes that impend in Albany, Harrisburg, Hartford, St. Paul and elsewhere could very well lead directly to his and his associates' retirement in 1956.

What is meant by those who say that the administration neither won nor lost much in the elections is, first, that the Democratic congressional gains were somewhat lower than those of the out party in most previous off-year elections, and, second, that in terms of policy the Eisenhower administration will get as much of what it asks for from a Democratic Congress as it would from a Republican one. The first proposition is susceptible of statistical proof, and the statistics are imposing. Since a normal loss for the party in power would be something like forty House seats, it can be argued—and today is being argued by spokesmen for the Republican National Committee—that the administration has succeeded in keeping discontent to about half its traditional volume. In order to make this appeal to history, though, it is necessary to overlook the fact that this has been a unique, unprecedented season politically, in that whatever discontent developed received very little encouragement or prodding from the American press; at the time when the precedents were established, the press was divided roughly in the same ratio as the people, but today it is deeply committed to the administration and therefore reluctant to air any grievances against it. As for the contention that the President will get as much of what he wants from Democrats as he would from Republicans, there are few to dispute it. By and large, the Democratic candidates had every bit as firm a grip on his coattails as their opponents had. And if they should seek to embarrass him by opposing his wishes too strenuously, they would find themselves charged with failing to live up to their own campaign pledges, which, by a coincidence that is not at all strange, were also his campaign pledges. From the President's point of view, the danger is not that the Democrats will give him less than he wants but that they will give him more than he wants. He will, it is expected, find all his antes raised; his military appropriations will be as large as he wants them to be and, for good Democratic measure, larger, and, with perhaps a few exceptions, such as Mr. Brownell's Department of Justice, his executive agencies will be treated with a generosity he may regard as overdone. If he asks for tariff reductions, he may get all that he asks for and probably some that he doesn't want. The Democrats are likely to approach what Senator-elect George Bender, of Ohio, a recent and improbable convert to the President's wing of the party, last night described as "that splendid Eisenhower program" with a measure of zeal that its promoter will regard as excessive.

30 "The Universality of Potential Destruction"

Letter from Washington

January 20, 1955

The President, in the budget message he sent to Congress earlier this week, spoke of "a revolution in military concepts" that is currently in progress and that puts "an extra premium on military leadership." Actually, this is but one of several going revolutions. Wherever there is talk of foreign policy nowadays, the air is electric with a sense of change. There is an almost universal feeling that the world the United States confronts today—the whole complex of political, economic, military, and technological realities that constitute the environment in which the national interest must be pursued—is radically different from the world it confronted even as recently as last summer. Russian achievements in weapons research and development have brought into being a new power relationship between this country and the Soviet Union. Last year's hydrogen bomb experiments at the Pacific proving ground have led to a new view of the meaning that any future resort to war would have for human life and civilization. The emergence of a new style, if not a new character, in Soviet diplomacy has created for our diplomacy difficulties as novel and as formidable as those that might be created by the sudden emergence of a new adversary. "It sometimes seems as if the very context of history has altered," Senator Hennings, of Missouri, observed the other day. "Our problems may be the same in substance, but they are different in form, dimension, and perspective. In any case, none of yesterday's assumptions can go unchallenged today."

Some of yesterday's assumptions are already in the discard. The one that lies there most conspicuously, perhaps, is the assumption of our superiority in nuclear weapons. Our military planning is no longer based on the premise that we enjoy any useful advantage. Senator Knowland, tirelessly urging a more militant policy on the administration he sometimes serves as a spokesman, often refers to a future in which an "atomic stalemate" will have been reached—the implication being that by that time militancy might be ill-advised—but Senator Knowland appears to stand alone in regarding atomic stalemate as a thing of the future. The majority of experts, led in eminence by the President himself, are convinced either that stalemate is here or that it is a condition so rapidly being approached that we must act as if it were already upon us. This is not to say that anyone assumes the Soviet capacity for the manufacture and delivery of hydrogen bombs to be precisely equal to ours. We probably have more and better bombs than the Russians have, better means of delivering them and superior defenses against attack. No one, of course, really knows. There would be uncertainty in this matter even if we had complete and authentic data on Soviet stockpiles and production, because we lack the criteria for evaluating such data. The working theory, though, is that the Russians have achieved and are maintaining a rough equality in research and development and that their ability to damage us is approximately as great as our ability to damage them. Since it has been frequently and authoritatively estimated that the United States has sufficient nuclear power to destroy every worthwhile military target on the face of the earth, it is clear that whatever we may have that the Russians lack is in the nature of surplus, or atomic fat. And while this surplus may be valuable in providing government officials with a warrant for asserting, as H. Struve Hensel, an Assistant Secretary of Defense, asserted a couple of nights ago, that the United States is "militarily stronger by far than its challenger," it weighs little or nothing on the scales of power.

"Atomic stalemate" is, in any event, a phrase now heard everywhere here, and one whose meaning a good many people are trying to plumb. If it is taken to describe a state of affairs that exists between the Russians and ourselves, it does not mean that our atomic and nuclear power can no longer be effective as a deterrent to general war and aggression; provided that Malenkov and his associates exercise any kind of rationality, the fact that they can now give as good as they get will not increase their receptivity to the idea of being themselves destroyed. What Sir Winston Churchill has called "the balance of terror" is generally regarded as a fairly promising substitute for the balance of power. "It is to the universality of potential destruction that we may look with hope and even confidence," Churchill has said. But a new contingency, or at least a newly acknowledged one, is that our deterrent power has developed into so awesome a thing that we ourselves may be deterred from getting what political leverage we can out of keeping alive the possibility of its use—that we may, in other words, upset the balance of terror by forswearing the use of nuclear war under any circumstances. (It appeared to many here that President Eisenhower came fairly close to doing this when, in an extemporaneous speech before a group of State Department employees on October 19 of last year, he said that "since the advent of nuclear weapons, it seems clear that there is no longer any alternative to peace." He repeated the thought the following day at Trinity College, in Hartford, declaring that "war would present to us only the alternatives in degrees of destruction.") Apparently, no such prospect was in view last January, when the Secretary of State first expounded the doctrine of "massive retaliation." At that time, he plainly had in mind the use of our most destructive weapons against Russia and China in the event that one or the other of them resorted to aggression.

Dulles spoke before the three 1954 hydrogen bomb detonations at the Pacific proving ground. The fishing boat cruelly misnamed the "Fortunate Dragon" had not yet been heard of;

the term "fall-out" still belonged to the jargon of the technicians; little had been said (though evidently a good deal had
been thought) about the genetic consequences of widespread
radiation. In the view of Chalmers Roberts, a Washington *Post
& Times-Herald* correspondent who has been the leading historian of this period of change in American foreign policy, the
Bikini experiments and their aftermath powerfully affected
President Eisenhower—in part, it seems, through the agency of
the British Prime Minister, whose visit to the White House last
summer was the result of the alarm he felt on reading some
vivid dispatches about radiation and fall-out in the Manchester
Guardian—and led him to soften, if not to blunt, the Dulles
policy. That the President has softened it is a fact that was
clearly established in the eyes of most people by our failure,
only a few months after Mr. Dulles's speech, to apply massive
retaliation, or even to threaten it, in the crises over Indo-China
and Quemoy. It would be going too far to say that the policy
has been withdrawn and that terrror is therefore already out of
balance; no one believes that the President interprets "coexistence" or the "modus vivendi" of which he has several times
spoken as meaning peace at absolutely any price. But there is
enormous confusion now over exactly what price, in terms of
Communist victories, we are willing to pay for peace, and a
certainty that whatever that price may be, it is—with even Mr.
Dulles advising the nation to "be slow to anger"—a good deal
higher than it was last year.

The balance of terror would not be upset if the Russians
followed us in placing an increasingly high valuation on peace,
or if some system of controlled disarmament could be put into
effect. There were indications last year that the Russians were
as appalled by the thought of using their deterrent power as we
are by the thought of using ours. In March, Premier Malenkov,
in a speech that seemed to qualify him as a premature fellow-
traveler of the President, said that "with the existence of modern
means of destruction . . . [war] would mean the destruction

of world civilization." In many quarters, this statement, along with others that came out of Moscow in 1953, quickened the hope that a selfish interest in enjoying life a while longer would incline the Soviet leaders to accept some practical scheme for disarmament. In July, when the United Nations Disarmament Commission began its sessions in New York, it was possible, despite the discouragement engendered by the five-power talks that had just been concluded in London, to think that some reasonable scheme of inspection and control could, with patience and energy, be made attractive to the Soviet Union. It was felt that even if the effort failed, the attempt by the anti-Communist powers was worthwhile to the extent that it would reveal Communist obstinacy and be read as an earnest of the West's good intentions by the neutral and neutralist powers, many of whose leaders were disarmament enthusiasts. In October, when the General Assembly proposed a resumption of the five-power discussions, the American delegates still felt that the pursuit of disarmament served the national interest. However, recent developments—or, rather, recent appraisals of earlier developments— make it plain that no matter how much the Russians grow in amenability, disarmament is a blocked road to peace and security in 1955. Even in theory, it seems, atomic inspection and control is no longer a realizable objective; its advocacy, for propaganda or any other purpose, has, in the opinion of many observers, become a fatuous expenditure of time and words. "The technical feasibility of atomic disarmament," Eugene Rabinowitch, the editor of the *Bulletin of the Atomic Scientists,* wrote recently, "now depends on a reliable inventory of existing stocks of fissionable materials. Considering the extremely small bulk of these materials, and the absence of penetrating radiations emanating from them, the only possibility of inventorying them is for the agents of the U.N. control body to be led to their stockpiles by national officials who know where they are located. Neither the West nor the U.S.S.R. can be expected to base its own atomic disarmament on the trust that the other side has not concealed a substantial part of its stockpile. . . . If this conclusion is true, then we must add to the appalling knowledge of the material and biological damage of a future atomic war the sad recognition that effectively controlled atomic disarmament has ceased to be possible and that all attempts to find a compromise solution are therefore bound to remain futile. Mankind will have to live, from now on, with unlimited and unchecked stockpiles of atomic and thermonuclear explosives, piling up first in America and the Soviet Union, then in Great Britain, and later in other countries as well." As someone here has pointed out, the day may come when humanity will look back on the Cold War as a time when one could live with nerves relaxed and confidence in the future high—the day being the one when we learn that Egypt, say, or Nicaragua, or Iran, has acquired a small cache of thermonuclear weapons.

Under the impact of our dizzying technological advance, the validity not only of military and political strategies but of basic ideas is often almost as short-lived as the design of a fighter plane. Concepts that once seemed as if they might endure at least through our epoch are ready for mothballs a few years or months after they have been grasped and disseminated. One notion that has lately come to seem obsolete is the industrial-potential theory of national power. It was only during the Second World War that Americans began to understand and accept this theory. In the late thirties, we were, as a nation, pretty well committed to the kind of force-in-being theory that, for example, led Colonel Charles A. Lindbergh, fresh from his guided inspection of Nazi air power, to take a despairing view of the capacity of the Western democracies to overcome it; impressed with the Luftwaffe's ability to darken the German skies in its consummately staged demonstrations, he maintained that the Allies could never hope to match the German power already in existence. The lesson of the war that followed was that it was not what a nation had on hand that counted but what it could produce in the course of a conflict. By the time the war ended, the idea had taken hold everywhere that the chief element in the political power of any given nation was the readiness with which it could lay its hands on raw materials and transform them into militarily useful objects. Diplomatic and political discourse became very largely essays on the measurement of factory floor space, machine-tool production, kilowatts generated, and the available supplies of coal, oil, and steel. These were, in the long run, the decisive factors, it was felt, and no policy that put them in a subordinate position was worthy of consideration. The whole Europe-first idea that has been fundamental to our strategy in the conflict with Communism has rested on the industrial-potential theory; the principle has been that while democracy could survive the conquest of vast, hugely populous parts of Asia, it could not survive the absorption of even a fraction of Western Europe, since the control of this area would tip the world balance of industrial power in favor of the Soviet system. But the development of thermonuclear weapons has made the industrial-potential theory passé and, along with it, certain of the strategies it seemed to require. One or two hydrogen bombs can take a gigantic bite out of any nation's capacity to produce; a brisk day's work by the air force of one nation could start another nation on the road back to the Stone Age, and an extra day or two could finish the job. "The nostalgic idea that our industrial power is our greatest military asset could ruin our military planning," Thomas K. Finletter, the former Secretary of the Air Force, wrote last fall in *Power and Policy,* a critique of American strategy that demonstrates time and again how relative a thing nostalgia may be. "We must build our military force on the exact opposite of this industrial-potential notion." In the view of many people here, however, Mr. Finletter's "exact opposite"—in a word, air power—has been rendered almost as obsolete by stalemate as the industrial-potential idea has been by the hydrogen bomb. Through the balance of terror, it is believed, air power can prevent defeat and destruction, but it cannot be the guiding or organizing principle for any sort of victory. Still, without it neither victory nor even survival would be possible, and there is almost universal agreement that the basic measure of military strength today is the speed with which a nation could, if sufficiently provoked, drop hydrogen bombs on its enemy. Thus, the force-in-being theory that was fallacious in the late thirties seems again to be valid—temporarily, at least—in the mid-fifties. Indeed, as long as there is parity in the major departments of thermonuclear warfare, the United States could double, triple, or quadruple its productive facilities and the Russians could revert technologically to the age of Basil IV without there being any fundamental change in the power relationship.

Needless to say, neither Mr. Finletter nor any other man with his wits about him would advocate a foreign or military policy based wholly on thermonuclear power. In fact, there is a growing tendency here in Washington to think that stalemate and the balance of terror (provided the balance is kept) will eventually lead us back to something resembling the world of a decade ago, and that any wars that many actually be fought—as distinct from the wars that will merely be talked about and threatened—will be conflicts whose outcomes are likely to be determined by productive capacity, manpower, and the other familiar elements in the equations of armed combat. But this would not alter the fact that thermonuclear power is the basic register and the ultimate resource of every nation that has it.

This fact, it is becoming clear, is of enormous consequence to the whole structure of our diplomacy. For one thing, it forces a reconsideration of the entire question of the balance between commitments and strength. The policy we have pursued all through the Cold War was based on an appraisal of American power as insufficient to enable us to function effectively except in the framework of a coalition. Both the Truman and the Eisenhower administrations have accepted and justified restrictions on our sovereignty and our freedom of action on the ground that our strength, to be felt, has to be augmented by the strength of other nations. Isolationists, unilateralists, and other dissenters and heretics have been disposed of with the argument that without allies we would inevitably find ourselves crushed by the growing industrial power of the Communist world. A moral and political claim was also advanced in behalf of the coalition strategy, but the first consideration has always been industrial. It is not for their leadership in virtue that we have regarded Germany and Japan as the two countries that must at all costs be kept out of the Communist orbit. But if power is calculated, however uncertainly, in deliverable megatons, then the gain or loss of an industrial nation here or there would not be crucial, or even important. If allies are valuable chiefly for their contributions to our military strength, then we no longer have any need for them, since our strength is already absolute. The fact that our absolute strength is matched by that of our principal adversary does not in any way change the situation. As a nation placing its main reliance on thermonuclear weapons—and the 1956 budget makes it plain that we do place our main reliance on them, even though our determination never to use them grows from day to day—we are able now to go it alone, if it is our wish to do so; our position in a general atomic war with the Soviet Union would not be improved in any degree by our being able to count on the use of someone else's machine tools or rolling mills or skilled-labor force. If such a war were to break out, we would be little better off with the whole non-Communist world ranged on our side than with it ranged against us. The last remaining use for allies in the kind of conflict we are armed for is to provide bases for our Strategic Air Command, but now we are assured the development of our bombers has very nearly reached the point at which bases outside this hemisphere will be no longer needed; with the coming of pilotless intercontinental missiles bearing hydrogen warheads, the need will disappear altogether.

The State and Defense Departments, grappling with the questions raised by the existence of a power that is at once absolute and useless, maintain that the situation creates a new need for allies at the same time that it obviates an old one. They concede that allies are no longer necessary in a general atomic war, but they argue that because the hydrogen bomb reduces and almost eliminates the likelihood of a general atomic war, it requires us to plan for all the other eventualities this new state of affairs may give rise to. These eventualities—limited wars of the Korea type, ideological conflict, diplomatic offensives, and economic warfare, to name a few of them or, it is hoped, all of them—not only demand a strategy of coalition but actually make such a strategy more urgent than it was in the period when our chief concern was to assure victory in a general war. No one here seems to have any disposition to quarrel with this view; obviously, it is important to have allies in what General Alfred Gruenther calls "wars of flesh," and it is impossible to conduct economic or ideological wars without them. But the strength of coalitions of the kind now needed cannot be adequately reckoned in the old terms of industrial potential. It can, however, be partially reckoned that way. The ability of this country and Western Europe to produce an abundance of conventional weapons would be valuable, and perhaps decisive, in the event of another Korea or Indo-China, and, of course, this ability continues to be the foundation of the strength of the North Atlantic Treaty Organization, which is still regarded as the cornerstone of our policy in Europe and the most impressive achievement of Western diplomacy in the Cold War period. But as the prospect of general war recedes, the prospect of future Koreas and Indo-Chinas, and the prospect of NATO's ever being forced to meet the test of aggression, appears to be receding along with it. We are evidently determined to stay out of all small wars that we can honorably avoid. The Vice-President has explained that the Communists have a plan for "nibbling us to death" and that we must not fall for it by being drawn into counter-nibbling operations. If this line of reasoning is difficult to comprehend, it is by no means difficult to comprehend the President's objection to limited wars, which is that under present conditions they are likely to become unlimited ones. And there is reason to believe that the Communists, too, share the view that any limited war developing at this stage would inevitably lead to the crowning catastrophe of general war. All their recent maneuvers have been in areas like the Tachen Islands, where we have expressly said we perceive no national interest and will not resist nibbling.

For the forms of conflict that remain, our industrial potential and our whole system of alliances are, like the hydrogen bomb, virtual irrelevancies. They will help us very little in countering the assault by infiltration that threatens Southeast Asia or the assault by astute diplomacy that threatens other regions. To prevail against these offensives, we unquestionably need allies, but we do not need them for the same reasons as formerly, nor do we in all cases need the same allies. There is a feeling here, as there is in some parts of Western Europe, that the closer we come to forming a military alliance with Western Germany, the more our need for that partnership diminishes. It is expected that the administration will be able to advance some vigorous arguments in behalf of the cuts it plans to make in American ground forces this year, but it is not seen how it will be able to reconcile these cuts with the claim that we need twelve German divisions for the defense of Western Europe.

What has happened in the last year or so, a good many people believe, is that the Cold War has been maneuvered completely away from the battlegrounds on which it was fought in the late forties and early fifties. Its character has changed almost entirely. To some extent, this change has been ordained by technology. But it is also to some extent the triumphant work of Communist diplomacy. Observing our unquestioned success in building the "positions of strength" that would, we thought, eventually enable us to negotiate an acceptable settlement, the Communists have deliberately sought to engage us in areas where our "positions of strength" would do us little good. Some of their new strategies

were forced upon them by the same events that have given us
pause—the arrival of stalemate, the revelations of the previously
unimagined horrors of war, and the passing of the industrial-
potential theory. But they have responded to these events with
great flexibility and imagination, and it is the Malenkov regime's
revealed ability to make such responses that gives Washington
a feeling of facing a new antagonist, and one far more resourceful
than the old one. A major asset of Western policy in the first
years of its conflict with world Communism was the predictabil-
ity of the Stalin regime and its gift for political blunder. We
derived huge advantages from its footless diplomacy. It drove
France, where Communism was strong, into the arms of the
West by its pointless insistence on denying that nation a great-
power role. It made a success of the Marshall Plan, which no
Congress would have continued if the Communist countries had
accepted the original invitation to participate. Its doctrinaire
rigidity cost it Yugoslavia and the second most powerful army
in Europe. Its attack on South Korea and its bluster and postur-
ing in Germany brought on American rearmament and frightened
Western Europe into joining us. The demeanor of its representatives at the United Nations and in international conferences
served constantly to remind the free nations of the arrogance and
brutishness of Communist power. Since Stalin's death, though,
the West has been deprived of the unsolicited but valued aid
it received from Moscow and has been forced to acknowledge
that the Russians are as much our equals in diplomatic adroitness as they are in the various arts of war. Their recent handling
of the Yugoslavs, their management of Communist interests at
last year's Geneva conference, their recent felicitous approaches
to Paris and Bonn, their establishment of their own Point Four
program, and their recent attempts to outbid us in sharing the
benefits of atomic energy suggest that from now on they will
tax the cunning and imagination of Western statesmanship as
heavily as they have already taxed our military strength. Thus,
in the very period when we have to face atomic stalemate and

a host of new problems created by advances in technology, we must also face the fact—wholly unrelated to technology and caused simply by the accident of a tyrant's death—that the enemy combines with his old malevolence a proficiency and craft that were not apparent when the Cold War began.

In the circumstances, it is hardly surprising that no one here seems to have any clear idea of where we are going next. A democratic leadership cannot react to a new situation as rapidly as a totalitarian leadership, and in this new situation there is no special need for haste. Although the possibility of thermo-nuclear destruction will doubtless be with us more or less permanently, no one feels that it is, just now, a fate to be awaited from moment to moment. Despite the appearance of a flock of new dangers, there is, in a way, more relief than apprehension here today, the relief being founded on a general acceptance of the view that, as the British military analyst Sir John Slessor recently put it, "we have at last arrived at the point when war—in the sense of total world war as we have known it in our generation—has abolished itself as a practical instrument of policy." If there is nothing else now, there is at least time for a certain amount of reflection, and the appropriate agencies of government—the State and Defense Departments, the National Security Council, and the foreign-relations committees of the House and Senate—are reported to be readying themselves for a prolonged siege of reflective endeavor. "What we call the 'long-haul' concept," Secretary Dulles said in his New Year's review of events, "has been brought into application both in this country and in others that had been operating on emergency plans." There is ferment and uncertainty here but no really deep sense of emergency.

There have been, here and there, some indications of a few of the trends of policy. Though the administration is seriously divided on China, with the President on one side and Senator Knowland, various members of the Joint Chiefs of Staff, and—some of the time—Secretary Dulles on the other, almost everybody believes that the President is determined to have his view prevail. His view appears to be that—in this area, at any rate— we have more to gain from making an active effort to reduce tensions than from merely exploiting them to our own advantage. This approach is implicit in his apparent eagerness to have the fighting in the Formosa Strait brought to an end, even at the risk of alienating the Nationalists and their supporters here, and it has been implicit in his reaction to several other recent occurrences. One of these was the shooting down of an Air Force B-29 by Soviet MIGs in the vicinity of northern Hokkaido on November 7th. The incident was similar in most details to half a hundred others that have occurred over the years. But the President's reaction was very different from any previous American reaction. Always, in the past, our spokesmen have sought first to establish Communist guilt, and after that to persuade world opinion to share our outraged view of the matter. This time, however, the President endeavored to put aside the whole question of guilt—even, astonishingly, to blur it. In his news conference of November 10, he explained that in dealing with shooting incidents of this sort it was well to bear in mind that "things were not always so completely clean-cut as they might look on the surface," and he went on to assert—on what evidence he did not say—that there had been "a very considerable different attitude shown [by the Communists] than there had been in the past."

The reducing of tensions could help to create an atmosphere conducive to the success of a new policy, but however commendable it might be on this and other grounds, it is not in itself a new policy, or any sort of policy at all. A disinclination to make things worse does nothing to make them better. It would be an error to say that all we are doing to meet the new situation we face is announcing the areas in which we refuse to be engaged, but for the moment these announcements appear to be the central feature of our strategy. For the rest, there is mostly talk—about striking a new kind of balance in military forces, about a new program of aid for the underdeveloped areas, about trade with the Communist powers, and about reduced tariff schedules. It may turn out that much of this is to the point, and that our own policy makers are being as alert and ingenious as the Communist ones. But these things have yet to be established.

31 Public Law 4

Letter from Washington
February 17, 1955

In his speech before the Foreign Policy Association last night, the Secretary of State did not give an altogether clear answer to the question of whether we are determined to hold Quemoy and the Matsus at all costs. He did, however, say that the administration has not yielded to the suggestion to abandon them. This is about what everyone had expected him to say, and this is about what everyone, including people who think it would be folly to be drawn into a war over these indefensible outposts, would have wished him to say, once he had decided to discuss the matter at all. He might have said nothing about Quemoy and the Matsus, in which case the situation would be precisely what it is now, but if he had said either much more or much less than he did, he would have invited a Communist attack on the islands. His one alternative might have been an attempt at a truly candid exposition of this vexed situation and the way it is being dealt with here. Had he chosen that alternative, he would certainly have confused the Communists. He might also have confused his listeners, and even himself.

It is at this moment a thoroughly mixed-up situation, and one reason Mr. Dulles could not have made a categorical statement, even if he had been so undiplomatic as to wish to do so, is that the administration itself has not settled upon a course. Or, at least, that is the appearance of things here at this juncture. One gets the impression that the only orders given the Seventh Fleet in regard to Quemoy and the Matsus are orders to check with Washington before doing anything drastic. One gets the further impression that the President is one member of the administration who is determined not to go to war over the offshore islands if he can find any possible way of avoiding it. His area of choice is being narrowed, however, not only by the Chinese Communists, who have the primary power of decision at this stage, but by the pressures on him here. There is, and for some time has been, a split in the administration that can be roughly described by saying that on the one hand there is a White House faction favoring a minimum of commitment in the Far East and a Pentagon-Capitol Hill faction favoring a maximum of commitment. This may do some injustice to the true delicacy of the situation, but by and large it is recognized that the President wants out and the Joint Chiefs of Staff and Senator Knowland want in. It may turn out that these differing points of view will have no bearing on what happens in the Formosa Strait in the coming weeks, for there is little doubt that if the Communists should launch an attack on Quemoy and the Matsus that was clearly preparatory for their promised assault on Formosa, we would be at war. The differing points of view would have extreme relevancy, though, in the event of an attack that was judged by our intelligence people to be an operation of limited scope, intended to assure Peiping's security and not to destroy Formosa's. They would also be relevant in the event of a Communist offer to bargain for control of the offshore islands in return for a promise to abstain from an armed attack on Formosa and the Pescadores. That the President is open to such a proposition was shown in his call for a negotiated cease-fire, which quite obviously could not be arranged unless there was a surrender of the islands within artillery range of the mainland.

Senator Knowland and Admiral Radford are opposed to any such deal.

The feeling here is that unless Peiping resolves the whole issue by making good on its threats to clobber the off-shore islands at an early date, this conflict will continue but will be settled before too long in a fairly clear-cut victory for the President. It is pointed out that although he does not wield the power of his office as forcefully as some of his predecessors, in this struggle he has won every contest so far. If Admiral Radford, who is becoming almost wistful in his repeated suggestion of a blockade of China, had had the upper hand in the last few months, it is of course possible that no one would now be concerned with weighing the prospects for peace. But in almost every case the President has pursued the exact opposite of the course recommended by the Joint Chiefs, and there is no reason to suppose that he has any different plans for the future. His independence of his military advisers has been in many ways remarkable, and quite a few people feel that he has been able to get away with it only because he is a military man himself. A civilian President who was told by his Joint Chiefs of Staff that the nation's security required a certain course of action would have to either take their advice or get himself a new set of Joint Chiefs. President Eisenhower has no need to do one thing or the other. He knows that he is at least the peer of any of his Joint Chiefs as a strategist, and if he should be disturbed by the possibility that his views are colored by his political background, he can recall the fact that the backgrounds of the present Joint Chiefs are no more innocent of politics than his. These men were more or less foisted upon him by Senators Knowland and Taft, because Senators Knowland and Taft felt that the country would benefit from having military leadership that rejected the Europe-first views of the group headed by the President's old associate General Bradley.

It is perhaps even more remarkable that the President has won most of his battles over Asian policy with Senator Knowland, for while a civilian President tends to be awed by generals, a military President tends to be awed by senators. Nevertheless, Mr. Eisenhower has usually had the better of the argument with the congressional leader of his party. There is clear evidence of this in the events of the last month. Senator Knowland did his part in seeking congressional approval of Public Law 4—the joint resolution on the defense of Formosa—and of the Mutual Defense Treaty with the Republic of China, but he did it with an unconcealed distaste for the only provisions in those documents that represented any sort of change from existing policy. These were the request for a negotiated cease-fire in Public Law 4 and what has been called the "re-leashing" section of the treaty—Article I, in which the Nationalist Chinese signatories pledge themselves to refrain "from the threat or use of force in any manner inconsistent with the purposes of the United Nations." If anything, Senator Knowland's objections to these provisions went deeper than Senator Morse's objections to everything else in the documents, but Senator Knowland had been maneuvered by the White House into a position that forced him to accept them, in order to get a reaffirmation of principles that would have been adhered to in any circumstances—the defense of Formosa and continued military aid to Chiang. The prevailing view here, then, is that if the President weathers this crisis, he will be pretty firmly in control of policy in his own administration. Provided the Communists have the good sense not to press their attacks in the Formosa Strait, the case of Admiral Radford and Senator Knowland will be greatly weakened.

Even if the peace is preserved there are bound to be difficulties growing out of the events of the past month. It is almost universally acknowledged here that Public Law 4 and the Mutual Defense Treaty have created fully as many problems as they have solved. Many people, including a large bi-partisan group of the senators who voted for it, feel that Public Law 4 will haunt the executive branch of government for many years to come. For what the President did in requiring Congress to approve in advance a course of action for which he already had full authority under the Constitution was to act as if the Bricker amendment, which was narrowly defeated in the last Congress and might be narrowly passed in this one, were so sound in principle that its provisions should be honored even without its being enacted into law. The President, of course, opposes the Bricker amendment in practice, and it was not because he endorses it in theory that he asked Congress to allow him to do what he had a full right—even an obligation—to do under existing law, and what, in fact, he had been doing all along. He wanted, for one thing, to impress Peiping with the degree of unity behind American policy, and for such a purpose a congressional resolution is effective; he also wanted, it may be assumed, to share with Congress the responsibility for the large risks that were being run. "Eisenhower is passing the buck," Senator Morse said at one point, and no one, even among the administration's supporters, took issue with him. The President was doubtless mindful of the reproach that met President Truman's failure to consult Congress before ordering air and sea support for the Republic of Korea in June of 1950. With the Communist armies slicing down the peninsula, President Truman did not have time to ask Congress to approve his action (it is unlikely that he would have done so even if there had been time), and there will be crises in the future when President Eisenhower and those who follow him will not be able to sit back and wait for the Senate, with all its pride in its tradition of unlimited debate, to grind out a resolution. But any future President who neglects to ask Congress's leave in a matter of this sort will be accused of ignoring the admirable precedent set by Mr. Eisenhower in 1955.

It is ironic that the President's surrender of executive power in this case is one that Congress, normally eager for whatever it can get, would just as soon not have received. For although the President seemed to be taking Congress into partnership in the making of foreign policy, the really important thing he was after was its approval of a particular piece of military strategy. He wanted Congress to approve the Seventh Fleet's participation in the evacuation of the Tachens; he wanted it to join with him in making the threat to break up troop and aircraft concentrations on the mainland; and he wanted it to underwrite his scheme for containing Chiang Kai-shek on Formosa and the Pescadores. (This last was not part of the resolution, but it was implied in the section calling for a cease-fire to be negotiated by the United Nations.) While Congress has always treasured its right to conduct post-mortems over military decisions and to raise general hell over military blunders, it has never revealed any wish to be an accessory before the fact. It has—since the Civil War, at any rate—been altogether content to have the chain of military command come to an end at the White House, and there is no doubt that if there had been any quiet and passably ethical way of rejecting the President's generous offer of a share in the determination of strategy in the Formosa Strait and the East China Sea, Congress would have made a grab at it. But once the President had told the country what he planned to ask of Congress, there was no way out. Congress has now been made a party to strategic decisions, and this, too, is a precedent that many people here expect will reverberate down through the years.

The Mutual Defense Treaty also broke new ground. Though the majority of observers, like the majority of senators, felt that more could be said for it than against it, there was widespread agreement with Senator Morse's view that it is a most peculiar document and one that we may very well live to regret ever having negotiated. During the floor debate, the proponents of ratification made no reply to Senator Morse's contention that what was under discussion was not really a treaty at all. "I do not believe the document before us meets the legal tests of a treaty," he said. "It is not a treaty with a sovereign power." In law, as he pointed out, a treaty is defined as a compact between two or more sovereign and independent nations. The Chinese signatories to this agreement represent no sovereignty whatever; they have no title to Formosa, which was wrested from Japan, after fifty years of possession, by the United States and now has the status, if it can be called that, of a *de-facto* American protectorate whose fate will some day be decided by the United Nations. The Nationalists are merely guests there. Chiang Kai-shek has scarcely any better claim to the island than General de Gaulle had to the United Kingdom when he was using it as a base of operations during the war. Mr. Dulles affirmed that this was also the State Department's view of the matter, and the Senate Foreign Relations Committee was so alarmed by the prospect of the Nationalist rulers' acquiring illusions of sovereignty from the treaty that in its report it incorporated the statement "It is the understanding of the Senate that nothing in the present treaty shall be construed as affecting or modifying the legal status or sovereignty of the territories referred to in Article VI." Article VI provides that "the terms 'territorial' and 'territories' shall mean in respect of the Republic of China, Taiwan [Formosa] and the Pescadores." Formosa and the Pescadores are geographical realities, but in the American understanding they are no part of the Republic of China, which is not a place but an idea. The Republic of China does not mean the Chinese mainland; one of the main purposes of the treaty is to prevent the Nationalist armies from touching off a war by attempting to return to the mainland. It is true that the Senate Foreign Relations Committee's expression of "the understanding of the Senate" is not part of the treaty proper— as many people feel it should have been—and thus may have no legal meaning. It is also true that the Nationalists are arguing that a resumption of the Chinese civil war on the mainland would not be a use of force "inconsistent with the purposes of the United Nations." Nevertheless, the American point of view, as expressed by both the Secretary of State and the Senate Foreign Relations Committee, is that the Nationalists have no title to Formosa, where they reside, and no business attempting to force a restoration of their authority in the mainland. In fact, the only territories to which no one here disputes their legal claim are the offshore islands like the Tachens, which we have urged them to evacuate.

"How can you sign a treaty with a government without recognizing that it has a habitation as well as a name?" Herbert Elliston, a distinguished critic of American diplomacy, wrote in the Washington *Post & Times-Herald* the other day. No one has dealt with this question. (In fact, the advocates of the treaty left almost all questions unanswered—doubtless because they knew from the start that they had the votes. The debate, especially on the administration side, was not on an elevated plane; a fair sample of what passed for argument and fact was the suggestion made at one point by Senator Goldwater, of Arizona, that "we might start with a consideration of the massive land-attack theory of Genghis Khan and its subsequent improvement by Alexander the Great.") The answer to Mr. Elliston's question seems to be that we have entered not into a treaty, which the Supreme Court has held to be "primarily a compact between independent nations," but into a military alliance of the sort that has sometimes been made by this nation and other Western nations with nomadic chieftains. Whatever we have entered into, most people believe that, with things what they are at the moment, the alliance is to our advantage, and that, far from increasing the chances of war in the period directly ahead (as Senator Morse contends), it will decrease them. Not very many found it possible to disagree with Mr. Dulles's statement that "failure to conclude this treaty would have the gravest consequences." But some of the consequences of concluding it also seem grave. Chiang Kai-shek regards the agreement as a recognition of his authority on Formosa and the Pescadores. His state of mind does not alter the realities, but the majority of people here think that his reading of this particular document is an entirely legitimate one, and that if the issue were to be tested in international law, the language of the agreement would be said to uphold his point of view more strongly than that of the Senate. And the importance of this, as was pointed out in the memorandum prepared by Benjamin Cohen, former counsellor of the State Department, and circulated without endorsement by the Democratic National Committee, is that whatever strengthens Chiang's case necessarily strengthens that of the Communists. If Formosa is legally part of the Republic of China, and if the Republic is legally superseded by the People's Republic, then Formosa is legally part of the People's Republic. If the defense of Formosa is a defense of Chinese territory, then an attack on Formosa by the Communists would not, as the Cohen memorandum puts it, be "international aggression on their part but civil war, in which the right and purpose of other nations forcibly to intervene would be open to serious doubt and question." The memorandum adds, "What we recognize as territories of Chiang's China other countries, including our allies [who] recognize Mao's China, may feel compelled to recognize as territories of Mao's China."

There is another bit of distasteful logic that follows from the alliance. The State Department has signed what most people concede to be an advantageous contract with Chiang Kai-shek, the one Nationalist leader in whom the department has confidence. Chiang, however, is sixty-eight years old and not in the best of health. It is expected that when he dies, the struggle for the succession will be as intense and as difficult to interpret as the struggle now going on in the Soviet Union. It is more than likely that the United States will not wish to be bound as closely to the victor or victors in that conflict as it has been bound to Chiang, and this is unquestionably the reason the State Department wrote into the agreement a provision, in some ways insulting, that makes the document subject to termination on a year's notice. (Twenty years is the normal period for which we obligate ourselves by treaty.) The Chinese signatories are surely not unaware of the apprehensions that caused us to insist on the provision, but they would be derelict in their duty if they did not claim that despite the provision we are morally bound to defend not only Chiang Kai-shek but his heirs and successors in the government he now heads. It is, indeed, their duty to recall and emphasize the high-flown sentiments of the treaty preamble, which speaks of the "mutual pride" in "the relationship which brought [these] two peoples together in a common bond of sympathy," and to ask where the United States acquired the right to negotiate an understanding with a single leader or faction. Mr. Elliston, in his comment on the lack of clarity in respect to the status of Formosa and the Pescadores, quoted the British historian A. J. P. Taylor, who recently observed that "diplomacy is an art which, despite its subtlety, depends on the rigid accuracy of all who practice it." Of the treaty as a whole, Mr. Elliston wrote that it "comes perilously close to the disingenuous. It is wrong in every sense of the word if the parties to a transaction are not at one over the meaning of it."

32 The Bone Shortage

Letter from Washington
March 17, 1955

The tax battle is over, and the Democrats have lost. Their scheme to let every taxpayer compute his obligation to the Republican government and then whack off twenty dollars, courtesy of the Democrats, and ten more for each dependent, courtesy of the same party, was rejected by the Senate, 50-44, with five Democrats, all from the South, joining forty-five Republicans and one Republican, from North Dakota, joining forty-three Democrats. Defeat, of course, was certain from the start. If the Democrats' bill won the Senate floor, it would have been killed by a stroke of the President's pen. The President goes along on this matter with George Humphrey, who said the plan was "silly" and a "quickie gimmick."

The impression is widespread that the loss does not sadden the Democrats much. Some of them, no doubt, were convinced that the economy needed the extra consumer purchasing power that would have been released by the cut, but the idea of tax relief in 1955 was always a political one, and the experienced politicians who favored it made no effort to conceal this fact. "You think the eggs are fertile and hope that a full nest of chickens will be hatched," Alben Barkley observed, apropos of politics, in the course of the debate. From the Barkley point of view, defeat is often more rewarding than victory. (In his earlier career in the Senate, Mr. Barkley reached the pinnacle of his fame when he resigned as majority leader because President Roosevelt vetoed a tax bill.) For one thing, the voters have an unfortunate way of forgetting all about the benefits they have received. Close students of the American mind assert that a man buying a new suit of clothes with money that might have been taken for taxes thinks of the money as a sum he himself earned by work—rather than as a sum that under other circumstances might have been used to defray part of the national debt. Moreover, those voters who do feel that they owe politicians a debt of gratitude are as likely as not to pay it off to the wrong ones. It is a stubborn fact of political life that voters tend to associate all good things with the party in executive power, even when the good things have been won against that party's opposition. Thus, while the administration very much wished to be able to help the French at Dienbienphu a year ago and was restrained largely by the disapproval of the British, the continuing popularity of the President is said to rest largely on the voters' gratitude for his having avoided that war. If the plan for a twenty-dollar cut for every taxpayer had gone through, the chances are that it would have done the Republicans as much good as the Democrats. At election time, a few citizens would have remembered, dimly, the alignment of forces in the dispute and would have simply recalled that at one point while Eisenhower was President someone in Congress did something about cutting taxes. Chalk one up, then, for Eisenhower.

But a tax cut that *didn't* come to pass—that has possibilities as an issue. It is somewhat easier to arouse a voter with a tale of twenty dollars stolen from him by one group of politicians than to persuade him that he has been given twenty dollars by another group. From the appearance of things here now, the Democrats plan to spend a large part of the next year and a half reminding the voters of the missing twenty dollars. One may assume that they realize this is not the perfect issue, for with things as they are these days a double-sawbuck really isn't a great amount of money; even those in the lower brackets can lose that much on a game of chance or a piece of unworthy horse flesh without feeling that disaster has struck; twenty is the price of a night on the town or a good Sunday dinner out for the family, figuring in gas and oil and tips and a drink or two. Nevertheless, the Democrats can be counted upon to keep talking about it because there isn't a great deal else that they want to talk about. The principal fact to emerge from two months of the Eighty-fourth Congress is that, apart from taxes, there is nothing of a controversial nature the Democrats wish to discuss. Washington, which the President feared would take on a Donnybrook atmosphere if the executive and legislative branches were controlled by different parties, has suffered since the beginning of this year from an unprecedented shortage of bones of contention. Of the battles that were said to impend when control of Congress changed hands last year, not one, aside from the battle over taxes, has been joined. Though the Democrats were, almost to a man, uneasy about the Asia policies set forth in the resolution on the defense of Formosa and in the treaty with the Nationalists, they supported the policies almost to a man. They have some well-known misgivings about many other administration policies, but up to now little has been heard of them. Nor have they chosen to take the offensive on any of the issues they regard as their own and used in the campaign. The promised investigation of the Dixon-Yates contract and of trusts and monopolies in general has failed to materialize. No one expects that it ever will materialize. Sidney M. Davis, the brilliant young anti-trust lawyer who, as a Senate Judiciary Committee attorney, exposed the Dixon-Yates affair in the Republican Eighty-third Congress, has been getting nowhere in his efforts to persuade the committee under Senator Harley Kilgore of West Virginia to move ahead with its investigations. The inquiry into the employee-security program has likewise failed to come to anything, even though the Democrats swore to avenge the traduced memory of the Roosevelt and Truman administrations and to undo the injustices they claimed government employees had suffered under Republican rule. A subcommittee of the Government Operations Committee has indeed been investigating the program (and the Post Office and Civil Service Committee has been awarded a hundred and twenty-five thousand dollars for another study), but those who have been steadily in attendance at the hearings of the Government Operations subcommittee have reported that when it is not serving as a forum for Department of Justice lawyers, it occupies itself with making molehills out of molehills. One day last week, for example, it devoted the better part of a session to a close examination of the possibility that young men are evading military service by swearing they are subversives, and ipso facto disloyal, when in fact they are just as loyal as anyone else. Defense Department officials insisted that, to the best of their intimate knowledge, nothing of the sort was happening, and they thought it unlikely in the extreme that anything of the sort would happen frequently enough to constitute a problem worthy of the attention of Congress. But Senator Humphrey of Minnesota and Senator Symington of Missouri were nevertheless deeply concerned, and they pressed the investigation hard. So far this oblique approach to the security program is the only one that has been made. "The whole trouble with investigating the security program is that the American people think of security as something pretty good," one Democratic leader has explained.

"They get the notion that if you criticize it you're against it, and the other fellow is for it. That's bad." A similar or at least a related line of reasoning has kept the Democratic majority from saying or doing very much of anything. It may be that later in the session they will launch the promised attack on the cut of a third of a million men from the ground forces, for in this case they may feel that they can exploit the popular conviction that defending the country is a pretty good idea, and make it appear that the Republican minority opposes this worthy principle. But even this is not certain; the Democratic charge that the Republicans are playing politics with national defense may well be held over a year, so that it can be used to maximum advantage in the 1956 campaign.

So far, anyway, this has been a thunderously dull session. There have been a few interesting and enlightening moments in the stock-market hearings, and it is conceivable that there have been some stimulating exchanges in the discussions of the brucellosis program, in the hearings on the nomination of John A. Hall as Director of Locomotive Inspection for the Interstate Commerce Commission, and in the inquiry into the future of beekeeping research, but by and large there has been less conflict and controversy in the Eighty-fourth Congress than in any other congress since the war. The only time any of the hearings have come to life was when a ghost walked in. The ghost is the junior senator from Wisconsin, who has stirred up some old memories now that the case of Dr. Irving Peress is being investigated again, and who one day last week made a sentimental journey that took him, according to a top-secret F.B.I. report, into every Senate hearing room where there were photographers of any kind. He would stroll in—pockets still bulging with papers, and briefcase still firmly clutched—and take up a position in the field covered by the cameras. A certain tension —nothing like the one he used to cause but discernible nonetheless—was felt wherever he showed up, but it broke as soon as he left, which was generally after five or six minutes, and was replaced by the ennui that seems to have become the prevailing mood on Capitol Hill. No one has spoken out flatly in favor of a Joe Must Come movement, but if things go on this way such a cause might well get considerable support.

There is no great mystery about what it is that keeps the Democrats from providing any excitement of their own. It is Dr. George Gallup's report that President Eisenhower enjoys the approval of a cool seventy-one percent of the American people. (Not all those who approve of Eisenhower would vote for him, if the poll is to be believed. Confronted with a choice between Eisenhower and Adlai Stevenson, those whose views were sampled give fifty-nine percent of the vote to the President. Against Senator Kefauver, he had sixty-four percent.) These figures, taken in conjunction with the now almost universal opinion that the President will run for re-election whether or not it is his personal wish to do so, have caused a state of near panic among the Democrats—as well they might, in view of the fact that never before, to the best of anyone's knowledge, has any President enjoyed so much esteem two-thirds of the way through a term. The Democrats attribute it to the circumstance that the press, being Republican by a heavy preponderance, has failed to call attention to any of the weaknesses of the administration. But, as a few of the Democratic leaders are willing to acknowledge, there is something of a cause-and-effect relationship between their own unwillingness to make so much as a pass at the dragon and the alleged oversights of the newspapers. If the Democrats—particularly those in the Senate—were to launch their own attack on the administration, the press would have to take notice of it, and there would then be at least some approximation of a balance between praise and criticism. In other words, the Democrats have it largely within their own power to redress the injustices they profess to be grieved by. They may get around to doing something about the situation at a later date, but right now they seem to be paralyzed by the fear that the President's popularity would survive their assaults and that the net result would be merely a diminishing of their own popularity. And some of the Democrats are restrained from mounting an offensive by their recollection of the fact that they themselves ran as Eisenhower candidates last autumn, and owe their success, as they see it, to the pledges they gave to support the President.

A good deal could happen, of course, in what remains of the session. At this stage of any new Congress, things are likely to be fairly quiet. But they are seldom as deadly as they have been these past two months, and the feeling right now is that there isn't going to be much change for quite a while. This may have its advantages for the Democrats in Congress, but it is rapidly depreciating the value of the Democratic nomination for the presidency next year. Unless something happens soon, that will be a prize no politician in his right mind will accept.

33 Getting off the Hook

Letter from Washington
March 19, 1955

There has been considerable bewilderment here over the eagerness of both the President and Mr. Dulles to get it on the record that we will use atomic artillery and cannon in the event of war. All they are saying, as far as anyone in Washington can make out, is that we possess tactical weapons incorporating atomic energy, that these are an improvement over tactical weapons of the past, and that if we have any need for them, we will use them. This scarcely seems worth pointing out to the American public, which takes it for granted that we would use weapons of an appropriate size and design if we had to use any weapons at all, and there is certainly nothing to be gained by drawing it again and again to the attention of the Chinese, who not only know perfectly well that we have up-to-date equipment but have been telling the world that we plan to subdue all of Asia with it. It has been suggested that the administration is determined to give the lie to Peiping's characterization of us as a "paper tiger"—the reverse side of its portrait of us as a nation of butchers. This seems implausible, too, since the administration knows that Peiping doesn't really think of us as a paper tiger—though, as someone has pointed out, it may be rapidly coming to the conclusion that we are a talking tiger. The likeliest explanation offered here for the President's discourse on atomic weapons at his news conference yesterday is that he was on the lookout for an opportunity to back up his Secretary of State. There has been much speculation lately to the effect that they do not see eye to eye on the Formosa crisis, and it increased, rather than abated, when Mr. Dulles told the press last week that he "wouldn't think there is any basis" for reports of a difference of opinion between the White House and the State Department. The press took this merely as an authoritative statement of what Mr. Dulles wouldn't think, and went right on publishing reports that the Secretary favored a more militant approach to Peiping and the President a more circumspect one.

If the President was indeed hoping to scotch talk of this sort, he has not yet succeeded in doing so. It is still the common opinion here that he stands almost alone in his administration as an advocate of restraint in language and commitments, and it is still the common opinion that when policy is made, and not just talked about, the President is quite firmly in command of the situation. At Mr. Dulles's news conference on Tuesday, his first since he returned from the Far East, he expressed his "foreboding"—which most of those present interpreted as his firm conviction—that nothing but "superior resistance" would stop the advance of the Chinese Communists. But then he went on to suggest that any advance they might make on Quemoy and the Matsus would not meet with resistance—from us, at any rate—if they gave us their assurances of future good behavior as they made it. It had been realized for some time that the administration was searching for a way to get off the hook on Quemoy and the Matsus, but it had not been thought—and certainly it had not been suggested by Mr. Dulles—that we would ever accept a mere assertion of good intentions on the part of Peiping as sufficient to this end. Yet Mr. Dulles said there was no reason we should not do just that, and he went on to say there was even some doubt as to whether the President would have the right to order the defense of those islands if an assault on them were accompanied by a Communist renunciation of plans to take Formosa and the Pescadores by force. He explained that under Public Law Four—the resolution that deals with American participation in the defense of Formosa—we could take action on certain unnamed areas described as "related" to the defense of Formosa, but that if the Communists put Quemoy and the Matsus in a non-related position by declaring they had no intention of going beyond them, the United States would then be trespassing and aggressing in any attempt to hold them. Would this be the case, he was asked, even if Peiping went on asserting a legal claim to Formosa? Mr. Dulles said that it would, provided we chose to accept Peiping's assurances about the use of force. It seemed a bit of casuistry that Mr. Dulles, who has often expressed his private opinion that we cannot afford to allow the Communists another square inch of free-world territory, must have had a hard time accepting; after all, the President's power to defend Formosa does not rest on the hastily composed resolution that Congress passed in January. As President of the United States, he has the right to take whatever action he deems necessary in any area he judges to be related to defense of this country, regardless of whether it is related to the defense of Formosa or anything else.

But Mr. Dulles, in his role as spokesman for the President, was clearly stating administration policy, and his words must be taken at their face value, at least until the next news conference.

34 The Peace Plugger

April 1, 1955

The President last week appointed Harold E. Stassen to a newly created job of Cabinet rank that the newspapers are describing variously as Disarmament Director, Secretary of Peace, and Special Assistant to the President "with responsibility for reporting on developments in the fields of armament and disarmament." It is Mr. Eisenhower's hope, we learn from a White House statement, that Mr. Stassen will "develop, on behalf of the President and the State Department, the broad studies, investigations, and conclusions which, when concurred in by the National Security Council and approved by the President, will become basic policy toward the question of disarmament."

The action symbolizes much that is good, bad, and indifferent about the Eisenhower administration. On the moral level, it is, of course, praiseworthy. It is even, in a way, bold, original, imaginative. We who have pioneered in so many fields can now post a claim to being the first nation on earth to have a peace ministry, an anti-war department, a twenty-thousand-dollar-a-year executive working at high pressure to get rid of the guns and bombs we have labored so mightily to produce. (The day after the announcement, though, the New York *Times* carried a reassuring story headed "Military Hopeful of Arms Build-Up.") No more will we Americans have to suffer in silence while Molotov, Mao, and Krishna Menon berate us for not loving peace enough. Which of their governments has a bureau that does nothing but search around for ways of abolishing war?

It is said that Mr. Stassen's job was the President's idea from the start. Maybe it was, but there is something about it that makes one suspect that the public-relations men, members of a profession that enjoys high standing with administration leaders, have been at work. The fact that the scheme is administrative nonsense encourages this suspicion. Peace plans and disarmament proposals should be the business of the Secretary of State. Peace is a function of diplomacy; diplomacy is a function of peace. Mr. Dulles has not been heard to comment on Mr. Stassen's new office, but it is perfectly safe to assume that he is not overjoyed by this development. For as long as Mr. Stassen has been head of the Foreign Operations Administration, he has been getting in Mr. Dulles's hair. Foreign aid should have been a function of diplomacy, too, but diplomats were in bad repute when the Marshall Plan was set up, and the Congress didn't want to entrust all that money to dubious characters from the State Department. As a consequence, the diplomats and the foreign-aid dispensers have suffered from a lack of liaison and coordination and have often worked and talked at cross-purposes. In recent weeks, for example, Mr. Dulles has been traveling through the Far East telling the leaders there that there is no excuse for their shilly-shallying in the face of the Communist threat, and Mr. Stassen, going over the same route, has been sympathizing deeply with the same leaders and saying that not much can be expected of them until they have more calories in their diet, more hydro-electric projects, more literacy, and so forth. Now matters will surely be worse. Mr. Dulles will be threatening war, and Mr. Stassen will be threatening peace, and neither, naturally, will be happy about what the other is saying.

It is perhaps the President's wish that Mr. Stassen and Mr. Dulles should embarrass one another—and particularly that Mr. Stassen should embarrass Mr. Dulles. The President is not a devious man, and there is no doubt that having a peace department, whether it was his idea or that of some advertising genius turned psychological warrior, appealed to him on its merits. (Incidentally, the idea is in a sense a triumph of the pacifist urge that was so strong between the two world wars. Those of us who went to school in that period remember well the idealistic civics teacher who was always saying, "We have a War Department. Wouldn't it be a splendid thing, boys and girls, if we had a Peace Department, too?") But an additional appeal of the project may well have been the opportunity it afforded to offset Mr. Dulles with Mr. Stassen. For Mr. Stassen's way of getting in Mr. Dulles's hair is as nothing compared to Mr. Dulles's way of getting in President Eisenhower's hair. Though the Secretary of State has changed his tune a good many times since 1952, when he wrote the Republican platform and in it promised the liberation of the satellite countries and just about everything short of the establishment of a town-meeting democracy in the Soviet Union, his pronouncements still do not come even close to the President's in terms of restraint and circumspection. If one tries to catch the rhythm of events in Washington, one observes that the periods in which our foreign policy, as it is laid down from on high, appears to reach the maximum of flexibility and sobriety are those periods when Mr. Dulles is out of the country and making the rounds of the chancelleries. Then it is the President who speaks and who gives a powerful sense of being profoundly aware not only of the danger of Communist expansion but of the danger of war. After these interludes, Mr. Dulles flies in for a few days, delivers a couple of dour Calvinist forecasts of doom and retribution, then heads back out to Bangkok or Rio or wherever.

It is believed in Washington that the President, who must retain considerable admiration for his Secretary of State, winces each time he is notified that Mr. Dulles is about to touch down at National Airport. He knows that there will be statements and speeches that will not in any sense contradict his own in substance but will place the emphasis where he has thought it unwise to place it. If the President is stressing his horror at the thought of an atomic war and his eagerness both to avert such a catastrophe and to prevent further Communist expansion, Mr. Dulles can be counted upon to bumble into town and say that if

there should be a war, it will be found that we have all manner
of atomic weapons and of course will use them if the defense of
the national interest seems to require it. If the President is trying
to let bygones be bygones and get along with the Democratic
majority in Congress, it is almost inevitable that Mr. Dulles will
choose the moment as an appropriate one for the release of the
Yalta papers. Mr. Dulles is something less than a master of good
timing.

In contrast to Mr. Dulles, Mr. Stassen, a practicing politician
since early youth, is never caught lagging behind the President
in any respect. It might be argued that he is not as straightfor-
ward or as tough-minded as Mr. Dulles, but if that is true it is
beside the point. Mr. Stassen listens attentively to what the
leader says and catches both the spirit and the letter of it. This
doubtless explains why he was chosen for the new job, and
it may explain why the job itself was created.

But it does not explain everything. For the fact is that quite
apart from how the President may feel about Mr. Dulles and Mr.
Stassen, the whole trend of American policy these days is away
from the point of view that characterized the early days of the
Eisenhower administration. Though the President's language
has never been as militant as that of Mr. Dulles, both of them
used to criticize their predecessors for a lack of militancy and
both were, in the jargon of the day, "liberationists." Every week
now brings some development that carries the administration a
step or two further from its original policy, and it is not unreasonable to say that it has long since been a good deal less militant—in practice if not in preachment—than the Truman administration. The world does not seem aware of this, the American people are manifestly unaware of it, and it may be that the
administration itself is uncertain about the direction in which it
has been headed. Yet any close inspection of policy makes the
matter plain enough. The administration wants coexistence and
has taken on Harold Stassen to talk it up.

35 Looking to Geneva

Letter from Washington
July 7, 1955

It is repeatedly being said here that no president of the United States, and perhaps no head of any democratic government in history, has ever undertaken negotiations with greater personal authority than President Eisenhower will have when he leaves for Geneva next week. In the Senate, the Democratic majority is behind him to a man. On the Republican side, he has new and valuable allies in Senators Knowland and Bridges. Only a few weeks ago, both these important leaders were saying that no meeting with the Russians should be held. Now they are all for the meeting, and Senator Knowland has said that he has "great confidence" in the President as a guardian of the national interest. No significant body of public opinion at present opposes the President's leadership in foreign affairs. The Gallup Poll finds only sixteen per cent of the people expressing dissatisfaction of any sort with the Eisenhower administration, and the causes of this trifling amount of discontent are thought to be almost wholly domestic. Senator McCarthy's following appears to have taken to the hills. A survey of the mail of senators who voted against McCarthy's recent efforts to torpedo the conference reveals that a mere ten communications from McCarthy supporters has been average, or slightly better than average. It is a decade at least since there has been anything approaching the present degree of national unity; it has been asserted here that neither Franklin Roosevelt during the war nor Harry Truman back in the days when every American was a Truman rooter had the kind of support that President Eisenhower has now. Whether this is so or not, the President is—for the time being, anyway—as free as a bird. At Geneva he can take any course that appears to him to be sensible. He can raise or lower the price of American consent to a settlement according to his own best judgment of what the price ought to be. All the power and prestige of the United States will be at his disposal, and although he must act in the knowledge that there will be a political reckoning late next year, he can be confident that anything he does at Geneva will now be accepted by the people and, if it should come to that, ratified by the Senate.

Broadly speaking, there are three views here of how successful the President can hope to be in the exercise of his extraordinary authority. One is the view of Mr. Dulles and of a good many diplomatic and military technicians, which is that no substantial benefits are to be gained at Geneva. Mr. Dulles is a righteous, godly man, and he is repelled by the thought of striking bargains with men as steeped in sin as the Russian leaders are. Certain of his State Department aides and a number of people in the Defense Department share his feelings about the conference without necessarily sharing the Calvinist foundations on which these are based. They believe, a good many of them, that no totalitarian society can afford to acquiesce in the easing of tensions. Mr. Dulles agreed to the Geneva meeting and persuaded the President to agree to it not because he thought any good would come of it but because he knew there would be resentment if the United States refused to participate. For quite a while, the President followed the Secretary's lead and spoke as if he thought Geneva could be useful only as an object lesson for deluded optimists. During the past couple of weeks, however, the President has been the self-appointed leader of the optimists. "I am trying not to expect too much," he told his news conference last week, and went on to make it clear that he is actually expecting a good deal, though not so much from Geneva itself as from a train of events he hopes Geneva will set in motion. "I personally believe from what I have learned in San Francisco and through my talks that the chances [for a settlement] are better than I thought they were two months ago," he said. What the President learned in San Francisco cannot have been very much more than what other people learned from the newspaper accounts of the United Nations festivities there, which was that Mr. Molotov was exploring the possibilities of conviviality and was insisting again that the Soviet position on disarmament is no great distance from the Western position. The President did not specify what he learned from, or even what he meant by, his "talks," but the general impression here is that he was saying that the sanguineness he is trying not to overdo rests in part on the reports he has been getting on the Soviet Union from his Intelligence services.

The burden of these reports is anything but a secret. On the contrary, the White House has been going to some lengths to acquaint people with its latest evaluations of Russian attitudes and behavior. It says it is now persuaded that the Kremlin has excellent reasons of its own for wishing a *détente* in the cold war, and that Russian statements on the reduction of armaments and the unification of Germany are to be taken pretty much at face value. In what appears to be a fairly risky procedure, embarked upon for currently unfathomable purposes, spokesmen for the President have been saying that Mr. Eisenhower will go to Geneva not to test the sincerity of the Russians—which was one way of putting the official attitude a month or so back—but to act on the assumption that in this and subsequent meetings an orderly pattern of peaceful coexistence can be established. It is rather an odd thing to hear people here discussing detailed systems of disarmament not as theoretical exercises or propaganda gambits but as programs that are well within the realm of the possible. It is also odd to hear American diplomats discussing free elections in a unified Germany not as something the Russians will fight to the death but as something they are quite likely to agree to if the proper approach is made and if some way can be found to establish for the new Germany an eastern border acceptable to Germans, Poles, Russians, and the North Atlantic

Treaty Organization. Yet such discussions are commonplace here now, and there is even serious talk by officials of the Republican administration of our joining with the Soviet Union in some sort of European security alliance in the event that progress is made on disarmament and German unification.

In his news conference yesterday, the President said that nothing was further from his mind than the thought that the Russians are negotiating from weakness. This, like similar statements by other Western leaders in the last few days, was an effort to reassure Mr. Khrushchev that we are not contemptuous of Russian power. Indeed we are not, but there has been a certain amount of disingenuousness in the Western pronouncements on this matter. It is believed here and in every European capital that the Soviet Union is having a severe crisis in agriculture. (Barely a month ago, Mr. Dulles told the House Appropriations Committee that the Soviet economy "is on the point of collapsing.") The main authority cited in support of this belief is Mr. Khrushchev himself, who in the past two years has delivered a series of speeches that paint quite a dark picture of Soviet agriculture and a not too glowing one of the Soviet consumer industry. Yet in another sense the President was striking a note of real candor when he disclaimed the suggestion that we regard the Soviet Union as weak. To many people here—the President almost certainly included—who argue quite earnestly for the optimistic view of Geneva, it is Russian strength as much as Russian weakness that makes the outlook hopeful. Strength and weakness are, of course, closely related; Russia's military power is one of the basic causes of its trouble with the rest of its economy. But it is the military power, in the opinion of a large number of observers, that makes the present situation favorable to us. They feel that if the Russians had not succeeded in their effort to catch up with the West in the development of nuclear weapons and long-range bombers, the prospects for a settlement would be much poorer. This is a fine piece of irony, since it has for many years been the basic premise of American policy that the West could arrive at

a settlement with the Communist world only when it could negotiate from "situations of strength" that the Communists would
recognize and respect. This premise has not been abandoned; no
one here is selling short the importance of Western power. But a
new premise has been added, for underlying the new American
line there is now a tacit assumption that the Western powers can
be the beneficiaries of the Soviet "situation of strength." Recent
Russian advances in the fancier types of explosives and the
fancier types of aircraft have, it is thought, relieved the Bolshevik
leaders of their sense of inferiority and have at the same time
demonstrated to them the awful cost of modern armaments. (It
has been estimated that in terms of the drain on the civilian
economy, an atomic-weapons program costs the Russians seven
or eight times what it costs us; even this, it is often pointed out,
does not measure the true difference, for its happens that such
programs stimulate our economy to new levels of consumption,
while in Russia their effect on both production and consumption
is necessarily depressive.) The Russians have now proved to
themselves that in the strictly technological sense they can do
anything we can do, and in the course of proving this they have
learned what a staggering job it is. With their anxieties lifted,
their common sense has a chance to function, not only in reckoning costs but in understanding that there will be no victors and
probably no survivors in the kind of war they have made themselves capable of fighting. When the prospect arises of the simul-
taneous death of capitalism and Communism, it is prudent for
Communists to be concerned for the survival of capitalist civiliation. And when the prospect arises of a strangulation of the
Communist economy by the mere effort to maintain the ability to
destroy all kinds of civiliation, it is prudent for Communists to
talk turkey on disarmament.

In general, this is the line of reasoning followed by those who
feel that, as the Washington *Post & Times-Herald* recently put it,
"there will exist at Geneva a major opportunity for great and
hostile nations to establish a way of living together in the nuclear

age." It is said by persons intimate with the President to be the view he is now taking, and all his recent public statements would appear to confirm this. Between his new-found optimism and Secretary Dulles's continuing pessimism, there is still another point of view. Its adherents do not challenge the analysis of Russian attitudes accepted by the optimists, but they are skeptical about the chances of ending or arresting the cold war by means of contractual arrangements with the Russians when it comes to armaments control and Germany. It is not, they think, a question of who is in earnest about peace and who is not but of the limited possibilities of solution inherent in the problems that everyone would like to see solved. It is a fact that the Communist leaders have lately been making large concessions to our point of view, and they may be prepared to make further ones. We for our part may be ready to yield a certain amount of ground. But the question raised here, and most specifically in regard to disarmament, is not whether the gap between the Communist and the Western proposals can be closed but whether any system at all is workable and enforceable. In the field of nuclear weapons, the opinion of many experts is that both sides have already gone too far for anything approaching foolproof control to be practicable, and that the world must now live through an indefinite period with the possibility of atomic destruction ever present, in the way that communities have lived with the ever present possibility of destruction by fire, disease, and similar catastrophies. To be sure, even in the absence of enforceable controls on nuclear weapons there might be a more or less enforceable system for the control of mobilized forces (whether at any given time it was in fact more enforceable or less enforceable would depend on the status of the United Nations Security Council or whatever supranational agency was in charge), and some reasonably effective "early-warning" system might now be possible. But these would in no sense be substitutes for atomic control, and they would not have much meaning without it. On German unification, the technical obstacles are less formidable, and it would appear that political obstacles from the Communist side are becoming fewer in number every week. Nevertheless, there are many people here who, without sharing Secretary Dulles's misgivings about negotiating with the Russians, are as doubtful as he is that when the chips are down the Russians will be able to bring upon themselves the shattering loss of prestige, to say nothing of the loss of millions of exploitable human beings, that would follow the sacrifice of the East German government.

By no means all those who have little hope of formal and specific settlements of large questions at Geneva, or even at post-Geneva conferences, are of the opinion that nothing will be accomplished at the Palais des Nations week after next. Obviously, it is in the interest of all parties to bring forth something concrete. There is very likely to be some specific agreement on the question of East-West trade, and there could be all sorts of understandings on some of the small issues that are fully as provocative as the larger ones—prisoners of war, for example, and border incidents and civilian travel. Beyond that, there can be an expression, in writing or otherwise, of a common determination to avoid resorting to war. Most people here take the view that the conference itself is bound to be such an expression and that nothing that may come out of it can be half so important as the decision to hold it at all. There is no form of armaments control, they think, that can be as effective as the determination by responsible officials not to use the armaments they have. Bombs that are not exploded don't cause much harm; there can be an easing of tensions in the world by the simple assertion of a desire for tensions to be eased. And in the aftermath of the President's recent press conferences and of Mr. Khrushchev's curious Fourth of July oratory in the garden of Spaso House, a large number of people here feel that Geneva will be this kind of assertion. If anything more happens, they will be gratified but surprised.

36 Four Heads of Government

Letter from Geneva

July 27, 1955

On May 11, 1953, when Sir Winston Churchill first called for a parley "at the summit of the nations," he said that it should be held "with a measure of informality and a still greater measure of privacy and seclusion." At the time, it might reasonably have been asked where in the world today the heads of the greatest powers on earth could hope to assemble in privacy and seclusion. They could, perhaps, meet undisturbed in an airplane or a submarine for as long as the fuel held out, or they might foregather in some totalitarian country whose government would simply shut off the supply of visas, but when it comes to free-world terra firma, there is nowhere the press and the lobbyists will not follow. Sir Winston's hope, as last week's muster of the heads of the British, French, Soviet, and American governments proved, was a vain one. Fifteen hundred correspondents, give or take a couple of hundred, were here, and the lobbyists, though uncounted, were plentiful—among them Ukrainian and a dozen other kinds of Irredentists, American businessmen impatient for the rise of the Iron Curtain, agents of the German Federal Republic, Bao Daiists, Esperantists, and two celebrated gentlemen of the cloth, Pastor Martin Niemöller and the Reverend Billy Graham. Pastor Niemöller held a press conference and Pastor Graham held a revival. He said that his being in Geneva at the time of the conference was, to the best of his imperfect knowledge, an accident, though he did not discount the possibility that "La Reunion Billy" held in the Parc des Eaux-Vives the Sunday before the meetings began had been arranged by Providence. Even so, he was full of conference angles, such as calling attention to the fact that Moses had long ago had a parley at the summit, and had there received a ten-point directive that the heads of government would do well to restudy.

Still and all, if there was any value in seeking even a degree of privacy and seclusion and of attempting the relaxation of international tensions in an environment in which local tensions had long been relaxed, this city last week approximated the ideal. Geneva provided an atmosphere as unobstrusive, as neutral, and as unpolitical as any that could be imagined this side of the moon. None of her citizens interfered. Few even showed an interest. Eisenhower, Bulganin, Khrushchev, Eden, Faure— none of them could draw more than a handful of gawkers into the streets. (Billy Graham drew 35,000 worshipers, according to the press.) The Swiss government and the canton authorities provided hotel accommodations, police escorts, a few simple military ceremonies, and an official and wonderfully tidy name for the event—Conférence à Quatre—but apart from fulfilling their obligations as hosts they did very little, if anything. They could not even be persuaded to show much interest in the proceedings. Long before the conference was set up, it had been arranged that the Swiss national television network would close down for two weeks, beginning July 19, in order to give the employees their vacation. This scandalized the public-relations men of the capitalist West and the Communist East, and they coexistentially pleaded with the Swiss to reconsider. After all, they said, just about every European sensed some connection between his own fate and the events of these historic days, and the least the Swiss could do was provide enlightenment through the most enlightening of mediums. For days, the Swiss were unmoved. They had promised their television people a vacation, and it would be bad for television morale if they reneged. There would be more conferences, they said, and if these chanced to coincide with the times Swiss television was in operation, something would be done. At the very last moment, the Swiss relented and a skeleton staff broadcast a few Conference shows to the rest of Europe. The Swiss were certainly right about there being more conferences. Chinese and American diplomats will hold a Conférence à Deux here next week, to be followed in a few days by a conference of sixty-six nations, or possibly more, on atomic energy, and in October the Foreign Ministers of the four governments that met last week will reconvene to do something about the bucks that were passed to them by their bosses.

Sir Winston, in the speech that fathered last week's conference, made a number of other suggestions about the arrangements. He recommended that it "should not be overhung by a ponderous or rigid agenda." It "should be confined to the smallest number of powers and persons possible." There should be present no "hordes of experts and officials drawn up in a vast, cumbrous array." To all these suggestions, as to the one about privacy and seclusion, it might have been objected that the then Prime Minister was calling for a kind of diplomacy that has not been practiced—certainly not "at the summit"—for the better part of a century. International conferences nowadays always have rigid agendas; whether or not they are ponderous depends on who prepares them. The number of powers involved is determined by the scope and application of the problems to be dealt with. The number of persons attending is necessarily large, for the best-informed of statesmen cannot be versed in all aspects of any major and controversial question. (On his visits to the White House during the late war, Churchill himself never showed up without a planeload of staff members.) Whenever important matters are under discussion, informality—in the sense of a free and impromptu exchange of ideas—is simply impossible. Even in our negotiations with friendly powers like France and the United Kingdom, the diplomats defend prepared positions from prepared texts and resist all temptation to extemporize.

Geneva, though inspired by Sir Winston, with a delayed assist from Senator Walter George, was to all outward appearances very unlike the meeting he had described. The agenda was rigid. Indeed, the first session of the Foreign Ministers was accounted remarkable and auspicious in that it succeeded in removing all flexibility—in other words, all possibility of meandering—from the number and sequence of topics to be discussed by the heads of government. (This feat was accomplished in exactly an hour and a half, which, according to the briefing officers of all four delegations, shattered every precious record in East-West negotiations.) No precise figures on the size of the delegations were ever made available, but each was certainly big. One of the most memorable scenes of the conference was of a vast, cumbrous array of possibly a hundred and fifty Soviet experts and officials in Oxford bags massed on the apron of Cointrin Airport to celebrate the arrival of Premier Bulganin, Grazhchanin Khrushchev, and Marshal Zhukov. The Western delegations, which never massed anywhere, were probably smaller. Of course, not all the members of any delegation participated in the sessions in the council chamber of the Palais des Nations, but quite a few did. At most meetings, each of the powers was represented at the council table by eleven or twelve persons, and there were seldom fewer than thirty or thirty-five additional staff people—members either of the secretariat or of the middle echelons of the delegations—in the chamber. An attempt at informality, or the circumvention of protocol, was made at the buffet dinners that followed the meetings of the heads of government, but it was said on excellent authority that the buffet conversations—apart from the generalized assurances of good will the President spoke about in his report a couple of nights ago—were of a sustained and formidable triviality.

Yet there is a sense in which the conference almost perfectly fulfilled the purpose its original sponsor had in mind. Sir Winston proposed the meeting within a month or so of Stalin's death, and it was clear that the opportunity he saw was not for a settlement of any kind, or even for serious negotiations, but merely for an exploration of the minds of the new Soviet leaders and an assessment of the new structure of Soviet power. He thought the West would be well served by a meeting if only it could learn who and what sort of people were in charge of things in Russia, and he no doubt wished to impart to those new and diplomatically uninitiated leaders some notion of what kind of men were in charge in the West. What he wanted was simply a confrontation, and as a confrontation Geneva was, from any Western point of view, a smashing success. Despite the fixed agenda, despite the cumbrously arrayed officials, despite the swarming reporters, the week was rich in opportunities for the kind of researches Churchill wished to make. Even the events that seemed to bear in no way on the issues in dispute provided clues to the great question of the structure of Soviet power. Doubts must still be raised about the nature and permanence of the structure, but theses are possible. A thesis that commended itself to many Americans who kept an eye on Nikita Khrushchev, as Nikita Khrushchev kept a cool and constantly appraising eye on Premier Bulganin, is that the relationship between the two men was approximately the same as that between a competent and self-assured prizefight manager and a heavyweight who is good but not so surpassingly good that the manager would have to retire if he lost him.

The merest spectator in Geneva could sense something of this from the moment Plane No. 001 of the Ilyushin-14 fleet opened its door at Cointrin. Khrushchev came down the ramp directly behind his heavyweight and, taking his place in the very center of the hundred and fifty or so earlier Russian arrivals, alternately chatted with Molotov and watched Bulganin while Bulganin was reviewing the crack infantry detachment the Swiss had produced for the ceremonies and, after that, while the Premier was delivering banalities into the microphone before the press stand. Then and on every subsequent occasion Khrushchev had the air of a manager watching his man in action not because he was curious about what would happen next but only because he was curious to see how the tactics he had devised would work out in practice. Unquestionably it would not do to press this analogy very far, for Khrushchev and Bulganin are Russians and Communists, and therefore not of the world in which such relationships obtain. Still, it did look as if a certain amount of Westernization has been taking place in Soviet politics, just as it has in Soviet technology and in a number of other phases of Soviet life. Back when the Russians were our allies and it pleased us to think that our allies were really very much like us, it was sometimes said that Stalin, though indisputably a tyrant, was made of essentially the same stuff as an American party boss. The late Edward J. Flynn, the Democratic leader of the Bronx, who once went to Moscow with what he and Franklin Roosevelt imagined was a promising plan for patching things up between the Kremlin and the Vatican, maintained that Stalin put him very much in mind of Charlie Murphy, the leader of Tammany Hall at the time Flynn entered politics. His case seemed pretty far-fetched, even in 1945, and a similar line of thought applied to the present Bolshevik leaders cannot be very profitable today. The differences between commissars and county leaders are almost certainly more numerous and more important than the resemblances. Nevertheless, in the aspect of the Khrushchev-Bulganin team in Geneva there seemed to be something Americans could relate their experiences to. Khrushchev—squat, tough, loud, indelicate, and altogether self-possessed—is the boss type. At the sight of him here, glad-handing the Swiss, shoving the deferential Marshal Zhukov ahead of him, snapping pictures of quaint scenes on the road to Lausanne, it was at last possible to believe that the American reporters had not been circulating a gag when they quoted him as saying in Belgrade that he subscribed to the doctrine of "live it up." (This was the day after he had got merry on Slivovitz and ordered Soviet visas for Western correspondents who had sought them in vain for a decade.) Whatever the actual relationship between the two, Bulganin seemed to complement

Khrushchev in a way familiar in Western politics. Well turned out, in an almost aristocratic style, and with hardly a trace of the appearance of craft and cunning that characterized Bolshevik top dogs from Lenin through Malenkov, he is distinctly the front-man or candidate type. He looks like a successful Kentucky horse-breeder.

To be sure, there is no one here bold enough to reject the possibility that Russians politics will take some Byzantine turn tomorrow or the day after. But the general impression of those who met with the Communist team in the Palais and of those who met with lesser Russians elsewhere in Geneva is that while basic things have not changed, a good many unbasic ones have, and that from several of these changes the West can hope to profit. The Russians are not talking a new language, but they are employing a new rhetoric, and it is one that Western diplomats find comprehensible, if by no means attractive. In the formal conferences, according to those present, Bulganin and Molotov seldom failed to address themselves to the matters that were commonly understood to be under discussion, and they never resorted to the infuriating illogic and incantations that were so common in the Russians' diplomatic discourse while Stalin was in power. In this fact itself there seemed to be some evidence of the stability of the present arrangements in Moscow, and thus of the value of negotiating with these leaders. In their use of Western techniques of controversy, the controversialists appeared to suggest that they were not trying to relieve or to stimulate the anxieties of their own people or to make time with somebody higher up; instead, it seemed that they felt assured of their own political security and of the backing of their own public opinion, and were therefore free to say and do the things that seemed best calculated to ingratiate them with non-Russians and non-Communists. An even more impressive indication of stability was the whole unhurried quality of the Russian strategy here. Far from seeming to be in need of quick victories or of defeats that could be presented at home as proof of the enemy's malevolence, they adopted the familiar Western approach of sweeping things under the rug. The briefest, broadest generalization that can be made about Geneva is that it was for all concerned an exercise in procrastination. The leaders of the mightiest powers on earth had their meeting here and, as far as such matters as boundaries and armaments and balances of power were concerned, they left the world exactly as it had been before the meeting. To this leave-it-lay, or mañana-mañana, diplomacy the Communist imperators assented in a most unrevolutionary manner. In fact, they led the pack. Of the four heads of government, all of whom were fundamentally of the view that some other time would be better than the present to attempt the unification of Germany, only Bulganin came out bluntly with what everyone felt. "The time is not ripe for unification," he said. The time, for the Russians, was not ripe for anything; European security they adjudged to be a nice idea, but they saw no need to rush headlong into plans for writing it into treaties or pacts. Disarmament they held to be a worthy goal, but they acknowledged certain practical difficulties in the way of attaining it; the question was put aside in the hope that time might reduce the number of obstacles.

This is by no means the first occasion on which the Russians have gone along with a strategy of delay, but it is just about the first occasion on which they have done it in good spirits and have elevated passivity, as distinct from cynical compromises, to the level of Marxist-Leninist principle. In doing so, Bulganin and Khrushchev seemed to be reflecting their conviction that they will be on hand when succeeding negotiations are held. And they seemed to be convinced, as their predecessors never were, that the society they rule is not altogether dependent on the maintenance of external tensions. Khrushchev, on his way back to Moscow, assured the East Germans that "neither side wants war," and *Pravda* and *Izvestia* have been saying the same thing to Russians. This is a really stunning concession. The Bolshevik leaders have never before allowed their people to believe that the rest of the world means them no harm.

The adoption of a Western approach to conference table technique or public relations does not alter anything of real substance in the Communist world. Yet the relaxation of tensions among the masters of the Communist world was, in Geneva, observable and easily measurable. At last year's conference here on Far Eastern problems, the Russians were withdrawn, uncommunicative, and security-conscious to the extreme degree one associated with the Stalin regime. They behaved pretty much as the Russians at the United Nations in New York have always behaved. When they yielded to Western bonhomie at all, they did so under conditions they could control—generally at receptions they themselves gave. They did not frequent the Geneva cafés, they did not walk the streets except in large groups, they did not, as a rule, even patronize the bar in their own hotel—the Metropole. (It was thought significant, though perhaps it was not at all, that they settled on a hotel bearing the same name as Moscow's most famous one for their Geneva headquarters.) At last week's conference, the Russians not only sampled the cafés and enriched the owners of bars and curio shops but fraternized eagerly on every level. On what was perhaps the lowest level—at the Maison de la Presse, the headquarters for correspondents accredited to the conference—the Communists from both the U.S.S.R. and the satellites were a conspicuous collection of Good-Time Charlies. It pleased them to talk and drink and relax with Westerners, and even to accept a certain amount of needling in good humor. It pleased them also to make poor but well-intentioned coexistence jokes, such as "Let us have a coexistence cocktail—vodka and Coca-Cola." Some of the things they had to say were revealing, and some were almost startling. It was quite an experience to sit in the Café Landolt, which is directly across the square from the press building and which once counted among its steadiest customers a Russian exile named Ulyanov, alias Lenin, and hear a son of Lenin's revolution explain how very much better life has been since the death of Lenin's putative heir, Stalin. The Russian and satellite correspondents could not be induced to pass any directly unfavorable judgments on Stalin's leadership, but neither could they be persuaded to praise him, and all of them were frank to say that they had found everything at home very much more to their liking since the spring of 1953. There might or might not be a connection they would say, between Stalin's passing and the improvement of their own lot; they purported to be too far from the sources of power (though some of them were actually very close indeed) to be sure of the exact causes of the change, but there was no doubt that the change dated from somewhere around the time of Stalin's death. It seemed notable that they were willing to go this far, and encouraging that they were so ready to concede that an increase in liberties is a measure of improvement. When pressed on this subject, they did not say that they enjoyed, or even wished to enjoy, anything like complete freedom of criticism; on the contrary, their line was that such freedom was not at all a good thing, and they would revert to type with the suggestion that the prospects for coexistence would be improved if certain Western journalists could be prevented from saying beastly things about the East and raising doubts about the integrity of the Communist leaders. Still, it was an increase of freedom they were talking about when they said that life was better. One of them, for instance, made the point that in the new atmosphere he felt able, as he had not before, to write about such undeniable actualities of the world as the resilience of the American economy. In the past, he said, he had been required against his own better judgment to propound some rather foolish doctrines, but now he could be altogether serious and realistic. When it was observed that some Soviet journals—in particular, a propaganda sheet named *New Times,* which was then on sale in the Maison de la Presse—were saying some altogether ridiculous things about American life, he acknowledged this with a shrug and said that surely an American should be able to distinguish between vulgar journalism and the more discriminating sort, which he professed to represent.

Whether or not discriminating journalism has any future in the Communist world, there are at least a few Communist minds that value the idea of discrimination. There was one quite important Communist writer (despite the camaraderie, one still hesitates to name names) who seized the opportunity given him by the presence of Americans to make a number of inquiries about the work of the American sociologist David Riesman, a man most widely known for his book *The Lonely Crowd*, which is a study of the effects that the increased productivity of the American economy and the increased leisure that this productivity makes possible have had on the American character. The Communist had read Riesman's book and had been fascinated by it—not, he said, because of its application to life in the United States but because of what he maintained was its extraordinary relevance to the present conditions of life in the Soviet Union. When he was reminded that Riesman, far from offering any encouragement to the Marxist view of life and society, held it up to ridicule and made a series of diagnoses, wholly incompatible with Marxism, the writer said rather testily that this was not the point, that Riesman still interested him, and that he would be pleased if one of the Americans present would be kind enough to have a New York bookstore send him, care of his home office, a copy of *Faces in the Crowd*, which is a kind of documentation of the ideas advanced in *The Lonely Crowd*.

In the minds of the Russian and satellite journalists at the Maison de la Presse one found a weird combination of a huge store of facts and statistics on the United States and an impenetrable ignorance about the quality and meaning of American life. The journalists seemed to have committed to memory the *World Almanacs* of the last twenty-five years. They could cite dates and sequences that had long since escaped the minds of their American colleagues. They knew what was in the Republican platform of 1948 and what General MacArthur said in an interview to the Arizona *Daily Star* in 1951. And they had an immense curiosity to learn more from the Americans. Yet when one attempted to explain so simple a thing as the fact that President Eisenhower had not really "changed" his line in the last few months, that he had never at any time been in favor of leading an aggressive war against the Soviet Union, and that, furthermore, it was not to be expected that his willingness to negotiate settlements, if settlements were possible, would make him any more tolerant of the Soviet Union's relations with its satellites, one got nowhere at all. The Russians were almost certainly better armed with mere information about the United States than the Americans were about the Soviet Union. But one felt that if our ignorance of the essential truth about Soviet life matched theirs about American life, it would be a shameful and dangerous thing.

The Russians worked away at scoring with Western opinion, even to the extent of giving a flattering imitation of Western ways. The leaders of the delegation scored most notably when they flaunted their unconcern with personal security and thus provided what many Europeans thought was a striking contrast to the Americans. When President Eisenhower reached Geneva, on the Saturday before the Monday opening of the conference, the European journalists who covered his arrival were shocked, or at any rate professed to be shocked, by the rituals that accompany the movements of an American President—the circling helicopters that attended his descent from the skies and the Secret Service men who dogtrotted beside his automobile. They quickly associated all these with the worst of our fantasies and the worst of our realities. The helicopters—were they, perhaps, to guard against unfriendly *"cadets d'espace?"* The Secret Service men they readily identified as "Gee-Men" and characterized as so many aspiring McCarthys. They would doubtless have milked the spectacle for all the ridicule it was worth even if the Russians had not provided an unexpected contrast. But when, the following morning, Bulganin, Khrushchev, and Zhukov landed with no helicopters, and proceeded to their villas in the rear of an open car with no dogtrotting guards, the subject became irresistible. The inevitable conclusions were drawn, and they continued to be drawn all week as each public appearance of the President brought out the Secret Service men and as the Russians took long, circuitous drives in their unattended touring cars.

For the Americans here, it was a consolation, though admittedly a small one, to reflect on the historical ironies of the situation—one of them, of course, being that the protection afforded our presidents by the Secret Service far, far antedated McCarthy and had been a response not to any silly obsession with subversion but, rather, to a public desire to see no more leaders of the Republic die at the hands of zanies. Another irony, unremarked by the European press, was that while American presidents have ridden in open cars since the invention of the automobile, Messrs. Bulganin, Khrushchev, and Zhukov had discovered the delights of the tonneau only a few weeks earlier. This was in Belgrade, when they made their state visit to Marshal Tito. It had been their plan to drive about that city in one of their Zis limousines, equipped with the standard heavy armor plate, bulletproof glass, and blinds. A Kremlin Zis was shipped to Belgrade in advance, but Marshal Tito took the Russians by surprise and led the way to an open car. No reporters were close enough to overhear any Russian expression of trepidation. But there were several who were well enough informed to know that Marshal Tito must have been a very jumpy Communist himself that day, for it was the very first time that *he* had chanced the streets of Belgrade in a touring car.

The Russians had this small triumph at the President's expense, but it was the only such triumph they enjoyed. No other judgment on last week's events so closely approached unanimity as the judgment that Mr. Eisenhower was the leading figure of the conference and a statesman whose behavior it was impossible to disapprove of. He radiated an earnestness and a pacific intent that forced Premier Bulganin to go on record with an acknowledgment of it, and either Bulganin or another Russian official to boost him for 1956. From the outset, he struck a note so appropriate to the occasion that even a journal as anti-American and as disparaging of mere sincerity as *Le Monde,* of Paris, was moved to something close to rapture. "Eisenhower, whose personality has long been misunderstood," *Le Monde* said, "has emerged as the type of leader that humanity needs today." The President drew bouquets of this sort not by doing anything in the least uncharacteristic but simply by showing to the conferees the same amenable countenance, the same yearning for conciliation and "tranquillity" (a word he has become increasingly fond of), the same willingness to grant the other man a rectitude equal to his own that he has shown in the past to Generals de Gaulle and Montgomery, to Senators Taft, Knowland, and McCarthy, and to a great many other men in public and military life. There have been times when the results of this method have not been as edifying as some people might have hoped, but this was a time when the Eisenhower technique was exactly what was called for, and it would not be going too far to say that it was enough in itself to make the conference a success—if not on his own terms, at least on the terms originally stated by Sir Winston and generally accepted by the other Western participants. In the weeks before Geneva, it seemed that the President had become confident of achieving here the unification of Germany and a workable disarmament scheme. Other people, though, apparently hoped merely to size up the Russians and to hammer into Russian heads the simple fact that the West doesn't want war; they wished more than anything else to persuade the Russians to forget all the nonsense in the books they read and write and to understand that the last thing the capitalist world wants at this perilous stage of history is to overthrow Communist governments by force and violence. Sir Anthony Eden and M. Faure made this point time and again, and often in more forceful language than the President's, but it was the President whose assurances seemed to count—in part, no doubt, because he spoke as the commander of the great citadel of world capitalism, but in part also because the man has an absolutely unique ability to convince people that he has no talent for duplicity.

His assurances had made a huge impression even before he backed them up, on the fourth day of the conference, with his astonishing proposal for an immediate bilateral exchange of military intelligence and the rights of aerial reconnaissance with the Russians. This offer was easily the most dramatic event of the conference, and, oddly, its impact was immediately felt and appreciated by everyone here but the Americans. To a large number of them, it seemed only a gimmick, and there was a good deal of hilarity on the subject of Batten, Barton, Durstine & Osborn's intervention in world affairs. When it was revealed that the President had interpolated his proposal into the middle of a speech that in its original form contained only a suggestion to "instruct our representatives in the Subcommittee on Disarmament in discharge of their mandate from the United States to give priority effort to the study of inspection and reporting," it was pretty much taken for granted by Americans that the President had not intended to make the outright offer he made but had intended, rather, to cite an extreme example of the kind of reciprocity the United States might be willing someday to consider, provided certain other agreements had already gone into effect. (The Americans, of course, could not put out of their minds the long detours our civil aircraft must make to avoid flying over the atomic proving grounds in the Southwest, or the elaborate security checks that must be run on our own nationals before they are made privy to the facts about our installations that Mr. Eisenhower was proposing to hand over to the Russians.) Spokesmen for the President insisted, though, that every word he spoke had been carefully planned, and that he had interpolated his remarks as he did only in order to make sure that no one would learn of them in advance. At any rate, while the Americans here, including some members of the official party, were asking niggling questions—such as whether the Russians would cruise about in our planes or theirs, whether by "immediately" the President really meant "right away," and whether any thought had been given to the problems involved in according the Russians the right to inspect our bases on other people's territory, all of which were answered by the official and far from helpful statement that the President had meant just what he said —most other observers here, and evidently most observers throughout the world, were hailing the President's offer as a master stroke of diplomacy. Exactly what made it a master stroke is a question that the Americans who remain here still find it difficult to answer to their own satisfaction, but very few of them are unwilling to accept the argument that if all the world thinks it's wonderful, then wonderful it is.

All the world seems to think that the conference itself was wonderful, even though, as everyone has noted, the powers failed to get anywhere with any of the three substantive problems on the agenda: Germany, European security, and disarmament. The view that no real settlements were reached is the orthodox one, and it is supported by the final communiqué of the conference, which passed everything along to the Foreign Ministers and their October meeting. There is another available view of the matter, however, and it accords more agreeably with the generally rosy estimate of the conference. It is that, far from finding themselves at loggerheads on such prickly questions as Germany and disarmament, the powers reached, with almost breathtaking ease, quite a substantial and significant meeting of minds. On the root question of the three—Germany—their decision was to ratify by inaction the 1945 division of that country, and the fact that this agreement seemed negative in character did not make it any the less solid or meaningful. A decision to accept a status quo can be every bit as important and, in certain circumstances, as helpful as a decision to rearrange things. In this case, the decision perfectly suited everyone except the Germans. The truth is that none of the powers represented at the conference had more than an abstract and theoretical interest in early unification. And in no case did what interest they had flow from any really deep attachment to the idea of unification for its own sake or for the sake of the Germans. Both sides want Germany as an ally, which is a way of saying that both sides have a continuing fear of Germany as an enemy; that is, as an ally of the other side. Though M. Faure twice employed his Gallic eloquence on behalf of a united Germany and was perhaps the most persuasive of the Western spokesmen on this question, he represented a power that, as everyone everywhere knows, would as soon see Germany divided into twenty parts as into two, and shudders at the thought of a Germany undivided. Sir Anthony Eden feels, as do the Americans, that Western defense requires a German contribution; this contribution, though, could come as effectively from Western Germany alone as from a unified Germany. The one spur to early unification felt by both the British and the Americans is the advanced age of Chancellor Adenauer; they fear that when he dies, he will be succeeded by some German who will strike a quick, unprincipled bargain with the Russians. Naturally, the Russians look forward to such a day, but they must look forward to it with as much dread as relish, for they have a lot to lose, as well as a lot to gain, in any such bargaining.

It was unmistakably clear here last week that both East and West regard the Germany that now exists not as the best of all imaginable Germanys but as the best of all currently possible ones. The Russians were almost brutally frank in acknowledging this, and the West agreed without being either brutal or frank. There was likewise general agreement that the existing security arrangements—our NATO and the Communists' Warsaw Pact—could be left undisturbed for the time being, because neither in point of fact threatened the security of East or West. Disarmament is evidently a real desire in both camps, but the sense of security that each side now has is not so great as to encourage anyone to undertake breakneck demobilization. It was decided to keep the bombs and the guns and the troops and to do a lot of proclaiming of determination not to use them. Agreements of this sort can be scornfully described as negative and as words, mere words, but a lot of history has been made by way of negative agreements, and diplomacy at its best has often been merely verbal.

37 The Vice-President

September 1955

The Vice-President of the United States is forty-two years old, robust, intelligent, conscientious, ruthless, affable, articulate, competitive, telegenic, and breath-takingly adaptable. He comes from a large state, leads an apparently blameless personal life, has an attractive family, has never been called a security risk, and is blessed with many friends and admirers—some of whom, as we learned from the campaign of 1952, have been willing to invest solid cash in his career. Those people showed good investor judgment. The actuarial tables and the laws of chance favor the Vice-President greatly. If he takes the elementary precautions with his health and does not squander the formidable political assets that are now his, he has ahead of him a full quarter-century of service to the Republic and to the good name of Richard Milhous Nixon.

What does this quarter-century hold? It would be rash to say that there is anything it does *not* hold. Nixon is even now a front-runner for the presidency in 1956. If the President declines the honor at San Francisco next year, Nixon will be the man to beat. The common opinion is that he would in the end be beaten. If the President accepts, though, Nixon is pretty certain to be Vice-President again—which is a way of saying that he is likely to be President, since Mr. Eisenhower, between 1957 and 1961, will not have the life-expectancy tables in his favor.

It is reported now that, in the 1956 Republican convention, there will be heavy opposition to a second Vice-Presidency for Nixon. He has powerful enemies as well as powerful friends, and he has in Senator Knowland a dedicated, resourceful rival. But if the President runs again and wants Nixon to run with him, the President will get his wish. "It can be stated authoritatively that Mr. Nixon is the President's only personal choice as a 1956 running-mate," Roscoe Drummond of the New York *Herald Tribune* wrote not long ago. On White House matters, there are few statements more authoritative than Mr. Drummond's. It is hard to see how he could be wrong on this one. The President has described the Vice-President as "one . . . of the great leaders of men" and "the most valuable member of my team." Why should the President of the United States takes second-best when the best is right at hand?

Nixon is ahead not only in the President's book but in that of the Republican masses. Although the Gallup Poll shows him as a probable loser if he were to oppose Adlai Stevenson or Estes Kefauver, and although he failed to place or show on the Poll's list of the ten men Americans admire most, it revealed him as being comfortably ahead of all presently available Republicans —the President, of course, excepted—in the estimation of his fellow Republicans. One unavailable Republican, the Chief Justice of the Supreme Court, would have an edge over Nixon, according to the poll. There are some who think that Mr. Justice Warren was only playing hard to get when he said he would not re-enter politics "under any circumstances or conditions," but the statement puts him out of the running for the time being and leaves Nixon leading the pack and hugging the rail. Thomas E. Dewey trails him by seven points, Harold Stassen by ten, Ambassador Lodge by nineteen, his bitter antagonist Senator Knowland by twenty-one, Senator Bricker by the same number, and poor Senator Dirksen by twenty-six.

Next year will be the last time around for some of these statesmen. But if Nixon misses in 1956, he will be conspicuously available in 1960. Indeed, almost as far as one can see down the corridors of time—1956, 1960, 1964, 1968, 1972, 1976, 1980, and even
1984—Nixon will be available. With giant strides being taken
every day in the field of geriatrics, it is even conceivable that
Nixon will be a hard man to count out in the Republican convention of 2000—held, perhaps, at some pleasant American resort
on Mars. Whether or not the prospect pleases, it imposes. And if,
for some now obscure reason, Nixon never does capture the
grand prize, we may be fairly assured that he will somehow or
other be part of our lives—an influence, a force to reckon with
in the affairs of the country for some time to come.

He is a first-class influence right now. In an administration
headed by a soldier and staffed by merchants, he is the ranking
politician—despite the fact that he has been in politics less than
a decade and, five years before he was Vice-President, was the
subject of an article in a Washington paper headed "Greenest
Congressman in Town." More than anyone else, he has set the
political style of the Eisenhower Administration, with its heavy
borrowings from the techniques of modern advertising and public relations, with its emphasis on the great modern virtue of Sincerity, and with its mobilization of energies against the opposition rather than toward its own objectives. He was the author of
the clever, shocking campaign formula of 1954, "K-1, C-3"
(Korea, Communism-corruption-controls), and he was the leading strategist of his party in that election. He serves a President
who has a powerful distaste for many aspects of the job and is
only too happy to let the spotlights play over his understudy.

The lights do not bother Nixon in the least. He is always willing and able to help the Republican National Committee dispose
of any radio or television time it gets hold of. He takes other
responsibilities in good spirits. He sits with the Cabinet and the
National Security Council, presiding over both in the President's
absences, which are frequent. He is said to be the first Vice-

President ever to chair a Cabinet meeting, and perhaps he is. He also attends the President's conferences with legislative leaders. He is the administration's leading fixer. On the President's behalf and sometimes on his own, he irons out conflicts and accommodates difficult personalities in the party and in the legislative and executive branches. Since the death of Senator Taft and especially since the development of mutinous tendencies in Senator Knowland, he has been the administration's principal organizer in the Senate.

It is an open question as to whether Nixon is quite the wizard in the manipulation of public opinion that some of his associates believe him to be. He has done well for himself in California, and he was an effective campaigner in 1952. But his most prodigious labors were in last year's congressional elections, and there the results were inconclusive. Most of the candidates he helped were losers. The help he gave them consisted largely of lectures on the "6,926 Communists and security risks" allegedly separated from the government by the administration and of broad hints about the subversive connections of some widely respected Democrats. There are some who think he did positive damage to his own party in 1954. There are others, though, who think he damaged the Democrats and that with a little more of Nixon in the right places the Republicans would have won.

On the subject of Nixon's gifts as a political claim agent and maneuverer, there is no dispute whatever. He gets results. His impact on events is sharp and altogether impressive. But for him, the President's first tax program—the success of which was vital to the new administration—might have been torn to shreds in the House Ways and Means Committee. The then chairman, Representative Dan Reed of New York, swore that he would never let the administration bill out. "When I fight, I fight," he said at the time. Nixon had words with him. The official version is that Nixon advanced the argument that some things are more important than money and that Reed was dazzled by this illumination. This has an improbable ring. It seems more likely that lures and threats were skillfully employed. Anyway, Reed called off his fight and has not made the front pages since the day, now more than two years gone by, when they were graced with a picture of the Representative—once head football coach at Cornell—clasping the President's hand so hard the President winced and himself wincing from a clap on the back administered by the Vice-President.

Nixon has been particularly useful at times when the President could not count on the regular Republican leadership. There have been many such times, and there is no doubt that Nixon has been a loyal and effective supporter of administration policies. It may well be that if it were not for this loyalty, the Bricker amendment or one of its variants would be part of our fundamental law today. He rallied and organized the thin Republican opposition and surreptitiously encouraged the Democrats. When a howl went up from the Asia-first Republicans over the Korean truce negotiations, Nixon went among them as a diplomat on pacific errands. He is generally credited with having won the necessary political support for the settlement that was to become the administration's most prized accomplishment, even though Senator Knowland called it a "peace without honor."

The credit or discredit that attaches to the administration's handling of Senator McCarthy can mostly be put on Nixon's account. He established and executed the strategy. In Martin Merson's *Private Diary of a Public Servant,* it is shown that Nixon not only laid down the line on McCarthy to appointed officials, but that he had to be consulted even on so small a matter as whether an administration member should or should not trouble McCarthy for an appointment. Nixon kept the peace between the President and McCarthy longer than most people thought possible, alternately persuading the Senator of his need for the President and the President of his need for the Senator. When Harold Stassen threatened to break loose and fight McCarthy for "undermining the State Department" (this was when

McCarthy constituted himself a Foreign Ministry and negotiated an agreement on China trade with Greek shipping interests), Nixon prevailed on John Foster Dulles to torpedo Stassen with a statement praising McCarthy's services to American diplomacy and the comity of nations. At the same time, Nixon was torpedoing McCarthy's investigation of the Central Intelligence Agency. It was Nixon who arranged the humiliation of Robert T. Stevens, the Secretary of the Army, at the celebrated chicken luncheon Stevens had with McCarthy and other members of the Subcommittee on Permanent Investigations. It was Nixon, too, who arranged McCarthy's humiliation by appointing hanging judges to the Select Committee that reported on Senator Flanders' motion to censure McCarthy.

It is vigorously argued in some quarters that Nixon intended and hoped for quite a different outcome to this affair. Maybe so, but he is nothing if not shrewd, and this would imply a great failure of shrewdness—to say nothing of an uncharacteristic maladroitness. At any rate, once the unpleasant work was done, it was Nixon who made a small amend to McCarthy by altering the "Resolution of Censure" passed by the Senate to read simply "Resolution." Nowhere but in the title had the word "censure" appeared.

Nixon was in the Senate chamber for the censure debate, but that was a rare occasion. He serves as presiding officer of the Senate less often than any of his recent predecessors. Moreover, he is seldom to be found in his office at the Capitol. That office—traditionally a repair shop for hurt feelings and broken friendships, a sanctuary for weary, fretful senators, a room that can quickly be filled with smoke and well-laid schemes—is closed most of the time nowadays. It is not by the practice of good fellowship that Nixon applies his healing touch. He has no gift for bonhomie and wisely leaves it to others. He does perform certain other functions that are more clearly in line with the public responsibilities of his office than his essays in fixing. Besides his sessions with the Cabinet, the National Security Council, and the legislative leaders, he does a good deal of official greeting, dining out, and good-will touring of the sort that requires not bonhomie so much as an iron digestion and powerful smiling muscles.

It is the work he does along these lines that emboldens his and his party's publicity agents to claim that he is something special in the way of a vice-president—that he has enlarged, dignified, and given new meaning to an office described by its first occupant, John Adams, as "the most insignificant . . . that ever the invention of man contrived or his imagination conceived." "Busiest Vice-President We've Ever Had!" the *Saturday Evening Post* called one of its several appreciations of Nixon.

He may be all of that, but the significance of his career does not lie in his handling of his public and ceremonial responsibilities. The fact is that what they say about Nixon they have been saying about every vice-president for years past. It was a proud boast of the Coolidge administration that Charles G. Dawes had given new meaning to the office. Every vice-president since John Nance Garner has been said to have broken the Throttlebottom tradition. (Garner's successor, Henry Wallace, may have had his short-comings, but he was a real ball of fire when it came to keeping himself busy.) As the presidency has become a more and more burdensome office, presidents have thrust more and more work on vice-presidents and on anyone else who happened to be around and on the payroll. Because Mr. Eisenhower is the last in line and because he has a more relaxed approach to the work than other recent presidents, Nixon may be putting in somewhat longer workdays than certain of his predecessors. But the difference is purely a quantitative one. It is as a Republican politician and not as an officer of the government that Nixon is noteworthy and perhaps unique.

One of the unique things about him is that he has achieved his present eminence by concerning himself exclusively with strategy and ignoring the whole broad field of policy. It is astonishing that when one thinks of Nixon in relation to the history of the past three years there is no single item of substantive policy that one can identify him with. In the administration he serves and helps to lead, there are a number of men whose names one associates, automatically as it were, with a particular approach to a particular problem of concern to the nation. The mere mention, for example, of George Humphrey or Admiral Radford or Harold Stassen or Douglas McKay calls to mind a point of view emphatically held and energetically defended. Their names are synonymous with policies.

Nixon's name connotes nothing. If such a term as "Nixonism" were given currency, it would suggest, perhaps, a manner and a mode of public behavior, but it would have no application to any vital issue. Nixon cannot be identified with hard money or soft money, with Asia-first or Asia-last, with preventive war or negotiation, with protectionism or anti-protectionism. As he has had no influence on policy, policy has had no influence on him.

Policy, it would seem, is something in which Nixon has only a mild, spasmodic interest. He can take it or leave it alone. He does not fear it and avoid commitment, as a great many politicians do. On the contrary, there have been few public issues in his time that he has failed to take a stand on. But there is no discernible pattern to his commitments.

This has greatly increased his utility as an administration spokesman. When someone is wanted to advocate intervention in Indo-China, Nixon is ready as a warhawk. When the plan for intervention miscarries, Nixon, eager to pluck figs out of thistles, is primed to speak of the superior wisdom and morality of non-intervention. Nixon can plead with congressmen not to wreck the President's foreign-aid program with a meat axe. Then, when the axe has fallen in spite of his eloquence, he brings to the voters the glad tidings that Republican government is cutting back on foreign-aid programs to save the taxpayers' money.

Indifferent to doctrine, he dwells somewhere apart from factionalism. He cannot be classified as either a right-wing or a left-wing Republican. He is therefore free to act as a kind of double agent—now the left's ambassador to the right, now the right's ambassador to the left. And when the need arises, as it did in the 1954 elections, he can be an honest broker between the two, campaigning for Clifford Case in New Jersey and Joseph T. Meek in Illinois and advising Republicans everywhere to compose their differences, as he has composed his differences. ("We've got to get forty-eight votes in the Senate, and let's get that into our heads.") Nixon is the hub of the Republican wheel, the joining place of all Republican tendencies. He turns as the party wheel turns.

Many people refuse to accept the view of Nixon as a man innocent of doctrine. The Democrats profess to see him as a Republican of the most reactionary stripe, and their National Committee has tabulated, charted, and graphed his House and Senate voting record in such a way as to establish him as a creature of the vested interests, an isolationist, a trifler with the national security, and a politician heedless of the plight of all the exigent. By its reading of the evidence, he is a begrudger of hot lunches to little children and of decent habitation to the ill-housed, a proponent of restrictive immigration policies and of legislation repressive of free thought and inquiry, an enemy of workers, small farmers, and small businessmen. Adlai Stevenson has called him a white-collar McCarthy and others have called him worse than that.

The record can be made to sustain this view of Nixon, but only by omitting significant portions of it and carefully tailoring others. By a different tailoring process, Nixon can be made to appear a very different sort of Republican. Between 1947 and 1952, he supported several aspects of Democratic foreign policy. On the crucial issue of troops to Europe, he accepted Senator Vandenberg's rather than Senator Taft's leadership. On such matters as price controls, federal funds for school construction, and the regulation of trusts, he often voted in a manner held to be correct and virtuous by the C.I.O. and Americans for Democratic Action. Some parts of his record could have commended him to civil libertarians. True, there was the Mundt-Nixon Bill, which he sponsored and they deplored, but his behavior as a member of the House Committee on Un-American Activities was, from their point of view, far better than that of most members and, in fact, just about irreproachable. On several civil-liberties issues he voted with the liberals and delivered himself of liberal platitudes.

But what stands out in any consideration of the whole record is the flexibility that suggests an almost total indifference to policy. Nixon appears to be a politician with an advertising man's approach to his work. Policies are products to be sold the public —this one today, that one tomorrow, depending on the discounts and the state of the market. He moves from intervention to anti-intervention with the same ease and lack of anguish with which a copy writer might transfer his loyalties from Camels to Chesterfields.

To be sure, his speeches and public statements sound like advertising copy. Their emotional range is narrow. "No one," Murray Kempton once wrote, "can remember him in a display of real indignation." Even when, in last year's campaign, he was accusing Democrats of harboring "diseased ideas . . . from the Marxist virus," he never managed to convey a sense of outrage deeper than that of a man describing the ravages of Stomach Upset. (When the Democrats—who, according to Nixon, had secreted somewhere in Washington "a blueprint for socializing America"—took control of Congress, he blandly recommended to his fellow Republicans that they "advocate vigorously the policies we think are best . . . without impugning the motives of those who disagree with us.") His enthusiasms have the same simulated quality—"And remember, folks, Eisenhower is a great man. Folks, he is a great man, and a vote for Eisenhower is a vote for what is good for America."

Unless appearances grossly deceive, what Nixon communicates is about all he feels. No doubt there is somewhere in Nixon's mind or psyche a moral imperative of some sort and a view of human possibilities. The pure opportunist is a very rare bird indeed; in fact, so eminent an authority as Dr. Samuel Johnson insisted that there was really no such thing. In Nixon's case, though, the moral sources of his behavior are so well hidden that he himself seems unable to find them or explain them. He has once or twice referred to Quakerism as the wellspring of his beliefs.

"I guess my Quaker background gave me a kind of internationist bent," he told an interviewer in 1952. In 1952, running with Dwight Eisenhower, an internationalist bent was the bent to talk about. But if this was the manifestation of Quakerism, what sort of anti-Quakerism accounted for the anti-internationalist bent—the votes in the then recently adjourned Eighty-second Congress against aid to India, against Point Four, and to override the President's veto of the McCarran Immigration Act? Nixon is a birthright California Quaker (the "California" is by no means supererogatory, for the gentle faith has undergone weather changes, too: there is, or was, a Los Angeles meeting house with a lighted cross atop it). He is a native of a Quaker settlement named for the author of "Snowbound," and a graduate of Whittier College, a Quaker school.

He may aspire to the grace and nobility of Quakerism, but if so he has yet to comprehend the core of the faith. It would be hard to think of anything more wildly at variance with the spirit of the Society of Friends than his appeal for the pity and sympathy of his countrymen, in his famous 1952 speech on his financial arrangements, on the ground that his wife didn't own a mink coat but was appareled in a "respectable Republican cloth coat." A certain amount of virtue might have attached to Mrs. Nixon, who is not a Quaker lady, for suffering the lack of such a symbol of worldliness and wealth as a mink coat. But it was Nixon who was filing this claim to virtue on his own behalf. The performance was in almost every respect an odd one, but the reference to the cloth coat was fantastic for a man who had asserted the rights of an heir to those devotees of plainness of whom Oliver

Cromwell is reputed to have said, "I see there is a people risen that I cannot win either with gifts, honors, offices, or places."

Although Nixon resists factional or ideological classification, there is nothing of the maverick about him; while he has moved from left to right and right to left inside the party, he has never moved beyond the limits of Republicanism in any direction. It could, perhaps, be maintained that what appears to be a highly developed form of opportunism is really a crusade for the welfare of the Republican party. Taking Nixon's checkered record into account, Robert Bendiner recently wrote: "It does not follow that he is a man without political principle. He has, indeed, an overriding principle, and it is altogether political. Quite simply, it is the unity . . . of the Republican party."

But even if one were willing to concede—as Mr. Bendiner of course was not—that the good of a political party constitutes in and of itself a moral end, one would be left with several questions about the origins and quality of Nixon's Republicanism. In what way is his Republicanism more than a vehicle for his own ambitions? What, in his view, should the party be and do? Nixon has provided no answers.

Nixon's Republicanism is not a heritage. According to the best available researches, his people voted the ticket, but in a rather indifferent and irregular spirit, and his father is said to have supported Woodrow Wilson in 1916, Robert LaFollette in 1924, and Franklin D. Roosevelt in 1932. Nixon has given a curious account of how he himself got into Republican politics. On the face of it, it would seem that his loyalties came into being only after the consummation of a contractual arrangement of much the same sort as those which turn advertising men into Oldsmobile enthusiasts and Muffets boosters.

In 1946, he was in Baltimore on legal business for the United States Navy. While there, he got a phone call from a California banker named Herman Perry who was on the hunt for a Republican nominee for Congress from the Twelfth District, which is part of Los Angeles County. The party was having a rough time finding a candidate. The incumbent was Jerry Voorhis, a popular New Deal Democrat. The Republicans had gone so far as to advertise for a candidate in the newspapers. No one acceptable had responded. Apparently no one in Los Angeles County could see that a great Republican sweep was coming. (The Democrats were to lose seven of their sixteen seats, or just about every one it was possible for them to lose.) "Are you a Republican?" Mr. Perry asked Nixon. Nixon recalls his historic reply: "I guess so. I voted for Dewey last time." That was enough for Mr. Perry. He urged Nixon to hurry out to California and prepare for action.

The commonly accepted theory of the Nixon phenomenon is that a shrewd hunch about Whittaker Chambers and Alger Hiss has been parlayed into a spectacular career. Nixon, alone among his colleagues on the Un-American Activities Committee, had a suspicion that Chambers was telling the essential truth and that Hiss was brazening it out. He also had the courage—and it does no particular violence to the word to use it in this connection, for the cards at that time were surely stacked the other way— to push ahead with what appeared to others to be an eccentric view of the case. He was fortunate in receiving information, advice, and encouragement from the late Bert Andrews, of the New York *Herald Tribune* Washington bureau, who had the same hunch and who suggested the legal means which Nixon employed to require Chambers to produce what were later known as "the pumpkin papers." But Nixon had the responsibility, and he must be given the credit. He has taken it and gone a very long way on it.

Apart from this, there is nothing that is not routine in his career up to 1952. Not even the most sympathetic and industrious of his biographers has been able to construct any record of achievement for Nixon in the years before he became Vice-President. His opportunities were, it must be acknowledged, limited. Two terms in the House and a third of a term in the Senate are hardly enough for the making of a Clay, a Calhoun, or a Webster. Still, it is a pretty thin history for a man who has received as much acclaim as he has.

His record as Vice-President has not been meager. If he has built no enduring monuments, he has served his party and his President as both wished to be served. Yet, taking the record as a whole, it is an unimpressive one, and taking Nixon and his career together, one cannot help wondering precisely what it is that his admirers—the President who called him a great leader of men and the rank-and-file Republicans who favor him over so many of their other leaders—admire. It cannot be his views, for they are indeterminate and perhaps nonexistent. It cannot be what he has accomplished, for what he has accomplished is wholly in the realm of maneuver—and, beyond that, it has been very little publicized.

One plausible answer remains: the admirers admire Richard Nixon himself. As a person and as a personality, he embodies much that is held to be precious by a large and growing number of Americans—especially in that segment of the middle class to which he belongs and which is recognized by the Republican party as its best source of cadres at the present time. He is young, he is enterprising, he is successful. He is loyal to his organization and to his boss. He lacks humor, but exudes earnestness and frankness. He has a weakness for dogs but not too many other weaknesses.

"Dick," Mrs. Nixon has written, "simply cannot stand Washington cocktail parties, which he regards as the greatest invention for wasting time since the introduction of the siesta." She has also explained that "Dick doesn't pay too much attention to how women dress." The skepticism that may greet assertions such as these works as much in his favor as credulity would; they draw approving nods and approving winks.

His sales-executive manner and his account-executive rhetoric are the very stuff of the good life to his constituency. The fact that his ideas are obscure and his positive achievements few detracts not in the slightest from the charm of the public image. As

David Riesman has pointed out, we are well along in an age in which our heroes and godlings are not Captains of Industry but "Captains of Nonindustry, of Consumption and Leisure." Production, accomplishment, creativity—in a society of abundance and superabundance, these are no longer so important as they once were. The arts of consumption are the valued ones nowadays, and in these Nixon is highly skilled. His general appearance, his dress, his whole style of living and being, commend him to the multitudes who share his aspirations for a clear title to a ranch-house, furs for the wife, and pets for the children.

Charm, of course, has always been an essence, requiring no philosophy and no particular exertions on the part of its possessor. Nixon, for some Americans, has it. It is nevertheless well to recall that he did not make the list of the Ten Most Admired and his admirers are not as yet numerous enough to make him a good thing to wager on if he were the Republican candidate for President next year. But he has a lot of time for building—and there are those who believe that time is on the side of men of his kidney.

38   The Confidence of Leonard Hall

Letter from Washington

September 22, 1955

No spectacle currently on display here is more engrossing than that of Mr. Leonard W. Hall, chairman of the Republican National Committee, deftly constructing a situation in which the President will have no honorable or patriotic choice but to run for re-election next year. Some people believe that Mr. Hall has in Mr. Eisenhower an eager and increasingly talented collaborator; they think the President has already made the choice—in favor of running. Mr. Hall encourages this view of the matter. Almost every day, and sometimes twice a day, he says he has additional reasons for being certain the President will accept renomination. Every time the President says something to suggest that he faces the prospect of another term with somewhat ambivalent feelings, Mr. Hall claims to have been newly strengthened in the belief that Mr. Eisenhower will head the ticket in 1956. In Denver, a couple of weeks ago, the President addressed the Republican state chairmen and reminded them of his own mortality. He stressed the hazards of relying on one man alone. Mr. Hall, asked if his confidence in the President's readiness to serve again had been shaken by this talk, replied that, on the contrary, it had been reinforced. "I feel better about it now," he said. "My assumption [that the President will run] has been strengthened by the trip to Denver." The impression Mr. Hall's statements create is that he has some kind of private understanding with the President and that the President's expressions of doubt and misgiving are only maneuvers in a pretty foxy game he and the President are playing. The spread of this impression suits Mr. Hall right down to the ground. If it didn't, he would do something to stop it. But it plainly serves his purpose, for it sets up one more obstacle in the path of a possible retreat by the President. Obviously, if people get the idea that Mr. Eisenhower has given his word to Mr. Hall to run again, then Mr. Eisenhower, if he happens to be even toying with the thought of retirement, must contend with the fact that a refusal to accept a second term would seem to many people to be a violation of a pledge to a trusted and trusting lieutenant.

Mr. Hall behaves for all the world like a man in receipt of such a pledge. He keeps insisting that he is so certain of the President's willingness to serve once more that he and his colleagues are not even considering what they might do in the event the President refused. He said earlier this month, as he has said on a half dozen other occasions, that "at the moment, I am thinking of no other candidate than Mr. Eisenhower." At the same time, he says he is in no hurry at all to have the President commit himself. Early this week, he told reporters he was sure the President would announce his plans "pretty well" before the Republican convention but that he could not say, and was not really concerned to know, whether this meant days, weeks, or months. Everyone is aware that time is getting terribly short and that if the President is going to decline renomination, the Republican leaders will have to scramble to find another candidate and build him up. Everyone, moreover, is persuaded that the Republican cause would be hopeless without the President; the public-opinion polls all seem to show that just about any Democrat could beat just about any Republican except Eisenhower, who can beat anyone anywhere. The shorter the time gets, the better Mr. Hall likes it; the more that word gets around that all is lost without Eisenhower, the broader and jollier Mr. Hall's engaging smile becomes. For with each passing day, he appears to be more and more on the spot, and the more firmly on the spot he appears to be, the greater and more numerous are the difficulties in the way of the President's withdrawal.

For all the assurance he professes, Mr. Hall will not tempt fate by presenting the President with an opportunity to pull out. The Republican state chairmen who, before their trip to Denver, gathered here to be lectured by advertising geniuses, public-relations wizards, and master minds of television wanted to make a direct appeal to the President to announce his candidacy. Mr. Hall said this would be inadvisable; in fact, he put his foot down on the project. He recalled the melancholy sequence of events the last time such requests were made. On July 11, fifty-four Republican members of the House of Representatives issued a formal public statement urging the President to announce that he would seek re-election. On August 3, a delegation of distinguished Ohio Republicans called on the President in the White House and presented him with a similar appeal. Mr. Eisenhower's reply was an impromptu speech, and a rather moving one, discussing the wear and tear of the presidency on presidents, the fact that no man ever reached the age of seventy in the White House, and the need, as he saw it, for more young Republicans. Party men from one end of Washington to another reacted to the speech as to a knife thrust in the heart. Senator George Bender, a man who is generally fecund of comment and observation, was able only to say, "I have faith in God and Dwight Eisenhower." Mr. Hall said that it was now clearer than ever that the President would lead the party to victory in 1956. But reporters noticed a slight tremolo quality in his voice as he spoke and a touch of alabaster in his normally ruddy complexion. The following day, at his news conference, the President amplified the remarks he had made to the Ohioans, explaining that he couldn't possibly have acceded to the request to announce his candidacy because he couldn't see far enough into the future. "If I were such an infallible prophet," he said, "that I could understand all about the world situation, the domestic situation, and my own situation, including the way I felt, and possibly with the health, and everything else, as of that moment, then there would be no great excuse for deferring the decision. I have not that gift of prophecy." There were more expressions of anguish and more statements from Mr. Hall to the effect that it was now practically certain that the President was looking forward to consolidating the gains of his first administration in the course of his second administration. Nevertheless, Mr. Hall, two weeks ago, was quick to discourage the framing of another request to the President to announce his candidacy. He helped the committeemen to draw up a simple telegram to Mr. Eisenhower saying that they were "looking forward to supporting you again in 1956. We like Ike better than ever." Such a message, he pointed out, would call for no reply, and this would make things easier for the President. Besides, he reminded them, no reply was really needed, since the Vice-President had visited Mr. Eisenhower only a few days earlier and had announced, on leaving Denver, that "the people who know the President . . . are more optimistic than at any time since he was inaugurated. I feel he's in tip-top shape physically and in his attitude toward his job, [which] has become easier for him."

Though the committeemen's telegram called for no reply, the President volunteered a few remarks on it. He said, "we don't believe for a minute that the Republican Party is so lacking in inspiration, high-quality personnel, and leadership that we are dependent on one man. . . . Humans are frail—and they are mortal. [Never] pin your flag so tightly to one mast that if a ship sinks you cannot rip it off and nail it to another. It is some-times good to remember that." It was after this that Mr. Hall said, "I feel better about it now."

It may be that, as quite a few people suppose, the President has already decided to run again and has given his assurance to Mr. Hall. Nothing he has lately said precludes this possibility. He is under no obligation to announce his decisions the moment he reaches them, and he would, indeed, be foolish to do so. What-ever his plans for the future, he has an interest in ending his first administration as successfully as possible. A leader firmly committed to a particular course of action has less authority than one who merely reserves his right to pursue it on his own terms. If Senator Bender, who has been less enthusiastic about the President's policies than about the President's candidacy, were certain that Mr. Eisenhower had eliminated the possibility of withdrawal, his reverence might sharply diminish. From the point of view of disconcerting the Democrats, it is also sound politics to defer any announcement of the President's availabil-ity. Yet it is the considered view of a number of the most thought-ful observers of events here that the available evidence suggests quite strongly that the President has not yet made up his mind, that he is experiencing a good deal of pain in his effort to reach a decision, and that he is at the present time leaning heavily toward withdrawal. It is taken for granted that he has heard and weighed all the arguments in favor of seeking the vindication of a second term. There is nothing *récherché* about these arguments; they force themselves upon the attention of every sitting President, and Mr. Eisenhower no doubt has them called freshly to mind by every Republican who visits him these days. The arguments in favor of withdrawal are another matter altogether. They are, as a rule, offensive to self-esteem and therefore have a way of escaping notice. In the President's case, though, the fact is that, with only one exception, his public references to his personal future have consisted entirely of the presentation of reasons for retirement. The single exception was a speech in New Hampshire last spring, in the course of which he made a little pleasantry to the effect that it might take another five years of daily association with Sherman Adams to exhaust Mr. Adams' store of anecdotes about New Hampshire. The statements that have dealt with the case against running again and that have appeared to reveal a reluctance to try for another term have been far graver in tone than this; they have, in fact, dealt quite somberly with such somber matters as death and the ravages of time and the follies of adulation. In them, the President has achieved a clarity and a modest eloquence he does not seem to command when he discusses flexible price supports or proposed revisions in the tariff schedules. These discussions have had, in other words, a ring of sincerity. Mr. Eisenhower is not much of a hand at dissimulation, and when he gives the impression of being in earnest, it is generally a correct impression.

Those who think the President is probably leaning toward withdrawal cite more than his words in defense of their conclusion. They think that something of his present state of mind can be learned from his present whereabouts—at the mountain ranch of his banker friend Aksel Nielsen, some seventy miles north and west of Denver, over the Continental Divide and in an area where the air is reputed to be the coldest in the country. He went there early this week for the purpose, according to his aides, of relaxing and doing an occasional bit of trout fishing in St. Louis Creek. Early next week, he will motor back to Denver to address some remarks to a group of authorities on body-building who comprise the President's Commission on the Nation's Physique. The Commission will hold some panel discussions in Denver under the direction of the Vice-President. When Mr. Eisenhower will return to Washington no one in Washington seems to know. At least, no one in the White House press office seems to know. Persons who inquire there are advised that perhaps Mr. James Hagerty, the White House press secretary, knows the date, but that Mr. Hagerty is himself on vacation. When Mr. Hagerty's vacation is over, he will go to Denver rather than return to Washington. For six weeks now, the President has been in and around Denver, most of the time putting in a one-hour work day in his office at the Lowry Air Force Base where he arrives about 8:00 in the morning and signs whatever papers have been sent out from Washington. In the late mornings and early afternoons he is at the Cherry Hills Country Club playing not less than eighteen holes of golf and more often twenty-seven. After golf, he naps and visits with Mrs. Eisenhower and other members of his and her family in the late afternoons, and spends his evenings dining and playing contract bridge at stag gatherings in his suite on the eighth floor of the Brown Palace Hotel.

It is doubtful in the extreme that Vice-President Nixon or Leonard Hall has advised Mr. Eisenhower that his presence is sorely missed in Washington and that a growing number of his subordinates, particularly in the agencies concerned with foreign and military policy, are grumbling quite openly about the difficulties of leading a great republic through a period of readjustment and reorientation with no President on hand to provide the guidance and direction that only the head man can provide. Mr. Nixon and Mr. Hall have troubles enough of their own, and it would be understandable if they felt no call to go beyond their own broad jurisdictions and borrow the troubles of others.

It is conceivable that the President is unaware of the fact that many people in Washington are disturbed by the length and frequency of his holidays. It is almost impossible to overestimate the degree of insulation men in his office can achieve. In Mr.

Eisenhower's case, it is particularly high, for he is not much of a newspaper reader. Besides, the newspapers nowadays approach the President with as much tact and delicacy as Mr. Hall. So far as is known here, the only newspaper that has discussed Mr. Eisenhower's vacationing in a questioning spirit is the Oregon *Statesman*, whose publisher, Charles A. Sprague, a former Republican governor of the state, recently expressed the view that the country would be better off if the President left Colorado for Washington. Mr. Murray Snyder, Mr. Hagerty's assistant in the press department, was asked for comment. He said there would be none. He did not say whether the President had been informed of Mr. Sprague's suggestion. Aware of criticism or not, Mr. Eisenhower knows that he is President of the United States, and he knows from almost three years of experience what staggering tasks await him. There have been times in the course of his administration when he has seemed to be developing a certain delight and enthusiasm for his work, and there have been occasions—this year's Geneva conference, for example, and the closing days of last year's congressional campaign—when he has driven himself as hard as any of his predecessors ever did. But delight in the work and intensive application to it have been infrequent, and it is, on balance, difficult to escape the conclusion that Mr. Eisenhower is ill at ease in the White House and hugely discontented with his lot as President. He arranges to escape as much as possible, and he has opened up new territory in the realm of the possible. Even when he is regularly in residence here, he manages to spend an unprecedented number of hours in other places. It is clear not only that he dislikes the presidental regimen but that he is bored by most of the problems he has to deal with. Whenever he shuts up shop, either for a few hours or for such a protracted period of recreation as the present one, he seeks out the company not of colleagues in government but of men whose daily concerns are remote from his. Most presidents, like most non-presidents, have chosen their personal friends, in large part at least, from among people engaged in pursuits related to their own. When President Truman went off to Key West or Independence to escape the Washington climate and the pressures of White House life, he was in the habit of inviting along a few people involved as he was in politics and administration—or at any rate interested in them. Mr. Truman's intimates were not always, perhaps, the most admirable of characters, but they were his professional peers, and with them, at the poker table, he could and did discuss public affairs, which he found endlessly fascinating. President Eisenhower does not find them endlessly fascinating, and it is seldom that he has any dealings with politicians or administrators beyond those his official responsibilities compel him to have—and a good many people are saying now that he is not meeting the minimum demands of his office in this respect. When government officials or men of high rank in the Republican Party call upon him in Denver, they state their business succinctly and catch an early plane out of town. Now and then, one of them may be asked to stick around for a few holes of golf at Cherry Hills or a few rubbers of bridge at the Brown Palace, but this happens very rarely. An exhaustive study of the "tightly-knit group of presidential playtime companions" published recently in *U. S. News & World Report* turns up no one more closely connected with government than two retired generals and a former governor of Colorado; those not connected with government included three bankers, two real-estate dealers, two oil executives, two cattle raisers, two golf champions, two distillery executives, one soft-drink man, and representatives of such diverse businesses as automobile tires, newspapers, insurance, hotels, and washing machines.

Many people here feel that the President's whole being must be in revolt against the future that Mr. Hall plans for him. He must realize, it is thought, that if he has found so few satisfactions in his first term, those of his second would almost certainly be scarcer. Since the passage of the Twenty-second Amendment, in 1951, the second term of any president is bound to be more difficult than the first, for the Twenty-second Amendment, which says that "No person shall be elected to the office of president more than twice," all but destroys the political influence of a man who has been re-elected. Once the President has been safely returned to office, Senator Bender could revert to the isolationism that characterized the earlier part of his career and led him to oppose Mr. Eisenhower's nomination in 1952. Mr. Hall could cease his sturdy endeavors to organize Republican support for what he calls "the Eisenhower program." In fact, he would be almost duty-bound to give them up, for his job, or the job of his successor, would then be to concentrate on party organization for 1960. After 1956, it might not matter very much whether or not the President had Republican support, for the public-opinion polls that foretell a smashing victory for him if he runs again also foretell the continuing growth of Democratic power in congressional elections. The prospect, in the event of Mr. Eisenhower's renomination, is for several more years of Republican control of the executive branch and Democratic control of the legislative branch. With the President unable even to threaten a third term, the foundations of bi-partisanship would be imperiled. Democratic criticism of administration policies, which has been so gratifyingly feeble throughout most of this administration, would be certain to mount, probably to the point of outright repudiation. It might be that the President's standing with the public at large would remain at its unprecedentedly high level, but it is certain that it could not increase, and the odds would seem to favor a decline. For the present heights have been reached in a time of extraordinary prosperity and of something approaching comity in international affairs. Not many experts believe these conditions are going to last forever. Unrest is already developing in the farm and mining states. There is dispute as to the cause of the slight decline that has been showing itself in farm incomes, but no one denies the fact of it or the difficulties it creates for a Republican administration—not the least of them being the doubling in the annual cost of farm subsidies reported by the Department of Agriculture yesterday. In foreign policy, there will be any number of vexed questions. The Geneva conference carried the great powers into a period of competitive coexistence, which was what all the great powers seemed to want but which has found this country, for one, poorly prepared. In a forthright speech in Moscow last week, Nikita Khrushchev pointed out that his government was very much in earnest about the "competitive" aspect of the new period and that it had not the slightest intention of taking the heat off the West. The President, though he is undoubtedly aware of the implications of recent developments, could not in good faith promise as much on behalf of the United States. There is already a clamor for taking the heat off. In high places in the administration and in both houses of Congress, the pressure for unilateral cutbacks in defense—undertaken not to make life easier for the Communists but to make the budget balance—is mounting. Substantial reductions in American defense spending would play havoc with the whole network of our alliances, for it would at once undermine confidence in our continuing capacity to meet our obligations and encourage other nations to cut their own military programs. With Republican senators marveling at the fact that Russia has balanced *her* budget and assuring one another that there is no longer any need for most of our overseas program, the maintenance of a vigorous foreign policy by a Republican President will be a challenging job.

All of these factors, it is felt, must weigh heavily with the President whenever he gives any thought to his future plans. Yet among those who are persuaded that nothing would please him more than to quit Washington when his present contract runs out, there are very few who expect his wishes to prevail. Early this year, in a meeting with a group of correspondents here, Mr. Hall set forth the strategy he has been pursuing ever since. He was quick to concede that the President, if he consulted only his own feelings and those of Mrs. Eisenhower, would be unlikely to seek re-election. But he argued forcefully that no president is ever really free to do this. He is the leader of an association of men, and he cannot consider his own interests apart from those of his followers. His retirement cannot be an individual act; when he goes, others must go with him. Moreover, a sacrifice of principles is often involved. The association a president leads is held together by the belief that its members are peculiarly well qualified, by their views and by their talents, to do the job they have undertaken. To be sure, if a gifted successor is available, and if there is reason to believe that the successor could be elected, the common principles are not put too much in jeopardy; indeed, they may be advanced by a well-timed and well-planned withdrawal. But in the present case, Mr. Hall said, there are no gifted successors, and there is no reason to believe that if one were found he could hope to win. Sooner or later, he went on, these facts would impress themselves on President Eisenhower's mind, and he would be forced to yield to the wishes of the party. To yield to his own desires in such circumstances would be to surrender an army to the enemy, and this would be intolerable to his soldier's mind and conscience. There was always the danger, Mr. Hall admitted, that a man might put himself irreversibly on the record against running before the solid arguments on the other side had had a chance to work. And there was also the danger that a man might think there were qualified successors about when in truth there were none. Mr. Hall, however, felt that these dangers could be rather easily averted. Mr. Eisenhower, he said, was not so innocent that he failed to see the disadvantages of making any premature announcement of his plans, and the Republican National Committee was prepared to keep reminding him of the disadvantages. As for the successor problem, he said, it was a knotty one, for Mr. Eisenhower, besides having a military abhorrence of the theory of indispensability, might, in his impatience for retirement, let his eyes deceive him. But, Mr. Hall said, as long as Republican leaders talked Eisenhower wherever they went and acted on the assumption that there could be no successor, then there would be no successor. As long as it was said everywhere that Eisenhower was the only candidate, then not even the President would be able to talk seriously of another—though he might, as he has been doing lately, talk plaintively of the need for developing cadres. Mr. Hall did not on this occasion say that the strategy of talking Eisenhower and only Eisenhower would also create the impression that the President had already consented to be the candidate, an impression that would make withdrawal appear to be the breaking of a given word, but many people here are convinced that that has been part of the strategy.

At any rate, the general view here is that Mr. Hall's analysis was accurate and that his strategy is almost certain to meet with success.

39 Without the President

Letter from Washington

September 29, 1955

The National Security Council and the Cabinet are meeting, as they have in the past, under the direction of Mr. Nixon, who a couple of days ago was identified in the Washington *Daily News* as the "unofficial 'acting president,'" an office not provided for in the Constitution. For several days now, it has been customary, in discussions of the difficult role Mr. Nixon has had to play since the President was stricken last Saturday, to employ adjectives expressing irregularity and punctuation reflecting the legal ambiguities. No necessary blame attaches to Mr. Nixon for the confusion. Although in the immediate aftermath of the announcement of the President's illness, there was a widespread feeling that Mr. Nixon was moving with somewhat more speed and audacity than the situation required, the general opinion now is that he acted quite circumspectly. The circumstances were unusual and the precedents were few in number and not very helpful. Someone had to create the impression of a functioning administration, and Mr. Nixon, besides being Vice-President, was just about the only member of the government in Washington or anywhere near it. His status, nevertheless, continues to be a rather cloudy one, and, as Walter Lippmann puts it this morning, he may for some time have no way of knowing whether he is usurping presidential powers or failing to exercise vice-presidential powers.

The impression of a functioning administration has now been created, at least to the satisfaction of some high-ranking Republicans, and an effort is being made to quiet all talk of Mr. Nixon as being anything other than Vice-President. There will be new questions, of course, if the President suffers a relapse or if his present convalescent regimen lasts for very much longer than a few weeks, but the encouraging reports now coming out of Denver seems to suggest that sometime in October it may be possible for Mr. Eisenhower to confer for brief periods with some of his principal advisers and to express himself on some of the matters of policy that will by then demand the attention of the highest authorities. These cheering forecasts have had something to do with restoring Mr. Nixon to the office to which he was elected, but they are not the whole story. What seems to have happened is that a number of Mr. Eisenhower's associates, both here and in Denver, came to the conclusion two or three days ago that although a time might come, and very soon, when it would be necessary to straighten out the question of the Vice-President's position in a situation such as this, it was most inadvisable to make the effort at present. By now, just about every accredited Republican spokesman has said his piece against even a preliminary exploration of the problem that over the weekend seemed of the utmost urgency. Immediately after the President was stricken, it was announced that the Attorney General, who was vacationing in Spain, had been asked by James Hagerty to return and prepare an opinion on what powers of the President could be delegated to Mr. Nixon and what powers, if any, could not. Speaking for the handful of presidential aides in Denver, Mr. Hagerty said that such a clarification was needed right away, and a number of people in Washington said the same thing. Mr. Brownell evidently thought the matter a pressing one, for he flew back immediately.

While Mr. Brownell was airborne, however, most of the people who had felt that a speedy opinion was necessary gave the problem a second thought and arrived—almost simultaneously, it would seem, and unanimously—at the view that it wouldn't be needed at all. Before the Attorney General was on the ground, almost every highly placed Republican had issued a statement to the general effect that the Eisenhower team, reassembled from the four corners of the earth, was back in business and that each member knew exactly what his business was. Sherman Adams said this, and so did the Secretary of State, the Secretary of the Treasury, the Secretary of Agriculture, and Senator Knowland. By yesterday, Mr. Nixon himself was saying it, and Mr. Brownell, once he got back to Washington, fell right in line and acknowledged that the job he had hurried home to do did not need doing. The suspicion is widespread that despite Mr. Brownell's change of mind, there is probably someone in some dark recess of the Department of Justice quietly working up an opinion on Article II, Section 2, Paragraph 6, of the Constitution, which deals in such an unsatisfactory fashion with the vice-presidency, but the word for public consumption is that nothing of the sort is being done or contemplated, even on a standby basis. It has been the source of some amusement, in a week that hasn't provided very much of it, that on Mr. Brownell's first full day back on the job, about the only news to come out of the Department was a jubilant announcement by the Attorney General of his success in indicting "a trade association, a union, six corporations, and three individuals for conspiring to eliminate competition in the sale and distribution of smoked fish."

There is in certain quarters here an inclination to assume that Mr. Brownell's quest officially ended—or, rather, never officially began—because the hope for the President's early recovery made it unnecessary. "Fear that the government might be paralyzed by the President's illness may be laid aside," an editorial in yesterday's *Post & Times-Herald* said. "After the two weeks in which he is to be shielded entirely from official business . . . his absence will not be essentially different from a presidential vacation or a trip outside the country." On the matter of obtaining a clear understanding of vice-presidential powers, the *Post & Times-Herald* recommended a leisurely approach by way of statute and constitutional amendment. It accepts the administration view that things were so well organized before the President's illness that what still seems to many a crisis of moderate severity if not of the first magnitude is really no crisis at all. It seems extraordinary that there should be talk of constitutional amendments at a moment such as this, when the very reluctance of administration leaders to achieve a clarification of the constitutional issue is itself a measure of the gravity of the problem. Inspiriting as the recent Denver bulletins have been, a few people have been pointing out, it is absurd to act as if the very best outcome to be hoped for were the certain outcome. Even if the probability was that the President would be assuming command in a couple of weeks, the possibility would remain that he would be bedridden and in no condition to transact government business for months on end—conceivably through the end of his term. The most elementary kind of prudence would appear to call for the establishment, though not of course the immediate application, of a policy, and the unwillingness of Mr. Brownell and his colleagues to go through with this can only suggest that all of the men around Mr. Eisenhower do not wish to take any step that could result in giving Mr. Nixon greater authority or even in giving Mr. Nixon the impression that greater authority was soon to be his. This reluctance, if that is what it is, would not necessarily reflect distrust toward the Vice-President as a person—

though there is in fact a certain amount of that—so much as it would reflect the ancient fear that has always attended this and related questions: the fear that a reshuffling of power, or, as in this case, even a discussion of it, will result in a loss of power to individuals. Mr. Brownell, Mr. Humphrey, and the rest are, it must be remembered, members of the *Eisenhower* cabinet, and their authority derives from the President. As Harry Truman has been pointing out in his serialized memoirs, there is inevitably a conflict of interests between a president and a vice-president, and an increase of responsibility for the vice-president, even if it left him a good deal short of the full powers of the presidency, might easily work to the disadvantage of certain members of the Cabinet and of such presidential appointees as Sherman Adams and James Hagerty. To be sure, Senator Knowland, who came in from California yesterday morning and promptly aligned himself with those who said there was no present need to look into the transfer-of-powers matter, owes very little to the President and frequently opposes him, but Senator Knowland is almost universally regarded as a presidential candidate himself and is in any case no admirer of the Vice-President. His enthusiasm for the status quo is readily understandable.

There is, then, a feeling here that we may very well be facing a fairly chaotic period. No one, to be sure, expects government services to break down or basic policies to be violated. The general opinion is that in the purely administrative sense things are very well organized; through most of the summer, the government ran itself without much direction from the President, and in recent weeks the heads of most of the executive agencies have been away. Moreover, this is, as Mr. Hagerty and several other administration people have said, a period in which the pressure of government business is not very great. Congress will not return until after the first of the year, and there are relatively few high offices to be filled by presidential appointment. The principal business before all agencies is the planning of budgetary needs for the fiscal year that begins next July, and while later on this

will call for intervention and refereeing by the President or whoever acts in his stead, all the departments have several weeks of
purely departmental work facing them. But although disaster, if
it had to strike, could have chosen a much worse time, the President's illness is an unsettling factor and it will continue to be
one even if he recovers sufficiently to devote part of his time to
the duties of his office. The mere fact that his retirement next
year is now expected by everyone greatly diminishes his authority within his party. He may be firmer than before in making
clear his views and his wishes, but the translation of views and
wishes into policies and legislation is a result of the bargaining
process, and much of his bargaining power will disappear if it is
believed he is soon to withdraw. Moreover, no amount of talk
about teamwork can prevent the growth of discord within the
highest administration circles; to suggest that it can is almost an
insult to the President, for if an administration can be effectively
held together merely by the spirit of cooperation among its members, then no President is needed. How deep the team spirit
really runs will be determined in the coming weeks, but even if
the will to cooperation is as strong as it could possibly be, the
developments of last weekend have set in motion forces that are
bound to be destructive in their effect. It may be that Mr. Adams,
Mr. Brownell, Mr. Humphrey, and Mr. Nixon trust and understand each other perfectly, are all imbued with loyalty to the
same objectives, and want nothing for themselves but success in
carrying on as they think the President would have them carry
on, but the fact is that on every hand here the seeds of mistrust
and misunderstanding are being sown. Washington is humming
with unauthenticated reports that Sherman Adams regards himself as the President's appointed caretaker and is doing everything he can to cut Mr. Nixon down to size; that Mr. Humphrey
has suddenly been seized with presidential ambitions and is
elbowing his way to the forefront; that Mr. Brownell has been
struck with the vision of bringing Thomas E. Dewey back into
national politics and that all his actions from this point on will be

directed toward this end. These and a hundred other stories, mostly unkind, are in circulation, and it is well known that the most ill-founded sort of political speculation can deeply affect political realities.

How this may be could be seen in an incident that occurred yesterday. For reasons best known to himself and the others involved, the Vice-President conferred with Mr. Humphrey, Mr. Adams, and Mr. Brownell in Mr. Humphrey's office in the Treasury. Why the Vice-President went to Mr. Humphrey's office, rather than have Mr. Humphrey and the others come to his office, is a question that could be answered only by someone who had been given the facts by Mr. Nixon or Mr. Humphrey. It could well be that it suited the convenience of one or both of them, or it could be, as some people immediately began to suggest, that Mr. Humphrey wished to demonstrate his power and independence and insisted that Mr. Nixon present himself at the Treasury; whichever it was, not many people besides Mr. Nixon and Mr. Humphrey would be in a position to say, and so far as is known no one in a position to say has said anything. Similarly, only the people involved could know whether the presence of Mr. Adams and Mr. Brownell had been expected by the Vice-President or was a surprise to him, and the people involved have not yet addressed themselves to this question. No sooner was the occasion known about, though, than the word went out that Mr. Humphrey, Mr. Adams, and Mr. Brownell had demanded that Mr. Nixon appear before them and render an accounting of what he had been up to the last few days. It was further reported that the three who received the Vice-President in the Treasury had constituted themselves a junta and that, as their power to summon the Vice-President revealed, they were henceforth to be regarded as a ruling triumvirate. The story gained enough currency to leave Washington in the form of newspaper dispatches.

The stories that went out may be true, though it would be a triumph of guesswork if they were, or they may be wholly untrue. If they are wholly untrue, if Mr. Nixon went to the Treasury merely because he happened to be headed that way and if Mr. Adams and Mr. Brownell were there because Mr. Nixon had requested them to be there, then Mr. Nixon and the others would know the facts and be uninfluenced by the rumors. But this is a city full of people who attach great importance to who calls on whom and where—and very often rightly so, since such things are quite frequently of significance—and it can reasonably be predicted that the circulation of the story of the meeting will fix in a good many minds the conviction that the Messrs. Humphrey, Adams, and Brownell are the people to be doing business with. What is more important, there are, between the possibility that the story is wholly true and the possibility that it is wholly untrue, a dozen other possibilities. The presence of Mr. Adams and Mr. Brownell could have been a surprise to Mr. Nixon but a perfectly innocent one so far as Mr. Humphrey's intentions were concerned, yet the construction placed upon it by outsiders could very well raise agonizing doubts in Mr. Nixon's mind about the kind of game his three teammates were playing. For their part, they could easily assume that the fuss over Mr. Nixon's visit had been stirred up by Mr. Nixon himself, who had in retrospect seen the incident as a chance to advance his own fortunes. This is a tense period for all members of the Eisenhower administration, and it is also a period in which each member of it has some responsibility to think about his own role and about the continuing representation in the government of whatever interests and viewpoints he stands for. The savage struggle for power that has been forecast by some people may never take place, but with the President hors de combat and conceivably on the verge of complete retirement, it is hard to see how a contest for control of the administration and of the Republican Party can be averted. A great deal is at stake, and to suggest that the President's withdrawal alters nothing is to suggest that his presence contributed nothing.

Mr. Dulles, in his statement of reassurance, said that "the policies and principles" of the administration were entirely familiar to those charged with carrying them out and that therefore the President's illness would not jeopardize "the steady prosecution of our national and international policies." It is in Mr. Dulles's field that most people here expect to see the first consequences of the changed situation. The fact of which everyone is now aware is that while American policy and grand strategy may be fairly constant, American diplomacy can be one thing when the President is firmly in command and quite another when he is not. This was observable as recently as the day before he was taken ill. Just a week ago, Harold Stassen, called upon to answer three Russian questions at the disarmament talks in New York, replied in language that was as unsatisfactory to everyone here as it was to the Russians. It was clear in Washington that the reason for Mr. Stassen's imprecision was that he had no clear directive from the President, who had removed himself to the Byers Peak ranch of his mortgage-broker friend Aksel Nielsen and was not available for consultation. With the President high in the Rockies, Mr. Stassen could do nothing but offer an untidy patchwork of his own views, those of the State Department, and those of the Pentagon—each part being wildly in conflict with the other. He and everyone else involved in negotiations will be laboring under difficulties of this sort for as long as the President is an invalid or for as long as the constitutional question is unresolved. In last week's case, the difference in terms of consequences was almost certainly negligible, but they could be staggering. On several occasions in the past, the President has felt called upon to overrule the majority decisions of the National Security Council, over which Mr. Nixon presided this morning. No doubt each member of the council was persuaded that his views were clearly in line with the administration policies and principles Mr. Dulles spoke of, but the President thought otherwise and on one notable occasion thought that the council's approach would in all likelihood lead to a catastrophic war. Mr. Dulles was reported to be among those who had seen the problem differently from the President, and, whether that is so or not, there have been numerous instances of the President seeing things differently from Mr. Dulles. Before the Geneva conference of last July, it was plain to everyone here that the President was determined to offset Mr. Dulles's dour and gloomy anticipations with some sunny ones of his own, and scarcely a press conference passed in that period without Mr. Eisenhower saying something quite contrary in spirit to what the Secretary of State was saying in his news conferences. Between the President and the Secretary of State, there is quite a considerable difference in outlook and method, and this has almost surely had its effect on the general situation. Whether the results at Geneva advanced or retarded American interests, they were results that were achieved when the President powerfully asserted his right to make policy and to speak for the nation. Most observers of diplomatic affairs are convinced that the outcome could not have been the same if Mr. Dulles had been the American spokesman.

Mr. Dulles will shortly return to Geneva for the meeting of the Foreign Ministers, and even if by that time the President is able to follow the transactions there and instruct the American team, it will not be the same thing. It is likely to be quite a while before he can subject himself to the rigors of the press conference, which he made so valuable an instrument of diplomacy last summer, and it may well be that there may not be enough time in what remains of his term to allow him to resume his role as spokesman for the entire nation. It was in that role that he was his most effective and will be most sorely missed.

40 The Power to Speak

Letter from Denver
October 27, 1955

Early this week, it was announced that the President would today begin work on the 1956 State of the Union message, and a few hours ago Mr. Eisenhower's press secretary, James C. Hagerty, reported with satisfaction, after a visit to Fitzsimons Army Hospital, that the schedule was being maintained. He said that Major General Wilton B. Persons, a White House assistant whose chief responsibility is liaison with Congress, and Kevin McCann, a public-relations man and speech writer, had arrived in Denver on the Columbine III and were assisting the President in the preparation of the report, which will be due in January. Mr. Hagerty's statement stressed, as did the earlier announcement, that this was the first work session—the first real presidential chore—that Mr. Eisenhower has undertaken since the onset of his illness on September 24.

To his auditors, Mr. Hagerty's talk about this event seemed of greater interest and importance than the event itself; indeed, there is a tendency to believe that the event was arranged so it might be talked about. Although the news that the President is at this moment working on next year's State of the Union message has gone out to the country and to the world, not many of the observers of political affairs who are now making Denver their headquarters regard this as an entirely literal statement of the facts. They do not for an instant doubt that the President is receiving General Persons and Mr. McCann, or that the three of them are discussing matters connected with the general welfare that might very well turn up in the January address. Nor do they question Mr. Hagerty's word that the State of the Union message has been put on the agenda for this meeting. But they find it almost impossible to persuade themselves that a President who has not been permitted to see a newspaper in over a month and has been shielded, on doctors' orders, from knowledge of any possibly unsettling developments is in any meaningful sense "working" on a policy report. Moreover, it is felt here that if the President were now able to participate actively in the affairs of his administration, he would be most unlikely to give a high priority to the State of the Union message. The preparation of this message has never been regarded as a particularly significant part of the Presidency. The Constitution requires that such a paper be submitted "from time to time," but most Presidents, while complying, have taken the requirement rather lightly. From Jefferson's day to Wilson's, the messages were sent to the Capitol by courier and listlessly read by clerks, often to an almost empty chamber. Wilson saw the message as a useful means of impressing his wishes on Congress, and he restored the practice of going before a joint session and delivering it in person. His successors have followed his lead. To a greater extent than most Presidential papers, though, the State of the Union message is an assembled, rather than a written, document, being in the main a catalogue of the legislative requirements of the executive agencies. In the normal course of events, it comes to the President's attention only in the final stages, and Mr. Eisenhower's involvement in it at this time could consist, one imagines, only of hearing his subordinates' suggestions on what they would like to have him endorse when Congress reconvenes in January.

According to earlier statements by Mr. Hagerty and others, President Eisenhower has been receiving such suggestions ever since he became well enough to have visitors. For example, Herbert Brownell spent some time at the President's bedside last week, and before flying back to Washington he informed the press that he had won the President's support for the construction of some new jails. Since Congress will be called upon to provide authorization for this construction, it would be fitting to mention the need for it in the State of the Union message, and no doubt the Bureau of Prisons has drawn up some description of its needs that could be incorporated in the President's report. Few people here, however, regard as plausible the supposition that the President or any of his leading advisers feel any great sense of urgency in joining the Attorney General's request for more penitentiaries to all the other reports and requests that the message will embody when it is submitted next year. The job has to be done by someone sometime, but it hardly seems the sort of thing that demands the attention and exertion of a hospitalized President just now.

It is more or less taken for granted here that there is and will continue to be a somewhat tropistic quality to many of the announcements released by Mr. Hagerty in the temporary White House offices at the Lowry Air Force Base. This does not apply to the medical bulletins. Most people have been enormously impressed by the candor with which the details of the President's condition have been made known, and no one has at any time cast doubt on the progress reports that are issued three times daily by Mr. Hagerty and at two-week intervals by Dr. Paul Dudley White. But there is a firm and widespread conviction that the official accounts of what occurs in the President's hospital room during the increasingly numerous visits of his associates in the government are not to be taken wholly at face value. The truth is that the President's illness and the circumstance that it struck at this time and at this distance from Washington have placed Mr. Hagerty and his colleagues in an unprecedentedly difficult position, one that seems to leave them no alternative but to speak on occasion in euphemisms and to resort on occasion to staging techniques. They are faced with the problem of accompanying the news of Mr. Eisenhower's daily headway as a convalescent with news of his recovery of political leadership. His physical progress does not have to be dramatized;

everyone recognizes the significance of his first sitting up in bed, his first steps, his first photographs, and all the other familiar markers on the path back to a normal state of well-being. It is not quite so simple to convey an impression of his return to the exercise of his presidential powers—in part because he is not making this return so rapidly, but in larger part because these powers, while mighty, are difficult to express in words. In one sense, Mr. Eisenhower is leading a more active political life now than he did in the period immediately preceding his heart attack. He sees two or three government people a day for a half hour each; within the last ten days, he has been visited by practically all the senior members of his administration. In the several weeks before he fell ill, he spent about forty-five minutes a day at his desk and saw very few of the people he is now seeing. It was, in the view he evidently took, a dry period in politics, which left him without much to do. But because he was then in full vigor, there was no need to remind anyone of his continuing authority. Now, however, though government business is still a good bit slower than it will be soon, the psychological need is great, and it has fallen to the lot of Mr. Hagerty and those working with him to impress on the public consciousness the notion that there is a center of authority in American government and that Mr. Eisenhower is it. Now and then, this can be done by promulgating statements from Mr. Eisenhower's bedside, such as his letter to the Vice-President asking him to go on calling and presiding over Cabinet meetings, and his memorandum of this morning on the Geneva Conference that begins tomorrow, but the feeling of presidential advisers here is that letters from the President's hospital room tend to emphasize his general disability and his absence from his accustomed place of power, whereas reports of visits with him, and of government business discussed and negotiated in the course of those visits, convey a sense of continuing command and control.

It may be that a certain amount of government business is in fact being transacted in these conferences, but the common belief is that the Cabinet members and other high officials who have recently been in Denver would have visited Fitzsimons whether or not they had anything of substance to discuss with the President. Moreover, it is believed that in a good many cases the matters of substance that are discussed with the President are quite different from those that are later reported on to the press. As a case in point, no one takes very seriously the idea that Herbert Brownell flew from Washington to Denver to burden Mr. Eisenhower with a discussion of the problem of housing prisoners of the federal government. No one supposes that a President who was not permitted to hear the news of the French withdrawal from the United Nations General Assembly was playing any very active part in the making of American foreign policy when he met with Mr. Dulles last week, and no one supposes that he is actively at work today on so routine a task as the preparation of an early draft of the State of the Union message. What seems clear from this vantage point is that the President has received the officials who are concerned with these problems, has been given their assurance that they are working on them, and has, in turn, assured them of his unfaltering confidence in them.

This exchange of assurances is a function of leadership and administration, and no one regards its recent manifestations as being in any way synthetic. Mr. Eisenhower's greatest gift has always been thought to be his ability to command the loyalty of his associates and to return their loyalty with trust and support. And there seems to be little doubt that he has the loyalty he needs now. His illness has—for the time being, at any rate—unified the Republican leadership and stilled the noisiest of the factional disputes. However, the assurances that are exchanged, if they are to be made known to the public through the news agencies, have to be somehow related to specific matters of government business, and it is this necessity that leads administration officers to appear here and to insist publicly that the President is thoroughly *au courant* on the jail problem, or—as Mr.

Dulles declared in the very conference in which he revealed that nothing had yet been said to the President about the French crisis—that Mr. Eisenhower is providing our Geneva delegation with the "counsel and advice [of] a President who fully knows the issues."

In terms of the inner politics of the administration, what really counts about the President's conferences is not the questions of policy that are discussed but the simple fact that a conference has been held. If Mr. Eisenhower spends half an hour with the Secretary of Agriculture and Mr. Hagerty calls a press conference at which the Secretary says he has had a good meeting with the President, then Mr. Benson's fellow-Republicans will understand where the President stands on Mr. Benson's policies. It does not matter in the slightest whether the President has or has not been led through all the complexities of the debate over flexible, as against rigid, price supports. Mr. Hagerty, though, cannot think solely in terms of administration politics. His province is public relations, and it would solve none of his problems merely to issue an announcement that this administration member or that one had seen the President and been encouraged by him to carry on. Headlines are not made of such announcements. And so, one after another, the dignitaries who have had audiences with the President are escorted from Fitzsimons Hospital to Lowry Field and there presented to the White House correspondents, before whom they customarily make lengthy asseverations and by whom they are invariably questioned in considerable detail about what passed between them and Mr. Eisenhower. These press conferences are an extraordinary innovation, and if they were to establish any sort of precedent, they would bring about some crucial changes in the institution of the presidency. As it is, they come perilously close to undermining the right of the President and his advisers to maintain confidential relationships. In his room at Fitzsimons, Mr. Eisenhower is at once more sequestered and more exposed than he has ever been in Washington. In Washington, the President is under public scrutiny

more than most men would wish to be—and more, certainly, than
Mr. Eisenhower relishes—but in a sense the seclusion he enjoys
there is almost monastic compared to what, despite his isolation,
he gets here. In Washington, the White House does not as a
general rule consider itself under any obligation to furnish public
information on the President's conversations with his callers. In
that setting, it would be unthinkable for Cabinet members to
follow the Denver practice of calling formal press conferences
immediately after their audiences with the President. It is, of
course, the practice of the White House correspondents to keep
a close check on the President's visitors and to press them for
details of their interviews, but the visitors thus pressed are free
to answer or refuse to answer as they choose, and unless the
subject of a particular meeting is raised at a presidential news
conference, no more is ordinarily heard of it. In Washington, too,
it frequently happens that people the President wishes to see are
shown in through a rear entrance to the White House and that
their names are left off the appointments calendar released daily
by the press secretary. There, under normal circumstances, the
President is able to retain at least a measure of his privacy and
to keep certain of his relationships on a confidential basis.

In Denver, with the President hospitalized, this would be
physically impracticable even if it had not been judged to be
politically undesirable. Although this is a large and busy city, the
presence in it of any distinguished figure in political life would
be just about impossible to conceal during the present crisis.
Within recent days, two friends of the President who do not
qualify as currently conspicuous figures in government—Paul
Hoffman, the automobile manufacturer, and Clifford J. Roberts,
the President's investment counsellor—came here unannounced
and evidently desirous of remaining that way, but they were
spotted in the Brown Palace Hotel within a few hours of their
arrival, and both they and Mr. Hagerty were questioned at
length as to the significance of their presence in Denver. In the
case of administration members, though, it is not the difficulty

of concealment that accounts for such novelties as press conferences under presidential auspices for Mr. Brownell and for such ordinarily retiring figures as Dr. Arthur Burns and Gabriel Hauge, a pair of White House economists who were here a couple of days ago. These are carefully staged productions, and they have arisen out of the need to create a substitute for the contact with American and world opinion that a President normally maintains through speeches, through news conferences, and through the public's mere awareness of his active presence. As one observer put it the other day, the President is retaining and exercising the most important of his powers—the power to speak to the country and the power to speak on behalf of the country—by delegating a small portion of it to each member of the administration who is invited to his room at Fitzsimons and led from there to a press conference at Lowry Field.

Nothing else about the Denver experience has been so impressive as the evidence it has afforded that the power to communicate is in fact the most important of the presidential powers. One gets a sharp sense of this in the offices at Lowry Field, where it is possible to see the presidency in far clearer perspective than one can achieve in Washington. The people who are considered to be essential to the smooth functioning of the presidency have been brought out here and given offices in the base administration building, an abandoned tuberculosis sanatorium in the southeast quarter of the city. These essential people are surprisingly few in number. No unenlightened visitor to this rather shabby military compound would guess that it is the staff headquarters for the President and Commander-in-Chief. Excluding clerks, stenographers, Secret Service men, and the like, the White House staff members come to no more than half a dozen, and even with everyone counted in, the total floor space they occupy seems comparable to that of a business of very modest proportions; not more than twelve or fifteen small offices are in use. The largest is that of Mr. Hagerty, and he, his staff, and the correspondents accredited here occupy on the first floor of the building almost exactly the same amount of space as that devoted to official government business on the second floor. In terms of strict protocol, the ranking figure here is Sherman Adams, the Assistant to the President. By any other standard, though, Mr. Hagerty, the top man in the communications department, is at the head of the Denver roster. Indeed, against this background Mr. Hagerty stands out as just about the largest figure in the administration next to the President himself, and there was a time, immediately following the President's attack, when he was here alone with Mr. Eisenhower and in a real sense *was* the administration. For several days he was even more authentically the spokesman for American power than the Vice-President, because the Vice-President was never duly authorized to speak for the President, as Mr. Hagerty was. It is believed that responsibility for the fact that nothing was done to increase Mr. Nixon's authority lies largely with Mr. Hagerty. It was he who discouraged the Department of Justice from conducting a study of the constitutional questions involved in delegating powers, and it is assumed that today it is he, as the spokesman's spokesman, who has the largest voice in such matters of high policy as which administration members shall see the President, in what order, and for what announced purpose. For the time being, these are about the only questions of high policy that the President or anyone on the White House staff is concerned with, and it is expected to be this way up until the President is removed to Gettysburg, and for quite a while thereafter.

41   Trial Balances

December 1955

The major phase of the Eisenhower administration ended in the autumn of 1955. The President's illness and the reaching of an impasse at the Geneva meeting of the foreign ministers provided imposing markers of a terminal point that would in any case have been there. Broadly speaking, every administration makes its record in the first three years; the fourth is given over to defending the accomplishments of the first three—or to explaining away the lack of accomplishment. The fourth year is a time not for doing but for backing and filling and talking.

In the instant case, though, unforeseen and unwelcome developments supplied large and vivid stress marks. On September 24, 1955, in Denver, Colorado, the President suffered a heart attack which a celebrated cardiologist, Dr. Paul Dudley White, described as "neither mild nor serious [but] moderate" in character. For about three weeks, such executive decisions as had to be made—fortunately, it was a period of very light governmental activity—were made by the Vice-President and a group of White House advisers and senior Cabinet officers. In less than a month, the President was holding bedside conferences in Fitzsimons Army Hospital and was once again the functioning symbol if not the actual wielder of executive authority. Seven weeks after the attack, he was keeping regular hours at a temporary White House in the United States Post Office at Gettysburg, Pennsylvania. In Gettysburg, as in the last days at Denver, he was as active a chief magistrate, by the measures of time and energy, as he had been before his illness, but no one could sensibly maintain that his leadership under these circumstances was as effective or as powerful as it had earlier been or as it should be. To say otherwise, as some Republican leaders did, was in effect to say that the President, as President, is not an essential presence in American government or at its seat, Washington. His absence certainly did make a difference, one so conspicuous that it would have marked the ending of the major phase of the Eisenhower administration whether or not it had coincided with the natural ending of legislative and policy-making activity in the four-year cycle.

The American people were fortunate beyond imagining that

the illness did not strike at some other time. It is awkward to speak of good luck and happy coincidence in connection with a coronary thrombosis, but there is no escaping the fact that any other time would have been worse, far worse than late September of 1955. By then, the better part of his work had either been done or was beyond the possibility of doing.

The October-November Geneva conference, the one just below the summit, was another milestone. Diplomacy does not follow the rhythm and beat of our domestic politics, and if the second Geneva conference signalized anything at all it was the beginning, not the ending, of a period of intense diplomatic activity, one in which the opportunities for victory and defeat were greatly increased by the new flexibility and imaginativeness of Russian policy. In strictly American terms, though, Geneva was also a culmination. When it was over, the record on the foreign policy of the Eisenhower administration was pretty much all in. The "bold new program" had been tried, found wanting, and replaced by a program that was neither very new nor very bold but that was informed by experience, a sharpened sense of reality, and the same morality that had characterized previous policies. By November 1955, in other words, the record on the Eisenhower foreign policy had been made, and it can be seen, despite what is almost universally described as the failure of Geneva, as a rather impressive one. Most post-Geneva judgments are too facile. Was it in fact a failure? It has never been within the power of an American government to bring the Russians to terms on Germany or any other matter of substance. The stalemate at the end of 1955 was of our making only in the sense that we did not choose to end it by war or appeasement. It was in some ways a more perilous stalemate than that which has existed for the last several years, for the sense of security it gave the Russians encouraged them to undertake bolder interventions in the Middle and Far East than they had ever before undertaken. But it gave them no more opportunities than it gave us, and both Geneva conferences could be judged a success insofar as they led to a Soviet commitment not to make war an instrument of policy and insofar as they bred in Russian minds and others an understanding of American policy.

The Soviet Union, Premier Bulganin said in an address before the Indian Parliament in New Delhi on November 21, 1955, "resolutely repudiates war as a means of settling international problems." The commitment may be worthless. Bulganin may be unmasked as an American agent day after tomorrow or he may find himself sixteen rungs down the bureaucratic ladder. Or he may simply repudiate his repudiation. Certain students of Bolshevik history assert that the iron Bolshevik will makes only strategic concessions and that no amount of Russian oratory counts for good in the real world. They insist that we got nothing of value at Geneva that we did not already have. They may be right, but their reading of events is in part a consequence of their belief that the Communist mind has no properties other than those lodged there by that malignant and ridiculous view of life known as Marxism-Leninism. They insist that it is idle to suppose that Bulganin, Khrushchev, and their colleagues could in any degree be affected by things undreamt of in their philosophy—the patent earnestness and good will shown by the President at Geneva, for example, or his truthful representation of American opinion as uninterested in the destruction of Communism by war. But there is in the minds of these students of Bolshevik theory and history at least a strain of the determinism that characterizes the thing they study, and a great many nonexperts, as well as quite a few experts, find it possible to believe that something well worth accomplishing was in fact accomplished when the cold-war belligerents were able to state before the world that they would not carry belligency to the point of bellicosity. This was the essential achievement of the first Geneva conference of 1955; it was intact at the end of the second one.

But these are questions apart from the consideration of the moment. Whether the administration's foreign policy is sound or unsound, successful or unsuccessful, the fact remains that its evolution is at this stage complete. The mysteries are dissolved, the ambiguities resolved. A *modus vivendi,* to use a phrase the President likes, has been found; it may not endure, it may be the death of us all, but it represents what the Eisenhower administration regards as tolerable and the best that in this epoch can be hoped for. We are on a kind of plateau that affords a clear view of the ground we have been over and a good, if in some ways disheartening, view of what lies ahead. The rhetoric is no longer an obstructing feature. No one now, for example, is in doubt as to what was meant by "massive retaliation," "liberation," or "agonizing reappraisal." Not very much was meant by any of them. This can be seen by an examination of deeds and of language that is not mere rhetoric.

All this is only to say, at too great length, that now is a fitting time to examine the record of the Eisenhower administration, to appraise the leadership of the thirty-fourth President of the United States during his first term in office.

II.

In the spring of 1953, not very long after his inauguration, the President, in a conversation that was casual but serious, volunteered an explanation of why he had entered politics. Early in 1952, he told a guest at one of his White House stag dinners, it had been his belief that if he did not accept the Republican nomination that was being urged upon him by so many Republicans of influence, Harry Truman would be returned to office. Eisenhower then felt certain that Truman intended to run again. He felt certain, too, that if he declined the Republican nomination, it would go by default to Senator Taft. In the contest he foresaw between Taft and Truman, Truman was bound to win, and this, he explained, had seemed to him about the worst thing that could happen to the country.

Although he had been privileged to see a good deal of the better side of the Truman administration, Eisenhower, it became clear in this conversation, had taken the conventional Republican view of the last Democratic President. He said that if he could possibly have known that Adlai Stevenson was to be the Democratic candidate, he would not have sought the presidency for himself. He said he had come to regard Stevenson as an upright and capable man; he believed Stevenson would have made a good president. This was a bit beside his point, though; his point was that what had troubled him deeply—what had, in fact, goaded him into political activity in his own behalf—was the prospect of another four years of Harry Truman.

One clear implication of this story, which is of unchallengeable authenticity, is that Eisenhower would have preferred not to be where he was when he told it: in the White House. Had his recent rival, or almost anyone else, been there in his place, he could have been taking his ease on his Gettysburg acres, his patriot's heart and mind untroubled by developments across the Monocacy River and over the green hills of Maryland in Washington.

The President is not a devious man, and the acceptance of a nomination for the presidency is not an act that requires apology or defense. There is no reason to think that the explanation he made to his guest in the early spring of 1953 was any different from the explanation he was making to himself in that period. He was trying to recall his 1952 state of mind a year later, and that could not have been easy. In the course of that year, he had led a hectic, crowded life. The regimen of a presidential candidate and president-elect is rough on memory and judgment. Adlai Stevenson, who was only a candidate, described the existence he knew in 1952 as "a continuous and disquieting menace to equilibrium."

The President's recollection was offered in perfect good faith, and the melancholy, almost self-pitying tone of it was one that came to be well-known to those who observed him up to the time of his illness last September. Still, there was a good deal, in fact a great deal, wrong with the story he told. For one thing,

Harry Truman had withdrawn as a candidate on March 29, 1952. "I have served my country long and I think efficiently and honestly," he had said. "I shall not accept renomination." After that assertion, no one of good judgment thought it remotely possible that Mr. Truman would be recalled to service. Republicans were not alone in thinking it time for a change; a great many Democrats—and loyal ones—were relieved by President Truman's retirement. At the time of its announcement, General Eisenhower, still at his NATO command at Rocquencourt, was by no means fully committed to a campaign. He had said in January that he would not "seek nomination" but that "a clear-cut call to political duty [would] transcend my present responsibilities." From January through April, he stuck to the position that he would serve if nominated but that he would not press any claim for nomination. On March 30, he was still far above the battle. Without fighting, he had won, on March 11, a smashing victory in the New Hampshire primaries, which were also the occasion of a humiliating defeat of Truman by Estes Kefauver. Eisenhower had not yet resigned as Supreme Commander, though he had probably made up his mind to do so, and he was not to return to this country until June 1. He was mustered out of the Army on June 3.

Thus, if his only interest had been in retiring Truman, he could have retired himself in April or May. It may be that he was too deeply involved for an abrupt withdrawal at that time, but he could at the very least, if Truman's elimination was all that he wanted, have foregone the vigorous pre-convention campaign he made. It seems clear now, as it seemed clear then, that without that campaign he could not have hoped to overcome the clear desire of most Republican leaders to give the nomination to Senator Taft.

The Truman theory of Eisenhower's candidacy simply does not hold up. It is, moreover, in conflict with another of his explanations—more widely reported than this one—of what induced him to run. In Denver, in the summer of 1952, he told a group of reporters that his single aim had been to serve the country by eliminating not Harry Truman but—Senator Taft. He used some rather biting language that he believed, mistakenly as it turned out, would be kept off the record. His general theme was that he had sought the nomination because he thought it would be a first-class tragedy if an isolationist like Taft were in the White House. He said he had given the best years of his life to the development of American leadership in the affairs of the part of the world that most concerns us, the North Atlantic community of nations, and that he could not bear to see that leadership pass into the hands of a man with Taft's views.

The Taft theory makes more political sense than the Truman theory. To anyone, though, who saw very much of the 1952 presidential campaign, neither theory can have much appeal. The truth is that no theory is needed and none can account for the facts. It was not to save the country from Truman that the General embraced Senator Jenner in Indianapolis or conducted furtive and sordid negotiations with Senator McCarthy in a Peoria hotel. Truman had been out of the picture for several months when those unattractive spectacles occurred. It was not to preserve Atlantic unity or crush a resurgent isolationism that he made all those breathless speeches about the hundred-odd taxes that were collected on every egg an American ate. In his own mind, subject as it may have been to "the disquieting menace to equilibrium," the embrace, the negotiations, and the egg speeches no doubt fitted into some noble scheme for rendering a service to the United States and to all mankind; it is characteristic of candidates to be fertile in the conception of exalted aims that justify the most questionable of political devices. But a clear and well-established sequence of events eliminates the possibility that Eisenhower in that time thought of himself as saving the country from Taft or Truman. We had already been spared both of them.

As a matter of simple fact, Dwight Eisenhower's presence on the hustings in that frantic autumn of 1952 was one of the few things that did not seem to require any explanation at all. The man wanted to be President because he wanted to be President. He had, as they say, the bug. The fever was upon him. In 1954 and 1955, when he often struck one as the most diffident and discontented of presidents, it was possible to wonder about the origins of that 1952 passion. It was especially possible in November of 1955, when, instead of returning to the White House, he chose to make Gettysburg, with its four-mile drive to an office and all of its other shortcomings and inconveniences, his headquarters. It seemed almost a gesture of hatred for Washington and the White House, and it was hard to avoid asking why in Heaven's name, if he disliked the office that much, he had been so desperate in seeking it in 1952? Perhaps the answer lay in his military training: facing the alternatives of victory and defeat, he chose victory. Anyway, in 1952 he was out for blood. He wanted to win the election, and he behaved as men bent on victory generally behave. In fairness, it must be remembered that Harry Hopkins dealt with Frank Hague, in Franklin Roosevelt's behalf, as Arthur Summerfield dealt with McCarthy and that Adlai Stevenson was uncommunicative on the subject of Pat McCarran.

It is curious, though, and certainly significant, that in two periods of relative calm the President should have put the responsibility for his plight on other men. It was during a breathing spell in what he described as "this great crusade" that he pinned the blame on Taft. It is unusual for a crusader to describe his undertaking in purely negative terms and, particularly, in terms of individual men rather than of substantive evils. And it is extraordinary that Eisenhower, after a few months spent in grappling with the problems of the presidency and learning the hard way how wrong Admiral Dewey had been in saying that "the office of President is not such a difficult one," should have been able to speak of himself, without any visible trace of irony, as a man who had sacrificed greatly in order to spare his countrymen another four years of Harry Truman.

III.

For there are very few things about the Eisenhower administration more striking than the numerous ways in which it resembles the Truman administration. It is commonplace, of course, to observe that the Republicans under Eisenhower, far from making the changes they said it was time for, have adopted and adapted nearly all of the basic policies of the Democrats under Truman. What John Foster Dulles once called "the immoral policy of containment" was pursued as regularly as it was denounced. In the aftermath of Geneva, it was not even denounced. The administration may still proclaim its hostility to "creeping socialism," but one hears little said in dispraise of the "welfare state," which is still intact despite the efforts of the reconstituted Hoover Commission to have it dismantled. All this was only to be expected. In a society as stable as ours, the kind of change that affects the basic structure of government is seldom sudden or drastic; to say that a new administration has carried on most of the policies of the old one is not to cite a remarkable or unexpected circumstance but merely to describe the character of the political order. It was only the political neurotics and romantics who looked forward, with exhilaration or with dread, to an end to what Eisenhower had called "wickedness in government" or to the early termination of the Century of the Common Man. It was always in the cards that wickedness and the Common Man would flourish—now in opposition, now in alliance—and those whose hopes and fears were not too much entangled with their intelligence understood that the election of a Republican president would not be the dawn of an entirely new day for rugged individualism, the gold standard, or Chiang Kai-shek.

But there are similarities between the Eisenhower and Truman administrations that are not at all of the sort ordained by the system. The two are a good deal alike in manner and method, in their patterns for the delegation of authority, and in the character of their respective leaders. The last resemblance is perhaps the most notable. As human beings and as political types, Eisenhower and Truman have more in common than either would in all likelihood care to admit. And they certainly have more in common with one another than either has with any of the seven men who held the presidency before them in this century. Both operate at low pressures. Both are moderate, middling, median figures in character and in doctrine. Neither has the vocation for leadership that the two Roosevelts and Woodrow Wilson had—or even, for that matter, Herbert Hoover and William Howard Taft. Their backgrounds are extraordinarily similar. They are products of middle-class families that lived close to the edge of poverty and close to one another—Independence and Abilene are no more than a hundred and fifty miles apart—in the center of the country. Both were brought up in a stern, semi-fundamentalist Protestant morality. Both are men of simple integrity and personal honor. Both have a kind of standard-American personality. Simplicity, frankness, and openness of manner commended each to his own following.

Truman is a somewhat brisker sort, with more bite and acid in what he says and does and a somewhat more bookish turn of mind. Eisenhower tends to be wanting in crispness and to lack Truman's sense of the concrete. Both, though, are essentially unideological, unintellectual, intuitive pragmatists, and feeble verbalizers. West Point left its mark on Eisenhower and made him more a respecter of rank and station than Truman, who was schooled in hard knocks and haberdashery. No man is a hero to his haberdasher—at least no man in mufti. Truman was almost as greatly awed by all generals except Douglas Mac-Arthur as Eisenhower is by all captains of industry. The difference, though, may be merely an aspect of the sameness—each, in his choice of heroes, has reacted conventionally to his own experience of life. Their taste in human beings, irrespective of vocation, is very much alike: both, for instance, admire the special wit of George Allen, the jolly hotel proprietor who had several small functions in the Truman administration, became a Gettysburg neighbor of Eisenhower's, and was his only companion the evening he was stricken. Except for Allen and a very few others, Eisenhower does not take well to politicians, but those who have taken the measure of such White House cronies as Kevin McCann and Harry Butcher find it within a fraction of an inch of several White House figures—scarcely the most revered ones—of five years ago.

Eisenhower was to some extent formed by his military experience, but what has always been thought notable about him is the smallness of the extent. It is his distinction and the source of much of the esteem in which he has always been held that he was never overwhelmed by the myths of his profession. He has been valued not as an illustrious representative of his caste but as a soldier remarkable for the many ways in which he was untouched and unaffected by his soldierly distinctions. It was, in other words, largely the Truman in Eisenhower that made Eisenhower a great world figure. It may even have been the Truman in him—the basic civilian-ness, the lack of dazzle, the resistance to *étalage militaire*—that led to his rapid elevation through the higher ranks, military and political, after only an average progress through the lower ones.

The simplest appraisal that could be made of the Truman administration was that it functioned intelligently and creatively—and at times courageously—in foreign affairs and rather badly in most domestic affairs. Because Truman, like Eisenhower, was not much of a hand at the formulation of policy, the character of his administration was revealed in its personnel. Truman put first-class men in charge of the State and Defense Departments and an assortment of incompetents, mediocrities, and boodlers in charge of the rest of the government. His major military and diplomatic appointments were superior to those of Franklin Roosevelt, who wanted men who would not talk back in the agencies he himself intended to run, but most of the rest of his advisers were men of few attainments, and his judicial appointments were almost invariably regrettable. Naturally, there were exceptions: Louis Johnson was a catastrophic Defense Secretary, while Oscar Chapman and Charles Brannan, Secretaries of the Interior and Agriculture, were men of professional competence and high standards of performance. But by and large the rule held, and one had the impression that the only way to account for the distinction that characterized one part of the government—the part spoken for by Dean Acheson, General Marshall, Robert Patterson, Thomas Finletter, Averell Harriman, Paul Hoffman, Stuart Symington, and Robert Lovett—and the lack of distinction that characterized the rest was in terms of a deal the President must have made with himself, a private resolution of the conflict between the general welfare and the demands of politics. Truman recognized that the over-riding need of his time was for a wise and politically disinterested diplomacy; he also recognized that in a democracy any kind of policy, wise or foolish, bears some kind of political price tag. It may be that he never acknowledged to himself that he was buying support for his foreign policies by giving their heads to men like Howard McGrath and Robert Hannegan and John Snyder, but there is reason to think that he did (could any president have failed to acknowledge the difference between the State Department under Marshall and Acheson and the Department of Justice under Tom Clark, Howard McGrath, and James McGranery?) and whether he did or not, that is the way he ran things.

The Eisenhower pattern has been essentially the same. It is not, however, so clearly manifest in terms of personnel. Eisenhower favors businessmen for any jobs that happen to be available, and on the whole his selections for the leading executive agencies have a quality that Truman's often lacked. This is not to make a moral, intellectual, or even political distinction between them: it would be a bold man who would say that George Humphrey is a better Secretary of the Treasury than John Snyder—or vice versa: what is evident, though, is that in George Humphrey Eisenhower is persuaded he has a man of high qualification for the job, a splendid fulfillment of his campaign promise to bring "the best brains in the country" to Washington. "In Cabinet meetings," he has said, "I always wait for George Humphrey to speak. I sit back and listen to the others talk while he doesn't say anything. But I know that when he speaks he will say just what I am thinking." The President has taken Humphrey's advice on matters as remote from currency and tax collection as mine inspection and atomic research, both of which Humphrey has favored less of. In John Snyder, Truman was persuaded not that he had a genius but only that he had a familiar human being, a known quantity. "He was one of my closest personal friends" he explained in his "Memoirs," "and I knew that I wanted him in my administration in a trusted capacity." Truman surrounded himself with cronies and the cronies of cronies, and his frank acknowledgment of a president's need for loyalty and friendship evokes a sympathy it is hard to feel for Eisenhower's view that a good practicing economist is a man who has made a lot of money.

Still, Eisenhower does deserve credit for the selection of men who appear to him to be qualified by experience and achievement for the offices they hold. There is nothing wrong in wanting the best brains. His judgment has not been confirmed in every case, but in a few it has worked out fairly well. Though Ezra Taft Benson has not been the most enchanting of public personalities, he has brought integrity and a determination to resist economic malarkey to his job. It is notable that in general Eisenhower's second choices have on the whole been superior to his first ones: Marion Folsom, Donald Quarles, and James Mitchell are distinguished public servants; they fill their offices in a way that their immediate predecessors—Oveta Culp Hobby, Harold Talbott, and Martin Durkin—never did. And no fair-minded critic can deny that Eisenhower's appointments to the Supreme Court have been better by far than Truman's. If, as Reinhold Niebuhr has said, Eisenhower has "rebuilt American conservatism into a viable political instrument," his court appointments have been the major contribution toward this end in the domestic field.

Nevertheless, there is an essential similarity in the approaches of the two presidents to the two major areas of policy. Truman gave his best to diplomatic and military affairs by commanding the services of the most competent and politically disinterested men he could find, and he found some uncommonly competent ones; at the same time, he played politics—sometimes in the common interest, sometimes not—with just about everything else. In Eisenhower's case, it is a matter of where he himself retains interest, acquires knowledge, and exercises firm control, and where he cedes all authority. In most things that bear on the larger interests of war and peace, the President has held on to the power of decision and has taken his constitutional responsibilities with increasing seriousness. He has over-ridden his Secretary of State, his Joint Chiefs of Staff, and the National Security Council on a good half-dozen occasions. On one occasion, during the crisis over Quemoy and Matsu in early 1955, his exercise of the veto power may well have meant the difference between an uneasy peace and a disastrous war, and for it the free world's gratitude may be as great as for Harry Truman's decisions to support Greek independence in 1947 and resist aggression in Korea in 1950. He provides his own emphases, which are often very different from those of Mr. Dulles and other subordinates, on major policy statements.

Toward most of the rest of government, though, he has been even more neglectful than Truman was. The executive agencies dealing with domestic questions are almost wholly autonomous; they make their own policies (or else freely neglect to make them, as was the case with Mrs. Hobby and the Salk vaccine) and execute them without interference or concern. Their failures and successes are wholly their own. Once Eisenhower has found a first-class automobile dealer, cotton broker, or razor manufacturer to head a department, he has acted as if the public interest has been satisfied and his own responsibility discharged.

IV.

The President has, to be sure, had a hand in the formulation of that curious thing which the Republican National Committee calls "the Eisenhower program" and which appears in restrospect to have consisted almost entirely of formulations: talk about such worthwhile things as good highways, increased school capacity, "parity in the marketplace," *mens sana in corpore sano*, Hawaiian statehood, trade-not-aid, fair labor and immigration laws. He has spoken an abundance of phrases to describe what he has said are his purposes: dynamic conservatism, progressive moderation, moderate progressivism. What, in institutional terms, they mean to him is most unclear ("I myself have used such phrases," he told a gathering of Republican state chairmen in 1955, "because we want to be known for what we are, the party of progress"), but what they clearly enough describe for Leonard Hall and his associates is the dilemma faced by politicians who must get their campaign funds from the rich and do their campaigning among the not so rich. It takes no advanced degrees in political science to perceive that the conservatism and moderation are for the comfortable, the dynamism and progressivism for the striving. The President unquestionably has some generalized notion of civic virtue and social welfare in mind when he speaks of the "program"—he has come quite a distance since the days when he said that true social security was to be found only in jails—but in point of fact the program has never been more than a pastiche of pieties, some of them borrowed from contemporary liberalism, some from the school of rightist uplift spoken for by Dr. Norman Vincent Peale, the *Reader's Digest*, and the public-relations industry.

As time for fulfillment runs out, the Eisenhower program remains programmatic. If an administration is graded by its impact on institutions, the Eisenhower administration has almost nothing to show. It has left the country almost exactly as it found it, with nothing added and nothing taken away. Its consequential acts have been those that have no platitude to represent them in the dogma as revealed through the official texts—such things, that is, as the Dixon-Yates contract, the deterioration of services in such service agencies as Commerce, Agriculture, and Health, Education, and Welfare, when it was headed by Mrs. Hobby; the repeated violations of the conservation tradition that had taken most of this century to establish; and the excesses of the internal security program. But even these acts have been pretty largely nullified: the Dixon-Yates contract was voided; goaded by the Eighty-fourth Congress, the service agencies restored their services and Mrs. Hobby retired; much of the conservation program was likewise restored; with the passing of Senator McCarthy, the internal security program became once again what it had been under the Democrats—making as much and as little sense in 1955 as it had in 1950.

Some of the cardinal weaknesses of the Truman administration reflected lack of authority and competence on the part of the President himself. Like Eisenhower, he presided over a divided party and never enjoyed large congressional majorities. He was unable to manage everything and everybody in his jurisdiction. Eisenhower may be similarly incapable of giving leadership in all departments—in all likelihood he is, since the job is not scaled to ordinary human capabilities—but this cannot be said with certainty, for the truth is that he has never put himself to the test. Where Truman failed, it was not for want of energy. He was an indefatigable worker. Every phase of government interested him, and he went to great lengths to keep himself informed. Eisenhower, on the other hand, has never been much interested. Though at times he has seemed to work up a certain zest and relish for the business of being President, it is plain that most of the time the whole operational side of government has bored him. He has his own views of what the results ought and ought not to be, but he is indifferent to administrative method and willing to subcontract everything in this line to George Humphrey, Herbert Hoover, and others he regards as managerial wizards. He makes no apparent effort to keep himself abreast even of those developments within his own administration that are items of widespread public knowledge. Time after time, his news conferences have shown him to have less awareness of events than might be expected of any reasonably conscientious reader of any reasonably conscientious newspaper. He is not a conscientious reader himself. It was said before his illness that he saw each morning the New York *Times*, the New York *Herald Tribune*, the *Washington Post & Times-Herald*, the Baltimore *Sun*, and certain other newspapers; no doubt that is so, but they did not grip his attention. Indeed, the matter of newspaper reading tells a good deal about Eisenhower's presidential style. In the first six weeks of his convalescence in Denver, he was given no newspapers at all. It was held that he would find them disturbing. Newspapers, of course, disturb all of us, but it is remarkable that a President well enough to produce oil copies of landscapes and do crossword puzzles (cut from newspapers) should be less agitated when deprived of newspapers then when given them. Most public men well enough to read would suffer far more from *not* knowing what was happening in the world than from knowing. But Eisenhower's lack of knowing has been so formidable that at times one wonders if it is not actually a revulsion.

He has often had a hard time identifying figures in his own official family. He has frequently been unaware of the leading bureaucratic conflicts of the day. When all of Washington, for example, was in a stew over the affair of Wolf Ladejinsky, the agricultural economist who was held to be a loyalty risk by Eisenhower's Department of Agriculture and a shining patriot by Eisenhower's Foreign Operations Administration, the President had only the dimmest acquaintance with the facts of the case, and of some widely reported aspects his ignorance was total.

One cannot, in such instances, ascribe his failings to a faulty sense of injustice, for we know very well that his instincts are sound and honorable. Nor can his defenders plead a lack of time and energies, for the record is clear that no president since Calvin Coolidge, who was a devotee of the afternoon snooze, has relaxed more or taxed his energies less than Eisenhower. It is possible only to conclude that the President finds the day-to-day problems of government tedious and fatiguing. He at no time made much of an effort to keep up with them.

This was never more apparent than in the Dixon-Yates affair, for which it was said that his personal responsibility was heavy. We may not for years, if ever, learn exactly what that responsibility amounted to, but we do know something of the extent of his ignorance and innocence. At the very start of the controversy, the President told a news conference that the public would be given the "complete record" of the transaction by the Bureau of the Budget and the Atomic Energy Commission. "It is all yours," he told the assembled reporters, and undoubtedly he meant what he said. The press—or that small part of it that thought the Dixon-Yates contract worth looking into—sought the "complete record" and, after innumerable rebuffs, got only scraps and pieces, with some pieces the worse for being tampered with. The President's help was once more sought by the reporters, who were told in a voice almost tremulous with irritation, that they would be shown "every document that was pertinent to this thing." Speaking on his own authority, without recourse to pertinent documents, the President assured the press that a certain Mr. Adolphe Wenzell, a noted banker and a man whose role in the affair seemed crucial, "was never called in or asked a single thing about the Dixon-Yates contract." Later, it was revealed that Mr. Wenzell was quite deeply involved and in ways that did not seem altogether wholesome; he had been at one and the same time a Bureau of the Budget consultant on the contract and a vice-president of the First Boston Corporation, which was to have played an important part in financing the project the contract authorized. All this was far outside the President's knowledge and understanding of the case, not only in its earlier stages, when there was no reason for him to be advised of every step, but at a time when the integrity of his administration had been called into question by responsible critics. Questioned about Wenzell's role and other puzzling details almost a year after his promise of the "complete record," the President said, "I don't intend to comment any more at all . . . I don't know exactly such details as that." And of course this was true. He went on to an even profounder truth. "How can I be expected to know? I never heard of it." Several months later, the Atomic Energy Commission announced that it was opposed to paying cancellation fees to the Dixon-Yates syndicate on the ground that Mr. Wenzell's dual role made the contract an illegal instrument.

There is a great deal of which Eisenhower has never heard, and he has organized his office staff and his Cabinet into a kind of conspiracy to perpetuate his unawareness. In no administration within memory have so few decisions been made by the President himself. Eisenhower parcels everything out to committees, commissions, secretariats, advisory groups, and task forces—to say nothing of individual surrogates like Sherman Adams, who perhaps wields more executive power than any man in history not elected to the presidency. The President has made it known that he wants to become part of the administrative process only when those below him have reached unanimity. His function thus is normally limited to veto and ratification—with ratification the rule. The pressure to suppress individual reservations is enormous, for lack of unanimity puts responsibility on the President and consumes his time. It is therefore not surprising that there is so much of which he has not heard. "Amid the mechanical apparatus," the London *Economist* observed in a study of Eisenhower's methods, "the presidency is insulated from the information and pressures which stimulate imagination, feed inspiration, foster insight, and develop sensitivity." Eisenhower has not, of course, wished to cripple his own imagination and sensitivity, but the mechanical apparatus is of his own making and the insulation deliberately sought.

One cannot avoid raising and re-raising the question of motivation. What did Eisenhower want in 1952? What sense can be made of his administration, as apart from his diplomacy, in terms of the man? What does he himself think he is doing as President of the United States? Clues are scarce. Few things are more difficult to get at than the human essence of the Eisenhower administration; frustration meets every attempt to identify it with recognizable attributes of character. The administration lacks the stamp of the President's personality and bears that of no one else—except, possibly, the collective one of the public-relations and advertising men who have provided its rhetoric and some of its policies. Still, the President is President, he fought for the office, and now and then he has shown signs of wanting to continue as President. Why?

A working hypothesis can be constructed on his record and on his few statements of purpose. Though his early career revealed no great concern for any particular theory of American defense or for any particular vision of American destiny, circumstances contrived to make him an historic figure in the building of the alliance between a free America and a free Europe. While the facts could not be made to support his contention that he went into politics against his will and only for the purpose of stopping Harry Truman or Senator Taft, there is in the Taft theory a note that seems to jibe with the known realities. Eisenhower's presidency has been continuous with his career since 1942 in the sense that he has throughout the entire period —first at SHAEF, then at SHAPE, and finally in the White House —addressed himself to the problems of the North Atlantic alliance. If he is concerned, as most public men sooner or later come to be, with the judgment of history, then it would be reasonable to suppose that the verdict he has hoped to win is that of the great unifier, the leader in war and peace of the coalition of Western democracies. He may have had secondary aims. No doubt he did find the Truman administration offensive —most men of his cast of mind did. But such views as he may have had about the organization of American life and government must have been lightly held, for there has not been the faintest glimmering of passion for any undertaking that has involved these views. There has at times been a kind of weary but admirable display of integrity—as, for instance, in the loyalty he has given his Secretary of Agriculture—and at times a warm response to other people, but more often there have been only indifference and impatience and how-can-I-be-expected-to-know?

"If only a man can have courage enough to take the leadership of the middle!" Eisenhower once said, or exclaimed, to John Gunther, who supplied the punctuation. No doubt Eisenhower was in earnest. The President has been in the middle, all right, and there is probably something in him that identifies moderation, the median, the avoidance of extremes, the halfway meeting-point cheerfully sought as Good. He has not "taken" the leadership of the middle, but he has found himself there. He is a middling type by temperament and a mediating personality by function, and it fits this hypothesis to have him a moderate sort, or even a radical in Republican terms, even though he is by instinct pretty far to the right. (One can get into all sorts of nonsense about where the middle is. Plainly, it is between the despised extremes, and each man has his own set of extremes.)

The point would be that neither Eisenhower's middle-seeking practice nor his rightist inclinations are crucial in his own view of himself and his mission. On domestic questions, such views as he holds he holds lightly—lightly enough to change and turn about when there is any gain in so doing. Look at the record. He has spoken disparagingly of the whole idea of social security, he has opposed federal aid to education, and he has described the Tennessee Valley Authority as "creeping socialism." He has seemed to regard the public lands as something the public came by wrongfully, and he is evidently convinced that the only way to redeem the great national investment in atomic energy is to convert it into private capital. This is the record of what he has said and seemed to be saying. But every point has its counterpoint. He has, in practice, favored broad extensions of social security and endorsed the principle of federal aid to education. His farm policy has not pleased Hubert Humphrey, but it has been by and large more to Hubert Humphrey's liking than to Herbert Hoover's. Confronted with his harsh judgments of public enterprises, he has invariably softened them.

Not to labor the point, his middle has been halfway, give or take a few inches, between his dislike of the welfare state and the electorate's liking of it. Where there has been nothing to lose by standing on conservative principle, he has stood. But he has bent before the wind—before, indeed, the gentlest of breezes. He has not been hard enough to be called a true conservative. That was only what he at first hoped to be—the promise of his early venture in politics. Nor is there any sense in regarding him as a Republican New Dealer. He has headed up an administration more liberal and more New Dealish than many Republicans would have liked it to be, but this was because he was forced to work within the realm of the possible in the United States in the fifties and not because he came into the Republican Party with contraband ideology. Ideological guilt can be imputed to him only by the association theory. Eisenhower has no particular view of American life; he has a not very powerful yearning and a quite formidable indifference, and it is the indifference that is characteristic.

In foreign affairs it has been quite otherwise.

V.

Truman and Eisenhower are the first American presidents who have had the opportunity—or better, perhaps, the need—to choose between foreign and domestic policy. The war presidents confronted no such choice, for when there is war, domestic policy, to the degree that it is separate from war policy, is simply shelved for the duration—just as between wars, in the past, foreign policy has been shelved for the duration of peace. Truman and Eisenhower have had to keep both going, and each has been successful only with foreign policy.

We now have enough perspective on Truman to realize that his delinquencies do not detract very greatly from his achievements. Some of the delinquencies of his administration, in fact, are becoming downright difficult to recall. Who today can identify James V. Hunt? Hunt was the prince of the Five Percenters, allegedly the overlord of all the influence peddlers and deep-freeze distributors, a man presumably as steeped in wrong-doing as Merl Young. And who remembers Merl Young? For months on end, the names of Hunt and Young, who was with the Reconstruction Finance Corporation and whose wife wore a mink coat she had acquired under circumstances that Congress thought peculiar, were writ large in the headlines as symbols of the degradation that Eisenhower was later to describe as "the mess in Washington." They are misty, impalpable figures now, gone with their bulging wallets and their costly pelts, and the only good excuse anyone will ever have for recalling them is that they and their kind were partly—but only partly—responsible for the break-up of the concurrent majority that governed this country, under Democratic leadership, for two decades.

Dixon and Yates and Wenzell are likely to elude the memory five years from now as Hunt and Young do today. This is not to say that they are headed for precisely the same chamber of oblivion. Hunt and Young were elements of the Truman atmosphere, as Harry Vaughan was, and as, later Wesley Roberts of the Republican National Committee, Harold Talbott of the Air Force, and Hugh Cross of the Interstate Commerce Commission were elements in the Eisenhower atmosphere. But none of them bore any particular relation to policy. Conflict of interest is as old as government and is no respecter of parties; there are instances which involve purely personal considerations and others in which policy is deeply involved. Because important policy issues were at stake, Dixon and Yates deserved all the attention they got, while Hunt and Talbott deserved less.

But unless we are in for a long period of Republican rule, in which Dixon and Yates might acquire the status of groundbreakers, this aspect of the Eisenhower administration is not likely to keep its present weight. Generally speaking, history strikes a rough rather than a delicate balance, and success in a single great endeavor is sufficient to win an approving verdict for an administration. Those who find much to praise in Harry Truman's stewardship look to the record in diplomacy and none too closely at the record in other spheres. (Truman's admirers, and even his non-admirers, appear to have forgotten that his administration, too, was vulnerable to charges of favoring the large corporations. Blair Bolles, one of the most fair-minded of Washington correspondents, published in 1952 a study of "the rich man's division of the welfare state" entitled *How to Get Rich in Washington,* and its melancholy and well-documented contention was that the New Deal agencies established to help the disadvantaged had been infiltrated by agents of privilege, most notably those representing the giant trusts.) What stands out sharply in retrospect is the leadership Truman displayed in organizing Western resistance to Soviet power. History thrust that organizing task upon him, and he responded well. History thrust a somewhat different task upon Eisenhower. The job of his administration was not to organize a concert of powers but to preserve one—not to build the strength of the free world but to help maintain it and prevent its misuse.

In this, the most crucial of his responsibilities, he has acquitted himself well. Almost to the limit of his power, the President has held the North Atlantic alliance together and has strengthened it, as James Reston has pointed out, by introducing an important new member, the Republican Party. Despite his enormous respect for George Humphrey, and despite Humphrey's contempt for any government undertaking that does not produce a revenue equal to outlay, he has kept more or less intact those shoring-up programs that Truman instituted and that the Republicans in Congress, and more than a few Democrats, hoped to liquidate. To be sure, he has not prevented depredations by Humphrey and by the appropriating depredating committees in House and Senate, but then Truman had difficulties of this sort, too. George Humphrey is only a rich man's John Snyder, and the sharpest meat-axe in Congress is Harry Byrd, Democrat of Virginia, at whose hands, or tight fists, three presidents have met frequent defeat.

It can be, and by Democrats often is, maintained that Eisenhower's retreats have been the really significant and characteristic things about his administration. But the so-called retreats were undertaken in fulfillment of the 1952 Republican platform, and surely the remarkable thing is that Eisenhower has held as much ground as he had. Though it was never to be expected that he would abandon the policy of his predecessors and replace it with Mr. Dulles's talk about liberation, the transfer of American power to the Republican Party put in prospect a deterioration in the Western alliance and a heightening of tensions in the Far East, where any number of Republicans felt that honor and self-interest combined to compel a heightening of tensions. Eisenhower held firm, and if our alliances have weakened in the past four years it is in spite of his best efforts and not because of them. They were in poor shape when he took office, they fell into worse disrepair in the year or so that followed, but as his administration draws to a close only the narrowest partisanship could lead anyone to deny that American prestige is as high today as it has been at any time in the last six or seven years. The restoration of American prestige is almost wholly the President's achievement and is very largely the work of a few months in the summer of 1955, a period culminating in his performance at Geneva.

What is perhaps most extraordinary of all is that Eisenhower, as the leader of a party committed to a riskier, more militant strategy in Asia, succeeded in pursuing one that was certainly not less circumspect than that of the Truman administration. He has pursued it in the face of opposition from some of the most powerful figures in his own administration, thereby opening up the possibility, suggested not long ago by Arthur Schlesinger, Jr., of his going down in history as the President who saved the country from his advisers. And of course it also opened up the possibility of his going down as the President who tried to save us from his advisers but didn't quite make it. At any rate, Eisenhower, though a statesman notoriously of the yielding sort, withstood considerable pressures. For two years, beginning when the administration was very young and Senator Knowland, having studied the terms of the Korean truce, announced that the President of his choice was negotiating a "peace without honor," he stood almost alone in his own circle. His Joint Chiefs of Staff, his Senate leaders, and as often as not his Secretary of State were ranged against him. In one Far Eastern crisis after another, they not only made powerful pleadings for a course of action that would ignore all calculations of the risk of war but sought to force his hand by making their own provocations and their own appeals to public opinion. Up to mid-1955, Senator Knowland kept up a steady drumbeat of criticism. (In the period just before the summit conference, when the air was thick with talk of coexistence and peace, it became plain that Eisenhower's leadership in foreign affairs had the support of the entire country, and this silenced almost all criticism, including, for a brief period, Senator Knowland's.) In those two years, the Navy and the Air Force were constantly releasing strategic appraisals that made the President's prudential tendencies look somehow menacing to the national interest. On numerous occasions, the commanders maneuvered ships and aircraft into positions of needless exposure. At the point of showdown, the Secretary of State stood, as he had to, with the President, but when decisions were in the making he frequently stood with Senator Knowland, Admiral Radford, Admiral Carney, and the rest.

His hand must certainly have been strengthened by the knowledge that public opinion would in the end uphold him and that the party politicians would be found on his side. From the simplest political viewpoint, it was not his course but that of the others that took moral courage. The side he was taking was the one that Walter Lippmann has called "the softer and easier side [that] reflects what we desire," while the others were taking "the harder side [that] reflects what is needed in order to satisfy the desire." (When it came to Asia, though, the author of *The Public Philosophy* was very much for the softer, easier side.) Nevertheless, the President's opponents enjoyed the kind of advantage few men like to yield. Their course of action could be represented as embodying the vigor and audacity and dauntlessness that we like to think of as properties of the national character, while his lent itself to being represented as appeasement and funk. But in every crisis, he held to his own view, and it is not beyond the realm of possibility that his uncharacteristic initiative saved mankind from disaster.

VI.

The Democrats who were bold enough to risk any criticism of Eisenhower—and such Democrats were not very numerous in those middle years of the administration—liked to point out that his troubles were very largely of his own making. Nowhere in the Constitution, they argued, does it say that John Foster Dulles must be Secretary of State, and there was really no reason why Eisenhower should not have repudiated Senator Knowland as freely as Knowland repudiated Eisenhower. It was the President who appointed the Joint Chiefs of Staff whose advice he so consistently had to reject—going even to the point of pressing Admiral Radford into service for still another term. If Truman could fire MacArthur, the Democratic argument ran, then surely Eisenhower could discipline an admiral.

It was all true and all largely irrelevant, for if one's quarrel with a President is that he ought to behave like someone he is not, then the complaint must be taken not to the White House but to the electorate. A Democrat had his reasons for urging a

Republican to demolish the Republican Party, but the rest of us can take proper note of the fact that Senator Knowland and Admiral Radford and John Foster Dulles are not altogether capricious men, that they spoke for a section of American and specifically Republican opinion that demands and deserves representation, and that the President is well known for his accommodating spirit.

For if there are similarities between Eisenhower and Truman, there are also crucial differences. Eisenhower is not mettlesome. He is not contumelious. He is the sort who hates nothing so much as a scene and shuns controversy on any plausible excuse. Millions of Americans have found this side of him the most appealing. To them, the Eisenhower who can coexist with Admiral Radford, who has nothing but praise for the wisdom of Senator George, who likewise finds much merit in Senator Knowland's outlook, who minimizes his differences with Secretary Dulles, and who can speak warmly of the Vice-President at lunch and glowingly of Sam Rayburn at dinner is an Eisenhower running true to advertised form. Throughout his career, from SHAEF in 1942 to Geneva in 1955, from Patton and Churchill to McCarthy and Bulganin, the quality his supporters have emphasized is his ability to get along nicely with all sorts of people. "He is a genius at personal relationships," John Gunther wrote in his admiring biography. "Genius" may seem too strong a word and "personal relationships" too imprecise a phrase to fit the facts, but there is no doubt that he knows a thing or two about the accommodation of personality. Certain attributes that were conspicuous and in many ways admirable in the characters of Franklin Roosevelt and Harry Truman are not among the hallmarks of the Eisenhower style.

A stronger-willed President could have avoided altogether some of the crises that plagued the Eisenhower administration. Certainly the agonizing crisis over the defense of Quemoy and Matsu could have been avoided altogether by a simple declaration to the effect that the United States had no intention of placing the peace of the world in jeopardy over a few islands of doubtful military value, even to the Formosa garrison, and clouded legal status. Such a declaration would not have ended the peril to these islands (on the contrary, it would have brought the Communist flotillas out in full sail) but it would have greatly eased the world's peril. Yet one may wonder whether any administration that could possibly have held office during the last few years would have dared issue any such declaration. We have been pledged to the defense of Formosa almost since Chiang Kai-shek removed what was left of his armies to the islands. Truman's order of June 29, 1950 put the Seventh Fleet in Formosan waters. While it restrained Chiang from making an assault on the mainland—which then, as now, he lacked the power to do—it committed us to far more than a simple defense of the Nationalist redoubt, since the primary mission of the Seventh Fleet was the maintenance of peace in the area. Had the Communists then been capable of launching an attack on any of the islands, the Seventh Fleet would almost automatically have become engaged. If a Democratic administration had been in power in 1954 and 1955, it would not have been subject to the same pressures from within for a military adventure in the Far East, but it would have been subject to heavy outside pressures. For all his grit and independence, Truman also made concessions to what used to be called the China lobby.

Eisenhower made some too, but they were quite as notable for their insubstantiality as for their number. Immediately upon taking office, he withdrew half of Truman's order and left Chiang free to reconquer China. On the first anniversary of this bogus emancipation, the New York *Times* summarized the results: eleven more coastal islands lost to the Communists. The leashing and unleashing of Chiang had an importance in American politics and American diplomacy, but they were militarily meaningless acts, since Chiang had at every stage been securely tethered by his own lack of strength. Only the real stuff of American power could have furthered his interests and thereby endangered our own. Under Eisenhower, Chiang was given somewhat more American materiel than he was getting before, but not a great deal more, and some rather poor advice. (Quemoy and Matsu had been reinforced at the recommendation of American military men, so that a decision not to defend them could be described as at once a double-cross and a service to the peace of the world.) A cold appraisal of Chiang's fortunes since January 20, 1953 reveals that their improvement must be measured chiefly in the number of visits he has received from the Secretary of State. For the rest, the whole trend of American policy, not as it has been discussed by Dulles but as it has in fact been made and executed by Eisenhower, has been toward disengagement. Eisenhower insisted that Dulles's treaty with Chiang contain no pledges on the offshore islands; the treaty was delayed while Dulles was getting Chiang to accept this omission. Eisenhower ordered the evacuation of the Tachens. Eisenhower compelled Dulles to seek a cease-fire through the United Nations. Eisenhower made it as plain as anyone could—or as plain, at all odds, as any Republican president could—that the United States would not, while he was directing foreign policy, engage in war to upset the power relationships of Asia.

VII.

One hesitates to attribute political adroitness to a man who has revealed as much political ineptitude as Eisenhower, but it happens to be a fact that he has achieved, through luck or good management, a number of things that are commonly thought to be the product of skill. He has not brought all Americans around to his view of foreign policy, but he has created an atmosphere in which the opinions of a man like Styles Bridges, which are really more representative of Republican thought than his own, are looked upon as deviationist in character. He has put Bridges and McCarthy and Knowland on the defensive. He has made preventive war a heresy. He has countered Republican disgruntlement with the United Nations with stout defenses of the organization and with what was for him powerful opposition to the Bricker amendment.

He has done as much as any man of his limited gifts could do in this era of bad feeling to maintain before the world an image of the United States as being still a nation of free men and free institutions engaged in an experiment of some splendor and one that derives its justification from the hope that it will be useful to all humanity. It was no fault of his that in recent years that image had become fuzzier than it used to be and that in some parts of the world it had been rejected altogether; it was by no means wholly McCarthy's fault, either, or the Republican Party's, or the American people's, though each of these bore some responsibility. But when Eisenhower has spoken for the nation, he has spoken, particularly in the more recent phases of his administration, with dignity and sobriety and has in general appeared before the world as a not unworthy successor to those few American presidents whom the world has known and respected.

"Eisenhower's greatest single contribution," Joseph Alsop wrote in September 1955, "has been bringing us all back to a sense of the true American style—setting that style, in fact, by his own example and in the most trying circumstances. . . . The American style is re-established." The proposition needs a certain amount of refinement. It cannot be overlooked that "the American style" which Eisenhower is said to have re-established was disestablished under his administration. We have put behind us, Mr. Alsop is saying, the time when McCarthy and Cohn and Schine were riding high, when an F.B.I. gumshoe named Scott McLeod was an arbiter of destinies among American diplomats, when the head of the Bureau of Standards was denied reappointment for not speaking well of a product he regarded as sleazy and thereby revealing "insensitivity . . . to the values of the marketplace." Happily, our foreign policy is no longer a series of posturings. Well and good, but it would be absurd to praise his administration for putting an end to politics of a rather squalid sort without acknowledging that it bore at least a measure of responsibility for the ills it had cured.

Yet the acknowledgement scarcely lessens the accomplishment. There was in the late forties and early fifties a reaction in this country. The signs were unmistakable long before Eisenhower's election. McCarthy was an issue in that election because he was already a mighty power in the country. There was nonsense in our foreign policy for which neither Eisenhower nor John Foster Dulles could be held to account. The Republican Party sought to take advantage of the reaction, but it sought a presidential candidate who embodied something of "the American style." The reaction, in all truth, was not an overpowering tide; still, it was a powerful current. Eisenhower had to deal with it; he had, in fact, to move with it, and this was not hard for him to do, for part of him was touched by it.

It flowed more swiftly in his administration, but in the end it died. The air was clearer in the summer of 1955 than it had been for most summers that Eisenhower had been in the White House. It is not extravagant to say that "the American style is re-established." One could feel it in Washington throughout 1955, and one could feel it in Europe at the time of Geneva. In a sense, of course, the reaction spent itself; this is really a definition of the American style—a saneness that has always, up to now, outrun reaction. But Eisenhower was the symbol of the style in 1955 and its agent. He must get the credit.

The American presidency is an endlessly fascinating and instructive institution. One of the many things to be learned from it is that the Actonian doctrine of power as an inevitably corrupting force, and a force that corrupts in direct ratio to its magnitude, is something less than a universal law. Generally speaking, in our society, the insolence of office is most frequently encountered among those of severely limited authority. The worst tyrants are to be found in sheriff's offices, the worst moral rot in city councils and state legislatures. Our presidents, far from having been corrupted by the power given them have as a rule been elevated by it. We have never had a truly corrupt president—a president, that is, who either used the office for purely personal gain or sought to broaden his powers merely for the satisfaction of their exercise. On the contrary, the lesson of experience is that men increase in stature in the White House.

This was surely true of Eisenhower's two Democratic predecessors. In 1932, Franklin Roosevelt was plainly a man of greater buoyancy and energy than his whipped and baffled adversary, but there was nothing about him to suggest greatness. He was an agreeable man who had done well, but not spectacularly well, as governor of New York and who appeared more likely than Mr. Hoover to try fresh and bold approaches to the problem of reviving the national economy. He rose to greatness on the job. And it was on the job that Harry Truman made that approach to greatness that was even more exciting to observe than Roosevelt's. In 1945, he seemed so unpromising a postulant for the order he was entering that thoughtful men were forced to ask themselves how we might remedy the defects in the political system that allowed such awful responsibilities as to be placed in such unskilled and trembling hands. He was thoughtful enough to ask the question himself. "Boys," he said to a group of newspapermen the day after his inauguration in 1945, "if you ever pray, pray for me now. I [feel] like the moon and stars and all the planets had fallen on me." But the office worked its magic on him, and not only the country but the world found itself in his debt.

In Eisenhower's case, the measurement of growth is more complicated than in Roosevelt's case or Truman's. For a decade before his election, Eisenhower had titles of greatness and seemed to much of the world to merit them richly. In one sense, then, he now appears a somewhat smaller man than he was at the height of his war and postwar career. The presidency may be ennobling, but politics is demeaning, and he has been in politics up to his neck. He seems smaller, too, because he has not made the kind of personal response to the presidency that others have made—he has not, unless appearances greatly deceive, found in the office the exhilaration and joy that others have found. He has seemed bored and tired and uninterested a large part of the time.

Diminished or not, he is blurrier. There was a kind of vividness about Eisenhower in 1952 that Eisenhower in 1955 lacks. His personal attractiveness is not today the quality that projects. The impression one cannot avoid having now is that of a distressed, flustered, put-upon man. No one now can believe, as many once did, that Eisenhower, because his heart is pure, is capable of lifting up the rest of Washington and putting an end to political squalor. Everyone has seen how Washington under Eisenhower wallowed in politics as it always had. He has not been a great unifier in his own house—his own party and cabinet have been rent by fractional strife as bitter and destructive as anything known under the Democrats.

Yet Eisenhower, like Roosevelt and Truman and quite a few others, has been a far better President than those who elected him had any right to expect. This is not the most flattering of judgments, since those who elected him really had no right to expect anything. His experience had been even less relevant than Truman's. He had, it would appear, less direct acquaintance with the realities of American life and politics than any president in our history, including Zachary Taylor, who was the only general officer to come to the White House with no civilian experience of any sort. Unlike his military predecessors, Eisenhower had spent the better part of his career outside the United States. He brought to his office not a knowledge of American life but a distant memory of life in Abilene in post-frontier days. His only knowledge of government was what he had picked up as an Army lobbyist when Douglas MacArthur was Army Chief of Staff and, later, when he himself was Chief of Staff and not a notably astute or vigorous one. These, together with some copybook maxims about "separate but co-ordinate branches," of government, were his qualifications for his present office.

In the circumstances, which were contrived partly by him

but more largely by a nation that has always had a tendency to confuse the categories of excellence, it is remarkable that he has been in any sense adequate as a President and in some ways admirable. Now that he has finished the meaningful part of his administration, we know enough to say with some confidence that the office had its way with him and that such challenges as he chose to meet he met well. We have not enough perspective to carry any judgment beyond that. It may be that time will work in his favor as it did in Truman's, making his weaknesses appear trivial and his successes large. Eisenhower, like Truman, has been fortunate in having no serious economic problems to face. The recession of 1953 and 1954 was mild, and the administration was able to bring it to an end by the application, as Elliott V. Bell, a leading Republican economist said, of "compensatory fiscal and monetary policies that some of its leaders would probably have denounced a few years ago as downright New Deal heresy." Eisenhower's only first-class domestic problem was Senator McCarthy, and he finally managed to get on top of that one. (It was not an elevating spectacle, but since McCarthy, when he was at the peak of his powers, was a demagogue of great ability, the task of dealing with him was never as simple as most anti-McCarthyites thought it to be.) On the other hand, Eisenhower's successes may very well be less enduring than his failures. As estimable an authority as John Foster Dulles has said that the summit conference at Geneva would be seen in retrospect as far worse than Yalta—Mr. Dulles takes the poorest possible view of Yalta—if the reduction of tension bred a reduction of American strength. Communism is still militant and still rampant; Soviet power is still a menace. Eisenhower—and Dulles, too, it must be added—dealt with it intelligently at Geneva, but the valuable results achieved there could be altogether destroyed if we were to fail to take seriously the competitive aspects of competitive coexistence. That would be to make a mockery of all the virtuous acts of the administration.

VIII.

It could turn out, as it has so often in the past, that the smallest, most dimly understood developments have the largest significance. But in making a trial balance we accept the moment for what it is, and what Eisenhower's moment most urgently demanded was the holding together of the Western alliance and a determined effort to avoid the destruction of Western civilization. Eisenhower attempted to meet these responsibilities in a spirit of decency and maturity that has been a credit to him and to the country.

Index

Academic freedom, Robert Taft's defense of, 110-111

Acheson, Dean, Dulles' statement about, 61; work under Truman, 81; announcement about Korea (1950), 145; views on "massive retaliation," 199; mentioned, 28, 50, 77, 91, 349

Acton, Lord, doctrine of power, and the presidency, 369

Adams, John, opinion of the vice-presidency, 299

Adams, Sherman, to head Eisenhower staff, 44; experience in government, 75; personality and career, 80-81, 83; responsibilities, 81-83; views, 84; influence on Eisenhower's nomination, 84-86; wife's views on, 81, 84, 86-87; Eisenhower's remark about, 312; and Eisenhower's illness, 323-326, 337, 356

Adenaur, Konrad, 168, 169, 170, 292

Agriculture, Department of, report on farm subsidies, 316; Ladejinsky case, 354; mentioned, 353

"Agonizing reappraisal," 341

Airplane travel, in presidential campaigns, 45-47

Aldrich, Winthrop, 143

Allen, George, 347-348

Allen, Leo, 104

Alsop, Joseph, on Eisenhower as president, 368-369

America First Committee, and Dulles, 58

American Civil Liberties Union, McCarthy's charge against, 135-136

American High Commission (Germany), and Hede Massing, 139

American Jewish League Against Communism, 131

American Legion, 229

American Legion Magazine, recommended by Cohn and Schine, 142

Americans for Democratic Action, 7, 301

Andrews, Bert, and Whittaker Chambers case, 305

Army generals, as presidents, 11

Army-McCarthy hearings, McCarthy's interference in the Malmédy atrocities case, 200; attitude toward *Constitution* at, 214; mentioned, 199

Aron, Raymond, views on McCarthyism, 95-97

Arthur, Chester A., 100

Asiatic policy, lack of knowledge of Eisenhower's views on, 22; Public Law 4 and the Mutual Defense Treaty, 247-256; new interpretations of, 262-264; Eisenhower's conduct of, 362-364; 365-367

Atlantic Charter, 62

Atomic Energy, Eisenhower's view on, 359

Atomic Energy Commission, and Dixon-Yates affair, 355-356

"Atomic stalemate," 234-235

Atomic warfare, Eisenhower administration announcements about, 262-263; mentioned, 166

375